10-10-60

ERNEST RENAN *as an Essayist*

ERNEST RENAN
as an Essayist

By Richard M. Chadbourne

UNIVERSITY OF COLORADO

Cornell University Press

ITHACA, NEW YORK

PRINTED IN THE UNITED STATES OF AMERICA BY THE

VAIL-BALLOU PRESS, INC., BINGHAMTON, NEW YORK

To my wife, Gisela

Acknowledgments

ACKNOWLEDGMENT is gratefully made to the publishing house of Calmann-Lévy for permission to quote, in French and in translation, from the *Oeuvres complètes d'Ernest Renan*, edited by Henriette Psichari (1947 to date). Chapter 2 appeared in substantially the same form under the title "Renan's Revision of His *Liberté de Penser* Articles" in *PMLA*, LXVI (Dec. 1951), 927–950.

I wish to thank Professors Kenneth Cornell and Frederick Pottle of Yale University for their advice on how to make a more readable book out of what was originally a thesis presented at that university and my former colleague, Professor Charles Donahue of Fordham University, for having read the manuscript at a still later stage of its growth.

I am deeply grateful to the members of the Committee of Award of the Modern Language Association–Crofts–Cornell competition for having singled out my work for recognition. The MLA–Crofts–Cornell prize for 1956 was awarded to me for this book while I was a member of the Fordham faculty. Professors Oscar Campbell and Justin O'Brien of Columbia University, members of the Com-

Acknowledgments

mittee, and Professors Albert Guérard, Stanford University, and Harold March, Swarthmore College, offered many constructive criticisms, for which I am greatly indebted to them, as I also am to members of the editorial staff of Cornell University Press for their gracious co-operation.

It is a pleasure to record all these acknowledgments; it is an especially keen pleasure, finally, to express in print my gratitude to Professor Henri Peyre of Yale University, without whose generously given counsel and unfailing encouragement all along the way the present book would most likely not have been possible.

RICHARD M. CHADBOURNE

Boulder, Colorado
September 1957

Contents

Note on References and Abbreviations

THE edition of Renan's works used for the most part is the *Oeuvres complètes d'Ernest Renan*, edited by Henriette Psichari (Paris: Calmann-Lévy, 1947 to date). All but one work in this edition, *Averroès et l'averroïsme*, are referred to frequently enough to call for the use of abbreviated titles in the text and notes, with the volume and page numbers of the Psichari edition following the title (e.g., *AS*, III, 1038, refers to *L'avenir de la science* in the Psichari edition, vol. III, p. 1038). Abbreviations are used as follows:

AS	*L'avenir de la science*
DC	*Discours et conférences*
DFP	*Dialogues et fragments philosophiques*
DP	*Drames philosophiques*
EMC	*Essais de morale et de critique*
FD	*Feuilles détachées*
MHV	*Mélanges d'histoire et de voyages*
QC	*Questions contemporaines*

RIM   *La réforme intellectuelle et morale*
SEJ   *Souvenirs d'enfance et de jeunesse*

Since not all of Renan's works are as yet available in this edition, other editions have been used as follows (the place of publication is Paris and the publisher Calmann-Lévy unless otherwise stated; abbreviated titles are used only for works frequently cited):

CJ   *Cahiers de jeunesse* (1845–1846), 1906
CRB   *Correspondance Ernest Renan et Marcellin Berthelot* (1847–1892), 3d ed., 1898
EHR   *Etudes d'histoire religieuse,* 7th ed., Michel Lévy, 1864
FIR   *Fragments intimes et romanesques,* 7th ed., 1914
NCJ   *Nouveaux cahiers de jeunesse* (1846), 1907
NEHR   *Nouvelles études d'histoire religieuse,* 1884

L'Antéchrist, 2d ed., 1873
Les apôtres, Michel Lévy, 1866
Conférences d'Angleterre, 1897
Correspondance (1846–1871), vol. I, 1926
Correspondance (1872–1892), vol. II, 1928
De l'origine du langage, n.d.
Histoire du peuple d'Israël, vol. I, 1887
Lettres intimes d'Ernest Renan et Henriette Renan (1842–1845), 1896
Marc-Aurèle et la fin du monde antique, 6th ed., 1891
Ma soeur Henriette, 1895
Mélanges religieux et historiques, 1904

Nouvelles lettres intimes d'Ernest Renan et Henriette Renan (1846–1850), 1923

Saint Paul, 15th ed., n.d.

Vie de Jésus, 13th ed., 1864

In Chapter 2, the following abbreviation is used for a periodical:

LP   *Liberté de penser, revue philosophique et littéraire*

Translations from these and all other French works quoted are mine, unless otherwise indicated.

Introduction

ERNEST RENAN?
It was once a celebrated name, as celebrated as Molière's or Victor Hugo's, known alike to the uneducated and to the cultured. But within the last twenty years, it has been slipping into relative obscurity. Albert Schweitzer has related how, aboard the French ship the *Ernest Renan,* he once asked a sailor if he knew to whom the name on his cap belonged. "No one ever told us," was the reply, "probably some famous general." Even in the minds of the educated, unless they happen to be specialists in nineteenth-century French literature or in Biblical history, the name is likely to arouse only the vaguest associations—oh, yes, Renan, the author of the *Vie de Jésus* and of some kind of prayer to Athena said on the Acropolis, an unfrocked priest (in reality, he never reached ordination) who wrote in an exquisite style, cultivating irony and skepticism, blaspheming with gentle good humor, and, above all, contradicting, contradicting himself to the point where it is impossible to define his beliefs, if, indeed, he had any. What is most significant about such recollections is that they are more likely to have originated in reading about Renan than in

reading his works. Neither outside France nor, I dare say, inside it, is Renan widely read today. Glorified during his lifetime (and even more, shortly after his death), as were Ronsard and Hugo and Anatole France, he is now passing through the dark night of indifference which usually follows on apotheosis or iconoclasm. Ronsard long ago emerged triumphant from this testing period, and Hugo is emerging, but Renan and his most famous disciple are still paying for their apotheosis.

Renan was wise enough to foresee at least a partial eclipse of his popularity. Apologizing for the frivolities contained in his last book, the *Feuilles détachees*, published not long before he died in 1892, he wrote: "The public, now indulgent, will one day take its revenge" (*FD*, II, 938). But he might have been surprised that posterity's vengeful neglect would affect his best work also and that he would succumb to a fate little better than being completely forgotten: the proud, sad fate of becoming an unread classic. Once one of the most controversial authors in the Western world, Renan has now been reduced to brief mention in nineteenth-century survey courses, where it is other writers, Balzac and Stendhal, Baudelaire and Rimbaud, who are given the living space, the chance to quicken the hearts of the young. Small fragments of his work have been enshrined in anthologies, or, at best, a limited number of his books, important but not too meaningful when isolated from the rest of his work, have been assigned as required reading. The books, furthermore, tend to be the same: the *Vie de Jésus*, now something of a museum piece, the *Souvenirs d'enfance et de jeunesse* (with its mercilessly anthologized "Prière sur l'Acropole"), perhaps *Ma soeur Henriette*. Significant as these are, they should not be assumed once and for all to be his masterpieces; they should at least be read with the understanding that they give a very limited, if not distorted, impression of the man and his achievement.

In reality, Renan's work is rich and varied and full of life. He was much more than an arranger of beautiful artificial sentences, a kind of French Walter Pater. He was no mere "dilettante"—a term often contemptuously applied to him but seldom precisely defined. Gustave Lanson, with much acuteness, was one of the first to warn against the injustice of seeing in him only "an incomparable entertainer, a bewitching dilettante, the greatest acrobat of the mind who ever lived" [1]—a warning which still needs attention, for his work is reduced by such deceptive praise to little more than bubbles and froth. We tend to forget that he was a serious writer of history. His *magnum opus*, comprising *Les origines du christianisme* (of which the *Vie de Jésus* is the most famous but not necessarily the strongest part) and the *Histoire du peuple d'Israël*, is one of the most ambitious syntheses ever attempted of Judeo-Christian and Roman history. Despite much that is outdated and questionable in its pages, it remains an extraordinarily readable work, an impressive example of that blend of scholarship and art which has always gone into the writing of history at its best. His *Dialogues philosophiques* and *Drames philosophiques*, in spite of his lack of logic and precision, his evasiveness as a philosopher, still have a curious power, still give off what an American critic, associating him with Plato and George Bernard Shaw, has called a rare kind of music, the "music of ideas." [2] As for *L'avenir de la science*, too often represented in meaningless fragments, it is a mine of ideas, a *summa* of the generation of 1848 (and, indeed, of the nineteenth century), a haunting dream of a world redeemed by learning and reason, which its author was never able to disavow.

It is, however, to another area of his work, as interesting as these and even more neglected, that we shall turn—his essays. Renan, as we shall attempt to persuade the reader, is one of the greatest French essayists. Of the several hundred articles he wrote over a period of some forty years, notably for the *Revue des deux mondes* and the *Journal des débats*, he collected the best in seven books, part of an eighth (the *Dialogues et fragments philosophiques*), and, if we extend the term "essay" a bit to include some of his speeches, a ninth, the *Discours et conférences*. As impressive as this production is in quantity and, even more important, in quality, Renan's special character as an essayist has never been defined. The advantages of approaching him from this angle are many. Not only are the essays highly readable in themselves, but they also give us a rich cross section of his life and work. Much of the drama of nineteenth-century France is reflected in them, from the Revolution of 1848 and the *coup d'état* to the *débâcle* and the rebuilding of a divided and humiliated country. A deeper intellectual drama is also mirrored in them, the widespread conflict between faith and science, of which he became an almost legendary symbol.

The essays assume added importance when we remember that, aside from the *Cahiers de jeunesse*, Renan kept no intimate journal, for, as the century progressed, this became a new literary genre which he despised as narrowly self-centered. His autobiography brings us down only to his break from Saint-Sulpice, and his correspondence, except for his youthful letters to Henriette and to his mother and those to his friend the scientist Marcellin Berthelot, is inclined to be conventional and unrevealing. Although his essays are hardly "intimate" in the usual sense, it is in them, nevertheless, that we receive the most substantial vision of the man in his many-sided personality—the scholar proficient as archeologist, epigraphist, philologist, and historian; the tireless and joyful voyager; the alert critic of contemporary affairs; the unsuccessful political candidate and acute political thinker; the marvelously gifted prose writer.

"Renan the Essayist" forms part of a larger subject which we can only touch upon but which must be borne in mind if we are to take his true measure, namely, the modern French essay. It was a Frenchman, Montaigne, who invented the classical form, the artfully rambling attempt at self-definition; but curiously enough, he won many more disciples of his form (though not necessarily of his thought) in England than in France. The French on the whole seem less conscious of the essay as a genre than do the English, who, cherishing its inherent empiricism and freedom, its possibilities for humor, have developed a variety of well-defined traditions. No Brunetière has yet appeared to trace the evolution of the French essay. For the older period, his task would be bewildering. There were, in the seventeenth century, a few works with the title, for example Pierre Nicole's popular *Essais de morale,* and in the eighteenth, a number of gazettes imitative of Addison and Steele. There was a profusion of unclassifiable *opuscules,* distant cousins of the essay. But the greater works—Saint-Evremond's letters and "*dissertations,*" La Bruyère's *Caractères,* the letters of Madame de Sévigné, Voltaire's *Lettres philosophiques,* and others—resemble the essay occasionally in spirit but seldom in form.

It is when we approach the nineteenth century that we

find the identity of the genre asserting itself, for then began the great era of modern French journalism, and it was serious, polished writing for periodicals which made the essay possible. While, in the 1820's, Lamb, Hazlitt, De Quincey, and others were brilliantly renewing the genre in England, an Anglophile by the name of Sainte-Beuve was creating the French critical essay. He accomplished this pioneer task by raising the magazine and newspaper article on literary subjects, broadly conceived, to the level of a fine art. The majority of nineteenth-century French essays, following the Sainte-Beuvian archetype, were critical rather than confessional in nature (though not always bearing on literature), centered about a book or books to be judged, and reached their destination between hard covers by way of great periodicals.[3] These *recueils d'articles*, whether they were called *études, mélanges, causeries, fragments, questions, variétés, curiosités, fantaisies*, or, occasionally, *essais*, became a prominent feature of the literary landscape. Most of them retain only a historical interest today; some have more life and readability; a very few, those of Sainte-Beuve and Renan, for example, are enduring works of art.

The new genre was recognized not only as a marvelous vehicle for literary or art criticism (especially of contemporary works), but also as an invaluable means of ranging out almost day by day over politics and history, ethics, sociology, and philosophy. Renan's own generation—Taine, Baudelaire, the excellent political journalist Lucien Prévost-Paradol, the translator of Emerson and very original and conscious essayist Emile Montégut, and others—set high standards in this art, and the generation which followed—Bourget, Faguet, Brunetière, Lemaître, Anatole France, Remy de Gourmont—continued the tradition with no less vigor and devotion. Apropos of Gourmont, James Huneker in 1913 wrote:

It is a holy and wholesale custom with certain French authors, to collect and publish annually in book form their fugitive essays. As a rule, the material, notwithstanding its heterogeneous nature, is worthy of a second perusal. It is hardly necessary to add that the essay as a literary exercise, almost as extinct as the dodo in America, is still vigorously cultivated in France.[4]

In this context, Renan's work appears as one of the most readable and most durable, and the reason may well be that artistically it is the finest. Nothing keeps a book alive quite so well as what Albert Thibaudet called "the incorruptible oil of style." [5] If Sainte-Beuve was the first to recognize the great promise of the *article de revue*, or periodical essay, it was Renan whom he acknowledged (this much-maligned critic was capable of modesty) to be *"le maître d'un genre nouveau,"* and this on the strength of the younger man's first two collections, the *Etudes d'histoire religieuse* and the *Essais de morale et de critique*.[6] Renan was as conscious as the author of the *Lundis* of putting his best efforts into a new literary form—new, that is, for the French—and he even went so far as to suggest that the new genre might one day be looked upon as "the one belonging most essentially to our age, and consequently the one in which our age has done its finest work" (*EHR*, pp. i–ii). In retrospect, we see that fiction and poetry were mightier rivals than he perhaps realized, but at least this much can be said in confirmation of his insight into his time: the critical essay as he and Sainte-Beuve practiced it revealed itself to be more truly creative, more truly a work of art, than all but the greatest of novels or poems or plays. What he called "*la critique universelle*," if not the most powerful creation of his age, may well be its most original.

To trace the growth of this new art in Renan's work, from the crucial phase following his break with Roman Catholicism through his complex maturity down to what Maurice Barrès called his "twilight musings" ("*songeries crépusculaires*"), may, we hope, provide a fresh approach to a writer whose notoriety, now a bit stale, has done him more harm than good. Recalling a remark of the historian Gabriel Monod, which gave us one of the original incentives for our theme, we shall try to discover exactly what were the qualities which led him to hail in Renan "the foremost of our essayists." [7] But how (this question is likely to be asked by English or American readers accustomed to the "personal essay"), how could Renan have been a true essayist, let alone a great one, when he once declared: "To speak about oneself is always evil" ("Parler de soi est toujours mal")? Isn't this cutting out the ground from under the most frankly subjective of literary genres? A hint as to the answer lies in the sentence leading up to his dictum: "I have on several occasions reproached the minds of our time for being too subjective, too wrapped up in themselves, not sufficiently carried away by, absorbed in, the object, that is, in all that lies before us, the world, nature, history" (*FD*, II, 937–938).

ERNEST RENAN *as an Essayist*

"The characters of some men are curious mixtures of truth and affectation, of pride, even vanity, of egotism and unselfish enthusiasm. God alone has the key to such souls. Jean-Jacques Rousseau. I myself am false sometimes and think of appearances. And yet there is also a great fund of truth in me."

"Il y a des caractères qui sont des mélanges bizarres de vérité et d'affectation, d'orgueil, de vanité même, d'égoïsme et d'enthousiasme désintéressé. Dieu seul a la clef de ces âmes-là. J.-J. Rousseau. Moi-même je suis faux quelquefois et je songe au δοκεῖν. Et pourtant aussi j'ai un grand fonds de vrai."
— *Nouveaux cahiers de jeunesse*, p. 88

Chapter 1

From Faith to Scholarship

"Criticism consists in maintaining contradictory elements opposite each other, in not letting a single component of humanity stifle any other."–*Fragments intimes et romanesques*

DURING the years 1845–1850, while Renan was still in his twenties, an extraordinary ferment of ideas took place in his mind. Outwardly he went about the business of withdrawing from the seminary of Saint-Sulpice, of taking his degrees at the Sorbonne, of building the foundations of his career as a lay scholar; in making this adjustment, which might have crippled or even shattered someone of less strength of will, he seems to have possessed great clarity of purpose, calmness, and self-assurance. Yet the intimate notes he kept of this experience, never intending them for publication, the letters to his sister Henriette, the *Fragments intimes et romanesques*, the *Cahiers* and *Nouveaux cahiers de jeunesse*, all published posthumously and all still much too little known even by scholars, reveal that he suffered a profound crisis of mind and heart.

1

It was once a fashion with critics to deny that Renan ever experienced any serious or deep *crise de conscience*. Of this paradoxical interpretation the source was probably Maurice Barrès, at his best a penetrating critic of the master who had influenced him so greatly, but not always a reliable witness: in the *Figaro* of May 1, 1896, he declared that Renan never had any real faith to lose and that his crisis was merely a *crise de vocation*, or the mild dilemma of deciding whether to be a scholar with or without the cloth. Victor Giraud republished this interpretation in a collection of Barrès' articles to which he gave the title *Taine et Renan, pages perdues* (1922) and developed a similar though more objective analysis of his own in *La critique littéraire* (1945), arguing that Renan's was less a *crise de conscience* than a *crise de carrière*. There is some truth in this point of view, but it would be inaccurate as well as pointless to deny the reality of Renan's religious crisis simply because his faith seemed not to have the intensity of a Pascal's or because his suffering was not revealed to the public in striking or dramatic terms. Sainte-Beuve came closer to the truth when he noted that Renan had indeed passed through a crisis but that it had been, especially when compared to the *"déchirement"* of a Lamennais, of a gradual, even serene nature: "Il avait eu son évolution, non sa révolution." [1]

Although the exact nature and causes of Renan's *crise de conscience* have been much debated, there is little reason to deny that the loss of his Catholic faith came to him as a very grave crisis; nor, after reading his letters of the period, can we doubt that he suffered intensely. In a particularly moving letter to his friend and fellow Breton, the seminarian François Liart, dated June 20, 1843, speaking of the sense of duty toward his mother which helped give him the moral strength he needed (he feared above all hurting her), he confided that he had "learned to suffer, which is the greatest good that can befall a man" (*FIR*, p. 233). What is more, his loss of faith, the central cause of anxiety in his soul, had repercussions in the form of painful uncertainty as to the value of the scholarly and critical vocation (to this extent Barrès and Giraud were correct) which he had chosen with such apparent firmness.

In reality, Renan's *crise de conscience* consisted of two phases. The first is the breakdown of his faith, the series of tremblings and vacillations which in the early 1840's had begun to disturb the soul of the lonely pious youth far from his Breton homeland at the seminary of Issy, and which reached their climax on October 6, 1845, when he walked down the steps of Saint-Sulpice "never again to reascend them wearing the cassock" and took a room in the nearest hotel. The *Souvenirs d'enfance et de jeunesse* tells this part of the story with a literary skill that has made Renan's name synonymous with the denial of faith for intellectual reasons. The second phase of the crisis is much less known. Extending roughly from 1845 to 1850, from the break with Saint-Sulpice to the return from his first trip to Italy, it consists of a search for new spiritual roots, a feverish questioning of the nature and validity of scholarship and criticism. An important part of this growth to maturity is Renan's formulation of certain ideals and principles for the scholar-critic, and insofar as these bear on his conception and practice of the essay, they are of immediate concern to us here.

It will be useful to go back a bit and to ask: What destroyed Renan's faith? The *Souvenirs d'enfance et de jeunesse* certainly throws some light on the problem; but by pointing out in his preface that "what we say of ourselves is always poetry" ("Ce qu'on dit de soi est toujours poésie" —II, 714), Renan forewarns us against accepting his autobiography as a factual record. It was written many years after the event and from a considerably softened perspective. Much more revealing are the intimate works to which I have already referred, dating from the critical period itself, and especially the letters to Liart, his former classmate at Tréguier.

If we reread the autobiography in the light of these frank, soul-searching notations and of the further texts and sober commentary provided by Jean Pommier (*Ernest Renan, travaux de jeunesse; La jeunesse cléricale d'Ernest Renan*), we discover that a combination of causes brought about Renan's separation from the Catholic faith. The piety he brought from home received poor nourishment in the thin humanistic fare of the Abbé Dupanloup at Saint Nicholas-du-Chardonnet and was further weakened by the curious mixture of Cartesianism, scholasticism, and Scotch utilitarianism taught as "philosophy" at Issy. He allowed himself to develop growing habits of skepticism and doubt, finding the refutations (*solvuntur objecta*) of Descartes and Kant less appealing than the arguments they were supposed to refute. Finally, despite his retrospective version discounting the importance of philosophy and metaphysics in the crisis of his faith and attributing it almost wholly to the influence of historical criticism and philology (*SEJ*, II, 849, 869), it would seem that Renan's faith was very seriously undermined by philosophical skepticism some years before it was completely destroyed by Biblical exegesis and *"critique historique."* One should add, almost completely destroyed, for it is part of the tragicomedy of Renan, as we shall see, that he never managed a forthright denial of Christian faith.

4

Does it appear, then, that his clerical teachers were largely responsible for his loss of faith? Such a facile paradoxical solution would never have been acceptable to Renan; his sense of justice toward them, his gratitude for what they had given him, his affection for them were too great. If there are numerous priestly professors in his autobiography who failed to recognize and arrest incredulity in their midst, there is also the unforgettable Père Gottofrey, who one day struck young Ernest Renan like a thunderbolt with the terrifying truth of his remark: "You are not a Christian!" (*SEJ*, II, 850). It is very clear, as well, that Renan's piety, which cannot seriously be denied when one has read his letters and notes, tended nevertheless quite early toward excessive rationalism. The object of his worship became less and less "the God of Abraham, of Isaac and of Jacob," the personal God incarnate in Christ, and more and more the God of abstract truth, and finally abstract truth itself. "Truth, Truth, are you not the God for whom I search?" (*FIR*, p. 280). He grasped firmly, as every Christian must, the real need for a rational justification of belief; his grasp became less and less firm upon the greater gifts of prayer, of penance, of faith. The living faith dried up within him.[2]

Although he ceased to believe without anything resembling the torment of the *nuit de Jouffroy* (a romantic thinker's famous religious crisis) or the turbulent apostasy of Lamennais and began immediately to reconstruct his philosophy, Renan's spiritual anxiety continued for some years in new form. The questioning spirit of criticism which had swept away his faith seemed to extend a desiccating touch to other areas of his life. Two years after leaving Saint-Sulpice, in a letter to Berthelot, he asked what human life really was, where one might find a cause to embrace wholeheartedly; he spoke of the courage the critic must have to remain detached, to hold himself aloof at the very moment when his enthusiasm is about to take fire.[3]

Renan was here expressing a recurrent nineteenth-century fear—the fear that the critical spirit might destroy all truly creative enthusiasm. In preromantic and romantic works this theme took on an anguish of almost pathological character: one thinks of Sénancour's Obermann grown old before his time from having "examined" everything; or Musset's *enfant du siècle*, Octave, tainted by the rationalism of his eighteenth-century ancestors, unable to embrace any ideal (or, perhaps symbolically, any mistress) without fear of being duped. The very year Renan was writing his *Cahiers de jeunesse*, Sainte-Beuve confessed in a letter to the Protestant theologian Alexandre Vinet, "I have passed into the state of a pure critical intelligence and look with saddened eye on the death of my heart." [4] In the 1880's Edmond Schérer revealed to the French public perhaps the most striking example in literary history of creative power sterilized by brooding critical intelligence, the *Journal intime* of Amiel. In England there are traces of this same conflict in the works of both romantics and Victorians. Matthew Arnold has given classic expression to it in verse in his "Empedocles on Etna," and it may be significant that he had absorbed his Sénancour as well as a great deal of Sainte-Beuve and Renan. Arnold believed, writes Lionel Trilling, "that the critical intellect, seizing the whole personality, splitting it into segments, making it doubtful, incapacitating it for poetry, was the force against which his poetic gifts must be protected." [5]

Except that the poetic gifts of Renan were never to find expression in verse, this, in almost exactly the same terms, was the dilemma he faced in the period of adjustment from the seminary to the world of scholarship and literature. He discovered the potentially destructive power of his critical and analytical mind. Criticism had released him from orthodox faith; would it destroy the possibility of all positive idealism? In asking this question he felt not *mal du siècle* or *ennui* or pathological strain, for these seem to be completely absent from his life, but a kind of vague impatience which caused him more acute suffering than anything he had ever experienced (*CJ*, p. 227).

The particular form in which Renan expressed these doubts about the value of criticism was the series of feverish academic notes on the meaning and future of literature which make up a large part of his *Cahiers* and *Nouveaux cahiers de jeunesse*. His contact, late in 1845 and in 1846, with the literary theories of university professors such as Désiré Nisard, Saint-Marc Girardin, Victor Le Clerc, and especially Victor Cousin, provoked him into formulating his own original viewpoint on literature. Under the influence of Mme de Staël and Cousin he outlined a theory of the history of literature which gave a preferred place to the German and French romantics, although it seemed to view the future of literary genius with considerable pessimism. History, according to this theory, had begun with the "*âge spontané*," an age of naïve primitive expression also known as "syncretism," because of the uncritical but highly poetic fusion of men's minds with nature which is supposed to have characterized it. Next came the "*âge réfléchi*," with its more conscious, calculated literary art, or "analysis." Finally, assisted by the romantics and obedient to Hegel's law of dialectics (Cousin was one of the first to introduce Hegel's thought into France), history, after the surfeit of

7

eighteenth-century rationalism, was now to evolve into the age of "synthesis," a kind of higher union of poetry and reason.[6]

As for the literary judgments derived from this cyclical view of history, which Renan took largely from Cousin, they are reflected faithfully enough in the *Cahiers de jeunesse*. The "*âge spontané*" alone was supremely creative, it alone had given expression to what Mme de Staël called the "*infini*," producing the genres so exalted by romantic theorists, the epic of Homer and Ossian and folk lyricism, including the Psalms. "*Littérature réfléchie*," on the other hand, is used as a derogatory term by Renan and its most deplorable examples he finds in Latin literature, seventeenth-century French classicism (Boileau enclosed in his narrow circle of the *fini*), and, worst of all, eighteenth-century neoclassicism.

Debatable as much of this theorizing is, it seemed to have for young Renan a clear and very disconcerting implication: the Frenchman of 1846 lived in an age so critically minded that it had made him incapable of poetry as great as that of Homer or the Psalmist and perhaps incapable of any true poetry. Once, so the nostalgic dream ran, men had communed intimately with nature and with God; they had expressed their deepest feelings in naïvely beautiful poetry. Now, they had reduced nature and even God to mechanisms whose laws they knew. Man had explained away the soul and had dissected beautiful things until he knew why they were beautiful but was no longer able to make them. What was the meaning of this dilemma for Renan, in personal terms? It was simply that he was uncertain as to how he could be a critic and scholar without doing violence to his nature. He knew that to create one must have enthusiasm.

His own nature, as any reader of the *Cahiers de jeunesse* or *L'avenir de la science* will be convinced, demanded the nourishment of some kind of poetry and faith. Yet he was painfully aware of the "great literary and moral disadvantage" of "analytical-critical ages." He was terribly afraid that no enthusiasm could be trusted to last when analysis had stripped it down to its springs and wheelworks, its *ressorts*. He was terribly afraid of being duped (*CJ*, pp. 112–113).

Cousin's theory of the three ages, however, left him with the vague hope that his own was to be a period of transition to an age of critical analysis which would not exclude enthusiasm, an age of fully creative activity. During the next few years this hope expanded into a prodigious testimony of faith which he called *L'avenir de la science*, various fragments of which were to appear in essays and other works before it was finally published in its entirety, little revised, in 1890. This work of a twenty-five-year-old agrégé has come to be recognized as one of the most significant in the history of European thought. On the whole it is certainly affirmative and optimistic in character; it is often lyric in its enthusiasm. But Renan has by no means dispelled his anxiety. He reveals, in fact, another aspect of the crisis we have been describing—his fear of being unable to harmonize within himself the various creative and critical gifts with which he had been endowed. In a striking passage of *L'avenir de la science* he declares that the secret of allying the diverse elements of human genius, its poetry, philosophy, art, and science, has not yet been found, and that the man gifted with "too rich a nature" (which he calls "*un supplice*") would really need one life in which to know, one life in which to feel and to love, and one life in which to act, or, rather, he would like to be able to lead at one and the same time a series of parallel existences and to be simultaneously conscious of each, in a kind of higher unity. . . . He wants to lose no part of this ardent, multiple life which slips away from his grasp and which he seeks to devour with haste and avidity. He moves from one world to another, or rather, discordant worlds conflict within his breast. He envies, each in its turn, for he can understand each, the simple soul who lives on faith and love, the virile soul who seizes life like a muscular athlete, the penetrating critical mind which savors the enjoyment of manipulating its sure, precise instrument [*AS*, III, 740].*

"*Une série d'existences parallèles*" united in one individual —such, expressed in the style of burning, impatient intellectual energy characteristic of his first major work, was the higher synthesis toward which Renan was striving. But the work itself falls far short of attaining the longed-for harmonizing and discipline of his "*trop riche nature.*" What makes it at once so difficult and so fascinating to read is that it represents precisely the "*mondes mal harmonisés*" colliding within him. On the one hand, we find a sensitivity to religious needs, a passionate idealism, a gift for poetry, which we know meant for Renan deep feeling expressed in rhythmical prose. The passage he later called "Résignation à l'oubli," the meditation on mortality inspired by his view of a Breton cemetery by the sea (*AS*, III, 904–905), is one of the earliest specimens of poetic prose in his work and, incidentally, fails to blend with the turbulent didactic prose that surrounds it. On the other hand, we are impressed by the author's rationalism and his *esprit critique*, which often jar with his poetry and idealism. Even his critical historical

* Renan, *L'avenir de la science*, III, 740, quoted by permission of Calmann-Lévy, publishers.

sense seems made up of two elements not always easy to reconcile: skill in precise erudition and facility for sweeping general views and hypotheses. *L'avenir de la science,* as Gabriel Brunet has pointed out,[7] is a critical work composed largely of dreams and dogmas about humanity, science, and progress; a eulogy in honor of the critical method, written with the method he calls "*enthousiasme.*"

The theme of the *trop riche nature* is developed further in two fragmentary "novels" in letter form, *Ernest et Béatrix,* written in November 1848, about the time that he was beginning work on *L'avenir de la science,* and *Patrice,* composed somewhat later at Rome. Both these curious confessions are published in *Fragments intimes et romanesques.* In *Ernest et Béatrix* the lament is at times worded exactly as in *L'avenir de la science (FIR,* p. 109). "I feel within me," complained Ernest, "a fullness of life which sometimes borders on intoxication, and which I am unable to channel satisfactorily into the narrow limits of learning" *(FIR,* p. 103). Yet he exclaimed: "How happy the scholar is! How I sometimes envy his fate, and how clearly it seems to me that such a life would constitute my happiness!" *(FIR,* p. 109). Renan had already received the Volney prize for his essay on Semitic languages when he wrote this, and he was soon to be sent by the French government on an academic mission to Italy; but it would appear that he had not yet defined his scholarly vocation in all its fullness or embraced it with conviction.

In *Patrice* there is a very thin veil of fictional disguise: a young man, the year before the French Revolution, writes from Rome to his sweetheart in Brittany describing the anguish he feels at not being able to share her childlike Catholic faith. We easily perceive, however, that this is Renan's own painful awareness, on entering the Catholic climate of Italy, of the great price he had paid for the development of his critical faculty. He even begins to fear that this faculty may rob him of the power to love: "The man who is too learned becomes impotent," "I have become incapable of loving," "I tremble in the presence of a girl" (*FIR*, pp. 69, 93). "The whole misfortune of my life," he declares, "is to have been too much a critic. . . . I have killed within me all youthfulness and naïve spontaneity; I cannot escape from myself" (*FIR*, p. 67). In terms harsher than he will ever again use in speaking of his critical faculty, he deplores it as "the weak side of my nature," "the cancer which devours me" (*FIR*, pp. 92, 72). He is especially pained to discover that the critical spirit, brought to bear on the study of the history of men's beliefs, might be the instrument that would deprive him of any firm or lasting belief. If there is no dispute of the past where we can recognize that either side was absolutely right or absolutely wrong, it must be assumed that future critics will not recognize that any of us are in possession of the truth: to know this is to find life "dried up at its source" (*FIR*, pp. 76–77).[8]

Patrice represents the trough of the crisis for Renan, a brief moment of despair and confusion as he considered the hypertrophy of his critical sense, the chaos of warring elements in his soul. In order to resolve this crisis, he had for some time been giving thought to a redefinition of scholarship itself, and of criticism, for the two things were always intimately associated in his mind. Gradually he conceived of the scholar-critic's art in the broadest and most humane terms as the very means which would enable him to harmonize his own contradictory intellectual and emotional, scientific and religious gifts. In this conception we touch upon one of the sources of all that is most characteristic and personal in Renan's subsequent literary art, particularly in his historical and essay work.

To put the matter once again in terms of Cousin's "three ages," Renan sought to make his own contribution toward the ushering in of the new age of "synthesis." His ambition was to bring together in his own work the poetry and idealism, the religious sense, of the "syncretic" era and the rational criticism of the "analytic" era, and to balance them in a fully creative equilibrium. Nor was this a vain, immodest personal dream. He took his cue for this vision of synthesis from a great collective reality of his time, the marvelous resurgence of a new historical learning which united the most solid erudition with a fine, lofty critical sense (*AS*, III, 834). In his notebooks he had squarely confronted the claim of Nisard, Le Clerc, and others among his proclassicist elders that French literature had entered upon a "decadent" stage; he was even willing to grant a little to their point of view insofar as he affirmed that his century was primarily a critical rather than a creative century. But he refused to admit that this so-called "decadence" meant sterility or lack of greatness and pointed above all to history as a truly creative art, in fact as *la création originale et propre de notre temps.*" [9]

Among Renan's romantic predecessors, several helped to fire the flame of his vision, although none provided him with a perfect model. He obviously learned much as a historian from the fusion of poetic beauty and erudition in the work of Michelet. He praised Lamartine for having already achieved "synthesis in poetry," especially in *Jocelyn*, with its blending of lyric, epic, philosophic, and religious elements.[10] From Sainte-Beuve—the only true essayist, it should be noted, among the many contemporary figures who influenced Renan—he certainly derived important critical notions and valuable practical lessons in the art of transmuting the raw material of erudition into the graceful prose of the essay. But Sainte-Beuve had much less of a positive influence on him than one would imagine: he had serious reservations about Sainte-Beuve's style and even more serious doubts about his philosophy and general attitude toward life.[11]

Two of the less great romantics seem to have contributed more to Renan's conception of scholarship: the philosopher Cousin and the historian Augustin Thierry. The great medievalist was an especially valued friend and literary mentor of young Renan, and his decisive influence on his style and historical method will be discussed at a later point. As for the famous Sorbonne professor, an extremely stimulating *excitateur d'idées* before he settled down to reign as pontiff of the official University philosophy, Renan drew heavily upon his eclectic method and his spiritualist, idealist thought. That, too, will be treated in a subsequent chapter. What should be noted here is that Cousin, never a dryasdust, indeed sometimes a gushing fountain of eloquence, had helped to broaden and revitalize the idea of scholarship: Renan admired his talent for bringing enthusiasm and a kind of poetic beauty into his writing of the history of philosophy (*CJ*, p. 111). But Renan early and late in his work took occasion to note the faults of Cousin: his lack of "*fermeté* (a similar leitmotif recurs in the criticism of Sainte-Beuve), the frequent vagueness of his scholarship, which was not always as reliable as that of researchers he himself had inspired; and of course his habit of sacrificing his critical sense on the altar of rhetoric, not to mention the altar of politics.[12]

The truest models of humane scholarship Renan found in his own field, philology, which was a tremendously vigorous, exciting, and far-reaching discipline in his day. Without the examples of the extraordinary sower of ideas, Claude Fauriel, and the great pioneer in orientalist studies, Eugène Burnouf, he might not have launched forth with such confidence and ardor into his vocation. His debt to Fauriel—philologist, critic, *comparatiste*, collector of Greek ballads, historian of Provençal literature—may perhaps be measured in a greater number of themes or ideas;[13] but it was a whole spirit Burnouf inspired in him.

This remarkable man, the son of a famous classical scholar, had taught Renan Sanskrit at the Collège de France, had befriended him and guided him personally in the early stages of his career. He was, in Renan's opinion, one of those rare men who are "both philosophers and scholars,"[14] a true "*philologue philosophe*," scrupulously erudite (Renan had already learned these high standards from the Abbé Le Hir, his Hebrew teacher at Saint-Sulpice), but also thoroughly aware of the wide significance, the philosophical implications, of his work. In the *Questions contemporaines* ("Trois professeurs au Collège de France") Renan devotes one of his finest portrait essays to Burnouf, delicately bringing out the contrast between his humane scholarship and the tendency toward petty pedantic virtuosity of his colleague in Persian, Etienne Quatremère. With Quatremère and Joseph Reinaud (Arabic) probably in mind, he declared to Henriette: "My life will never be absorbed by dry lifeless erudition. I refuse to be lost in the crowd of scribbling compilers who spend their whole lives without stirring up a single idea." [15] It was to Burnouf, in a letter filled with gratitude and with faith in the noble ideal of a scholar's life, that Renan dedicated *L'avenir de la science*.

Yet he looked even beyond such French scholars as Burnouf for a reality which would conform to his dream. There did indeed seem to be a country where learning and poetry, criticism and philosophy, rationalism and religious feeling, met in almost perfect union. The strong light of German scholarship filtered down to him, largely through such indirect sources as Mme de Staël, Cousin, and Fauriel. He discovered, with an effect he later described as a kind of intoxication, that in Germany there were scholars who wrote as beautifully as poets, who thought as profoundly as philosophers, and whose moral sensitivity was equal to that of preachers. In the work of Johann Gottfried Herder, preacher, poet, translator of the Psalms, collector of folk lyrics, scholar, philosopher of history, he found all these marvelous gifts united as though in a microcosm of humanity.

Renan was far from overwhelmed by the German influence. It is true that he later wrote to the Biblical critic David Strauss that coming upon German culture in his youth was like entering a temple (*RIM*, I, 438). But being Renan, he had a keen eye for the flaws in the temple. The historical views of Strauss and Friedrich Creuzer he had occasion to examine critically in the *Etudes d'histoire religieuse*. His conception of scholarship is obviously related to Friedrich Wolf's philology—the broadly synthetic, imaginative, artistic science of antiquity; but Wolf he found far from perfect, and even Herder, even his "*penseur-roi*" seemed to him often, as a scholar, "inexact, false, chimerical"

(*AS*, III, 832, 1132 note 56, 837). One virtue, however, he found especially strong in scholars beyond the Rhine: it is what Mme de Staël had called their *"esprit d'universalité,"* [16] their recognition that a poet does not betray his profession if he is also a scholar, nor a scholar sin if he is also a poet. From Leibnitz and Goethe to the most recent example, the geographer Alexander von Humboldt, but above all in Goethe and Herder, Renan felt the powerful attraction of this universality, this "happy combination of poetry, erudition, and philosophy, a combination which I believe constitutes the true thinker." [17]

Many currents, both French and German in origin, went into the genesis of Renan's ideal of scholarship. But it was nevertheless a very personal and original ideal as he developed it, for it became the solution of the dilemma which had grown out of his religious crisis and his loss of faith. Scholarship become the means of salvation is one of the central themes of *L'avenir de la science:* it is clear that the "science" of the title is much less the Anglo-Saxon notion of experimental science than historical scholarship, designed to replace metaphysics and theology as the way to truth and to life. Renan gives it a variety of names, each with its particular nuance, *"science," "philosophie," "critique," "dogmatique critique," "critique universelle," "philologie,"* and this may lead to some confusion. But his meaning is essentially the same in each case; he is thinking of a humane erudition broad enough to include the values of science, poetry, philosophy, and religion.

In the light of this discovery, criticism need no longer be feared as a purely negative, destructive force; it appears as the means for the individual to "embrace the whole from all its points of view" (*CJ*, p. 94), to become a microcosm

of humanity. "Criticism consists in maintaining contradictory elements opposite each other, in not letting a single
component of humanity stifle any other" (*FIR*, p. 78). The
true scholar must make his soul, in the words of Leibnitz, "a
mirror reflecting the universe" (*AS*, III, 741). He must
possess the form of critical sympathy which will enable him
to partake of the many-sided, contradictory gifts of humanity itself, so that he will become (Renan here quotes
Michelet) "both naïve and analytical, both child and adult,
man and woman, barbarian and civilized" (*AS*, III, 979).
Genius is to have both the critical faculty and the gifts of
the pure in heart (*AS*, III, 1103).

Within the context of Renan's personal evolution, erudition became the initiation into a kind of rationalistic *mystique*, a new faith to fill the void left by his renunciation of
Catholicism. It took on the values of an almost liturgical
communion, not with God, but with humanity. Yet this
communion, far from demanding, as he felt the Catholic
faith demanded, the suppression of his critical faculties, was
to be made possible only by their full use. The historian
alone can establish the authentic texts of the sacred story of
humanity and decipher them correctly; the historian alone
can wonder and venerate without fear of delusion; "the
scholar alone has the right to admire" (*AS*, III, 963).

There is in *L'avenir de la science* a key passage which
sums up perfectly this *mystique* of scholarship conceived
as the supreme synthesis:

Humanity will be truly learned only when science has explored everything down to the last detail and then reconstructed the living being after having dissected it. Do not ridicule, then, the scholar who buries himself ever deeper in these
thorny questions. Of course if this painful scrutiny were its

only aim, science would be nothing more than a sterile and debasing labor. But all becomes noble in view of the great definitive science, in which poetry and religion, science and moral wisdom will once again find harmony within complete reflection. The primitive age was religious, but not scientific; the intermediate age will show itself to have been irreligious but scientific; the final age will be both religious and scientific. Once again there will be an Orpheus and a Trismegistus, but they will come not to sing their ingenious dreams to childlike peoples, but to teach a wiser humanity the marvels of reality [*AS*, III, 974].*

Before Renan attempted to put into practice his extremely ambitious program of embracing the human spirit from many points of view, in a work which would have esthetic as well as scientific validity (*NCJ*, p. 260), he underwent two experiences of decisive importance in his growth toward maturity, especially toward artistic maturity. The first was his apprenticeship in journalism with the controversial and short-lived *Liberté de penser;* the second, his academic pilgrimage to Italy, which revealed to him a world of beauty he had known until then almost exclusively through books. He possessed already one of the guiding principles of his art, the conception of scholarship as a form of controlled but very real enthusiasm, a synthesis of the most varied creative and critical gifts. From this were to spring his historical work and a great part of his essay work, particularly the *Etudes d'histoire religieuse* and the *Essais de morale et de critique.* What he now had to do was to arrive at a more precise idea of style; to come to grips with a wider public than his purely learned paper on Semitic languages had

* Renan, *L'avenir de la science*, III, 974, quoted by permission of Calmann-Lévy, publishers.

reached; to test his thoughts with what Dr. Johnson called "the common reader." This was the function of his first periodical essays, which are the product of his experiment in polemical, or at least quasi-polemical, journalism. From this experiment he was to emerge a less undisciplined and a less dogmatic writer, but it left in his work a permanent residue of vigor and belligerence.

Chapter 2

Journalism and Artistic Growth

"I am not yet capable of defining my thought well. It lacks the necessary sharpness; I see it take shape like a dagger point beneath a veil, a statue under a veil."–*Cahiers de jeunesse*

THERE is no greater surprise for the reader of Renan's early work than to discover that the man we know as the master of airy equivocation and gentle evasion once complained that his style was insufficiently sharp and bitter. Yet this is the meaning of a series of self-criticisms, of cries provoked by the growing pains of style, that are recorded in the *Cahiers de jeunesse*. "Ah! how I stamp with rage at not being able to let all the acid of my thought transpire" (*CJ*, p. 329). His complaints sometimes take the form of those startling ejaculatory prayers which it is curious to contrast with the literary prayers he was later to develop into a minor genre of poetic prose: "My God! how I suffer! help me express my thought with the fire and gall which gnaw at my soul when I conceive that thought, for lack of being able to throw it out at the world!" (*CJ*, p. 340). Renan's unusual wish was, in a way, to be granted when his first important essays appeared, between May 1848 and September 1850, in the radically republican magazine called the *Liberté de penser*.

Acid, gall, and fire are hardly the elements customarily associated with the style of Renan; it is usually assumed that he was always the gentle intellectual coquette who declined to say either "yes" or "no." This is only one respect in which the traditional portrait of Renan, handed down from manual to manual, needs correction. It is true that avoiding polemical disputes was a stubborn point of honor with him,[1] which he set aside only rarely, as in his public controversy with David Strauss in the 1870's. But he had not yet formulated this rule when he wrote his first essays; nor did it ever prevent him, as his political work above all proves, from being at times an extremely aggressive and vigorous writer. This side of his work is closest to his conversation, which many observers have testified was surprisingly animated, forceful, trenchant, even authoritarian.[2] Taine recalled how Renan paid him a visit with Berthelot in the early 1860's and walked up and down his room as though in a cage, "*un homme passionné*," nervously obsessed with his ideas, expressing a wealth of thought in brief, jerky gestures and tones, "exploding," while Berthelot "fermented slowly, obscurely."[3]

In his articles for the *Liberté de penser* Renan attacked not any individual adversary, but the collective enemy of that review: Catholics of the political Right, the devotees of clericalism, the enemies of democracy or what their patriarch Count Joseph de Maistre called "*canaillocratie*." During his two years of apprenticeship for the *Liberté de penser*, Renan was much closer in technique to masters of the art of polemics like Maistre and Louis Veuillot than to Sainte-Beuve with his delicate critical shadings. He claimed to have known the *Soirées de Saint-Pétersbourg* by heart (*SEJ*, II, 812).[4] So vigorously affirmative and negative is the tone of his first articles that one wonders how the same man ever grew so sensitive to nuances of truth and error as fine as the color gradations in the pigeon's neck (the *cou de la colombe*). In terms of the polychromatic printing he once suggested for setting off the degrees of truth, from black (for certainty) to the most evanescent tints (for probability, plausibility, possibility),[5] it must be said that Renan's first ink was black with a vengeance.

In the preface of the *Etudes d'histoire religieuse*, Renan points out carefully that "Les historiens critiques de Jésus" [6] and "a few other pages" (probably "M. Feuerbach et la nouvelle école hégélienne") [7] were originally composed in a different manner from the one he has since adopted, but that he offers them to the public with some revisions since they still seem to conform to the truth (*EHR*, pp. ii–iii, xi). Similarly, he warns the reader about the immaturity of two essays in the *Questions contemporaines*, "Du libéralisme clérical" [8] and "Réflexions sur l'état des esprits (1849)," [9] which he does not disown, although their style is no longer his (*QC*, I, 19–20). Renan in fact revised these early essays much more extensively and in a much more significant way than he chose to declare in his prefaces. "Les historiens critiques de Jésus," in particular, underwent some striking alterations.

All this was part of a profound change which took place in the 1850's, not only in Renan's style but in his whole outlook on life. The change is well enough known in a general way, for Renan has told us in still another preface how Italy opened up to him a radiant and consoling world of art and sent over him a mild wind which caused his rigorous nature to unbend (*AS*, III, 716). Returning to France and rereading the ponderous manuscript of *L'avenir de la science*, he found it "bitter, dogmatic, sectarian, and harsh"; from its repellently wild overgrowth of ideas he decided, chiefly on the advice of Thierry, to cut out and trim certain portions for periodical readers and to delay indefinitely the publication of the work as a whole. At least two critics have examined in some detail the changes in the *Liberté de penser* essays,[10] but there is still more light to be shed on this phase of Renan's evolution, on the causes which lay behind it, and on the significance it has in the total view of his work.

The *Liberté de penser*, or *Revue philosophique et littéraire*, was one of the most interesting products of the period of intense journalistic activity and feverish socialist and republican aspirations between the February 1848 Revolution and the *coup d'état* of December 1851. Founded in 1848 by two professors of philosophy, Jules Simon, whose course in Roman Stoicism Renan had taken at the Sorbonne, and Amédée Jacques, it lasted until government opposition forced it to close down in 1851. Hospitable to a great variety of subjects including electoral reform, Christianity, and seventeenth-century Cartesianism, it had Lamartine for an *actionnaire* and numbered among its principal contributors the anticlerical lay prophets Michelet, Edgar Quinet, and Eugène Sue. Its fundamental message went deeper than any specific party alignments: it was simply liberty—liberty of thought, liberty of press, liberty of teaching. Its humanitarian fervor was perhaps purer than its literary standards, which were less exacting than those of the *Revue des deux mondes* or the *Journal des débats*—a fact explaining in part the relative formlessness and crudity of Renan's maiden essays. In its pages the brilliant twenty-five-year-old scholar, author of the *Essai historique et théorique sur les langues sémitiques* and already a member of the Société Asiatique, took his first bold strides into two fields which were to be of permanent interest to him and in which he was to make a resounding reputation: the history of religion and contemporary political and religious questions.

Renan may have rubbed elbows with some of the giants of the democratic revolution, but his own approach in this phase of his political thought was a timid and cautious one. Without committing himself to direct activity on behalf of republicanism, he accepted the Revolutions of 1789 and 1848 with what one might call an abstract enthusiasm. He seemed guided above all by the explanation (rationalization might be a more accurate term) Lamartine had given of revolution as a mysterious evil travail from which would issue something sacred for humanity. Several times in letters to the more conservative Henriette he quoted the celebrated verse of Lamartine about revolutions:

Woe to him who makes them	Malheur à qui les fait
Happy those who inherit them.	Heureux qui les héritent.[11]

Against the arch enemy, however, he threw himself into the attack without reservations. Clericalism, whether it involved maneuvers to obtain Catholic control of education or attempts of so-called "liberal" candidates to seize political power, was anathema to him.[12] In his first important essay, "Du libéralisme clérical," he defined the issue essentially as this: What happens to non-Catholics when Catholics take over the government? It is a question with a familiar ring in twentieth-century America. Renan's answer is succinct: "The Church, *when it can*, will bring back the Inquisition, and if it does not, *it is because it cannot*" (*LP*, I, 525). The theology of the Catholic Church—so runs his argument—makes it utterly impossible for any truly liberal political movement to grow up and remain within the orthodox fold. Renan hoped that this argument would brutally unmask and expose two kinds of enemies of the republic: orthodox Catholics, hypocritically disguised as "liberals," and so-called "neo-Catholics," naïvely supposing themselves orthodox. Of the two groups, surprisingly enough, it was the latter, the Montalemberts and the Lacordaires with whom he might have been expected to sympathize, who provoked his stronger contempt. At Saint-Sulpice he had been taught to view their "theological romanticism" with suspicion (*SEJ*, II, 811, 828–829); in leaving the Church he had made, in his opinion, too clean a sacrifice to logic and honesty to allow him to be indulgent toward those he considered (unjustly, certainly) to be halfway or theologically fuzzy Catholics.

Neither in its original nor in its revised form is this first essay free from serious weaknesses. It brings up many problems concerning the attitudes taken by the Catholic Church at various times in political questions, problems no sincere believer ought lightly to dismiss. But it has in common with polemical writing one fault, a fault, amusingly enough, which the mature Renan held in particular horror: it oversimplifies complex situations. The author cites, often in untranslated Latin, the authorities who prove his point and omits those who might tend to disprove it. The purpose of the learned quotations and footnotes seems to be not so much to open up all angles of the truth as to bludgeon the reader with the half-truth. We are referred again and again to ultraconservative, ultraroyalist Catholic thinkers, Bossuet, Maistre, Frayssinous; but no mention is made of liberal political tendencies in scholasticism or of such outstanding Renaissance theologians as the Jesuits Suarez and Cardinal Bellarmine, whose teachings were in sympathy with the idea of popular sovereignty.[13]

Given the bitterly partisan atmosphere of 1848, the one-sidedness of the essay on clerical liberalism is certainly understandable. Nor can one blame Renan, when he opportunely republished it in 1868, four years after Pius IX's Syllabus of Errors, for feeling that the papal condemnation of "liberalism" had strengthened his argument. Yet, should not Renan, as a scholar, have recognized in the work of many French Catholics the promise of a social and political liberalism not only compatible with orthodoxy, but, as Leo XIII was to show at the turn of the century, true to age-old Catholic traditions? It may be significant that in the revised essay he inserted, above a long footnote containing a violent denunciation of popular sovereignty by the preacher Frayssinous, a brief new reference to liberal tendencies in scholastic political thought.[14]

What this little addition, and many other more important changes, show is that Renan made an effort to attenuate the harsh tone of the original essay when he placed it before the public in his *Questions contemporaines.* He sought to remove some, though not all, of its sting. For example, he softened the wording of his description of a certain ecclesiastic whom he took to be the test case of the clerical liberal's good faith from:

We have got quite a howl out of the woeful discomfiture of a certain Reverend Father, who, in the midst of his democratic protestations, found himself insolently confronted by another passage of his work which was a little more orthodox and a little less republican. But does not the entire Church, in pretending to be liberal, expose herself to a similar contradiction? [*LP*, I, 512]

to:

We have smiled at the embarrassment of a monk who, in the midst of his democratic protestations, found himself opposed by a much less republican passage drawn from his previous writings. Does not the entire Church, in pretending to be liberal, expose herself to a similar contradiction? [*QC*, I, 285].

From one end of the article to the other, Renan polished rough edges, made his assertions less wildly universal, less hammeringly dogmatic. The sentence:

All Catholic writers, without exception, even those who have shown themselves most liberal, all theologies, all ecclesiastical philosophies, are in agreement in condemning our fundamental dogma of popular sovereignty [*LP*, I, 513].

was made both more concise and a little vaguer:

Treatises of ecclesiastical theology and philosophy are in agreement in condemning the principle of popular sovereignty [*QC*, I, 286].

Even more significantly, his enthusiasm for democracy having chilled in the intervening years, Renan has dropped the phrase "*notre dogme fondamental.*"

The most striking feature of the revised version, however, is the author's awareness of something a dyed-in-the-wool polemicist rarely grants, the sincerity of his adversary. The concluding paragraph of the essay, no mistake should be made about it, is still full of bite, with its comparison of the Catholic Church to a decrepit old man, innocuous and even worthy of some respect as long as he refrains from putting on the *bonnet rouge* of the Revolution. The Church should remain the representative of old ideas, but—and this important phrase has been added—"on lui tiendra compte de sa sincérité" (cf. *LP*, I, 531, and *QC*, I, 307). At one point Renan had accused theologians of duplicity in dealing with their opponents, especially with those unlearned in theology; even priests who profess respect for rationalism, he charged, are secretly contemptuous of it and, convinced in advance that their opponents cannot possibly be right, will use arguments they know to be worthless (*LP*, I, 525). In the text of 1868, besides softening these remarks, he adds a comparison which completely removes any suggestion that theologians are malicious hypocrites: the theologian is like the mathematician who, treating highly specialized questions, "allows himself many tricks of demonstration he knows are not exact but which he finds suited to his listeners" (*QC*, I, 299–300).

As for form and style, it is curious to note that Renan set out to prove, in a strictly logical, almost geometrical manner that the Church cannot produce truly liberal politicians. The basic structure of the essay, remaining unchanged, is practically a syllogism:

Major premise: The beliefs essential to liberalism are (1) popular sovereignty and the right of revolt; (2)

universal suffrage; (3) tolerance; (4) freedom of thought, speech, and press.

Minor premise: The Catholic Church officially repudiates each of these beliefs.

Conclusion: Ergo, the Catholic Church can never give rise to liberalism (*LP*, I, 513; *QC*, I, 286).

Exceptional as the essay is in this respect, it is still astonishing to find that the author who symbolizes relativism and nuance, defiance of all logic and all clear-cut argumentation, the author of the *Dialogues philosophiques* and the *Drames philosophiques*, once expressed his thought with this rigidity—especially when the matter was such a controversial and complex question. In this case his seminary training in *"scolastique cartésienne*," to which he later declared he owed the clarity of his mind (*SEJ*, II, 843), had engendered precisely the dogmatism from which he was trying to escape.

The syllogistic pattern of "Du libéralisme clérical" remained untouched, but there is a marked difference in style between the two versions of the essay: the original was often careless, awkward, insensitive to beauty of sound; the text of 1868 shows a writer alert to the refinements of prose harmony. Of the many judicious corrections the mature Renan made, one example will have to suffice. In writing of the insurgents who had died in the July Revolution (1830) and of the reluctance and bad faith with which—so he believed—the Catholic Church offered prayers for their souls, he recast a long, rambling sentence, full of awkward repetitions in sound,

Dans l'intimité on les damnait comme morts dans le péché mortel de la révolte, et j'ai ouï dire de mes oreilles . . . [the sentence runs on several lines], into

Au fond du coeur, on les damnait comme morts dans le péché de la révolte. [Cf. *LP*, I, 511; *QC*, I, 284.]

In an even more ambitious essay in the field of current issues, Renan attempted to sum up the state of mind of his own generation. What "De l'activité intellectuelle en France en 1849" represents is not the rigid form of an expanded syllogism but relative formlessness. It is in fact made up of loosely connected fragments of *L'avenir de la science*, especially of Chapter XXI. From its turbulent collection of vast general ideas and defiant paradoxes (this chaos representing perhaps all the more faithfully the period in which it was written), one theme seems to emerge, the defense of revolutionary storm and stress, unhindered political battle, as the only means to true social and intellectual progress. The enemy of Renan and the *Liberté de penser* here is not primarily clericalism but Louis-Philippism, the cult of order, calm, and security; the whole generation of bourgeois monarchists is cursed by the young journalist for having conceived, in their "tepid milieux," of life as a form of repose and of art as selfish enjoyment (*LP*, IV, 129). It is a young man attacking his elders with admirable enthusiasm.

In reworking this fiery apology for fruitful disorder, Renan sought, as he had done in the essay on clerical liberalism, to soften the dogmatic and anticlerical tone and to refine his prose style. He had to sweat much over his manuscripts to rid himself of the fever of repetitiousness, which was produced in him by the fear that unless he drove the nail in with repeated blows he would not be understood. "The art of composition, involving the felling of numerous trees in the forest of thought, was unknown to me" (*AS*,

III, 718). Even in the definitive version, his *coupes sombres* are not carried out with perfect skill: the revised text still reflects the time when his style, like the Renaissance in his own description, was a thick, luxuriant wood where art had not yet laid out her orderly paths (*LP*, IV, 126).

The earliest of Renan's ventures into religious history for the *Liberté de penser*, his "Congrégations *de auxiliis:* Episode dans l'histoire de la théologie," [15] is less an essay than a maliciously comic narrative of sixteenth-century disputes between Jesuits and Dominicans over *grâce efficace* and *grâce suffisante*. Curiously enough, it has a link with Pascal's ("Louis de Montalte's") polemical masterpiece on a later phase of this quarrel, for it was signed "Ernest de Montalte." But the differences in religious position are immense. The author of the *Lettres provinciales* was anti-Jesuit but not anticlerical, while the "Congrégations" is the most venomous product of this anticlerical phase of Renan's career. More significantly, Pascal believed in the reality of divine grace; Renan's purpose was to ridicule the proponents of papal infallibility (later defined as a dogma during his own lifetime, in 1870) by reducing the whole question of grace, the whole question of divine guidance of the Church, to a matter of clerical intrigue. One is hardly surprised, then, that almost forty years later this satire could be fitted perfectly, with no significant revision, into a book permeated with the mockery of supernatural beliefs.

Nowhere, on the other hand, is this former seminarian's development of a calmer attitude toward Catholicism revealed more strikingly than in the two essays which followed his debunking of high theological councils. When he wrote his brief essay–*compte rendu* on Feuerbach

("Qu'est-ce que la religion dans la nouvelle philosophie allemande?"), he had seen the Church in the light of Italy; he had perhaps also rediscovered, or at least allowed to well up from subconscious springs of adolescent reading, the work of Chateaubriand.[16] Although considerably revised for the *Etudes d'histoire religieuse*, this essay, even in its original form, pointed ahead to the new conception of the sensitive art of criticism he was to define in the 1850's. In its theme, the defense against Feuerbach of the artistic greatness of Catholicism (certainly an echo of the *Génie du christianisme*), and in several passages of poetic prose on the ruins of Mount Palatin and the bells of St. Mark's, Venice, the essay was already out of keeping with the anticlericalism and the somewhat rugged tone of the *Liberté de penser*.[17] Renan was, in other words, well on his way from partisan journalism to a more subtle criticism, a more conscious literary art. Of this evolution, the most remarkable proof is to be found in a much longer and more ambitious article, "Les historiens critiques de Jésus," especially when we compare its original and revised versions.

In a sense the ideas of the original text, which is a kind of *Vie de Jésus* in embryo, remained unchanged. After evaluating various interpretations of the nature of Jesus found in recent German and Jewish "higher criticism" (especially that of Strauss), Renan works out his own theory. It is substantially the same explanation sketched in his unfinished "Essai psychologique sur Jésus-Christ" (May 1845), written before his break from Saint-Sulpice when he still hoped to preserve his orthodoxy intact. Christ, according to this theory, was a *"miracle psychologique,"* an extraordinary historical event obedient, nevertheless, to certain psychological laws which human reason can estab-

lish. It is not my purpose here to examine these ideas critically, but rather to point out how, in the revised text of
1857, they were cast into such a startlingly different mold
that the thought is no longer really the same.

To feel this, we need only compare the opening paragraphs, which announce the function of criticism and set
the tone for what is to follow. In 1849 Renan wrote:

Criticism knows no respect; it judges gods as well as men. For
criticism, there is no such thing as prestige or mystery; it breaks
all charms, thrusts aside all veils. It is the only authority without
control, for it is nothing but reason itself; it is the spiritual man
of St. Paul, judging all, judged by no one.

This irreverent power casts its firm and penetrating eye upon
everything and is by very definition guilty of high treason
against man and God. Every sovereignty in the world must
give way before it, and, as its boldness increases with success,
there comes a day when it dares attack the God of the past
and look in the face him before whom generations of worship-
pers have bowed their heads in adoration [*LP*, III, 365].

Even allowing for the allusion to *"des générations d'adorateurs,"* which has the slight aroma of conventional rhetoric
about it, it would be hard to imagine a more blunt and harsh
statement of intention: we seem about to witness an exposé
by an *esprit fort* of the so-called "mysteries" of Christianity.

Here is the first paragraph of the essay as it appeared in
the *Etudes d'histoire religieuse:*

We are told that Fra Angelico da Fiesole painted the heads of
Christ and the Virgin only while kneeling: it would be well
if criticism did the same and braved the rays of such figures,
for centuries the object of worship, only after having adored
them. The philosopher's first duty is to join his voice to the
great choir of humanity in the cult of moral goodness and

beauty, which have manifested themselves in all noble characters and exalted symbols. His second duty is the tireless search
for truth, in the firm conviction that, if the sacrifice of our
selfish instincts pleases the Divinity, such cannot be true of the
sacrifice of our scientific instincts. . . . It is high time we
understood that criticism, far from excluding an attitude of
respect and implying, as timorous persons suppose, the crime
of treason against God and man, contains in itself the purest
act of worship. Least of all should criticism fear the charge of
irreverence when it seeks to define the true features of the
sublime master who said: "I am the truth" [*EHR*, pp. 133–134].

It is obvious that Renan's point of view has changed
radically, in some places contradicting outright what he
had said before. His style has also changed to suit his new
perspective. Some readers might find the harsh dogmatism
of the original version more effective than this "*culte de la
bonté et de la beauté morales*," extremely tenuous objects
of worship even at their source, the eclecticism of Cousin.
In places the style has indeed become uncomfortably vague;
but it is also better wedded to the thought. The first sentence is not only smoother; in a profoundly significant way
it invites the critic to approach sacred subjects with all the
technical skill, but also with all the veneration, of an artist.
In this one sentence is contained the whole difference between Renan and Voltaire (exception is made for Renan
in his less reverent moods) as critics of Christianity. There
is no longer any room for polemics. In the original introduction, furthermore, the thought is fired out as it were in
scattered shots; here there is truly organic unity, from the
allusion to religious art in the first sentence to the final quo-
tation (a curiously truncated one omitting "the way" and
"the life" from Christ's statement), which brings together

the various assertions of the critic's rights and duties and—in Renan's eyes at least—justifies them with an absolute solemnity.

The numerous other revisions he made in "Les historiens critiques de Jésus" were directed toward the same goal—to express his new conception of criticism in its most appropriate and most articulate form. The definitive essay still preserves some of the aggressiveness of the original, as can be seen in the passage ridiculing orthodox Catholic Biblical exegesis (*EHR*, pp. 205–206), or in the frontal attack on the type of "doctrinal" question that Renan felt historians should scrupulously avoid (*EHR*, p. xi, on miracles). No longer, however, is he content to coerce his readers with wild sweeps of the half-truth; he seeks now to insinuate into our minds, through the most subtle devices of style, his own complex attitude. Only a superficial critic would say that in revising his *Liberté de penser* essays Renan simply learned to write French more correctly. It was a much more significant change than that: his style not so much changed as came into being; his thought took on a carefully controlled and discriminating form so vitally related to its character that henceforth to separate thought and form in interpreting Renan is to risk doing violence to both. The questions which remain to be answered are: Why and when did this evolution occur?

The turning point seems to have been the years 1850 and 1851. The essay on Feuerbach appears to be the last article Renan had to revise to any great degree in transplanting from periodical to book. An important event in his life—it occurred in December 1851—explains why the later articles called for fewer revisions: I refer to his initiation as a contributor to the *Revue des deux mondes*. Unlike the *Liberté de penser*, this was a highly cultured literary review (though of equally broad interests) which had been in operation since 1829. In coming to it, Renan entered a milieu not unlike that of a literary salon and passed under the influence of one of the greatest French journalists, the controversial François Buloz. His firm editorial principle, as Henriette Psichari has remarked, was "to harass authors and, once he had obtained their prose, to harass them with criticism"; [18] more particularly, he sought to inculcate in his contributors two habits: excellence in literary form and the avoidance of any dangerous political radicalism. Renan's first articles for Buloz, "Mahomet et les origines de l'Islamisme" and "Les religions de l'antiquité" (December 1851 and May 1853), took their place in the *Etudes d'histoire religieuse* with very few changes.

By the time he had reached the *Journal des débats* and the lessons in French prose of an equally exacting editor, Ustazade Silvestre de Sacy, Renan was well into his mature style.[19] He had, in fact, already proved his true artistic and intellectual maturity with a masterpiece of scholarly writing, one of the great pioneer works in the "history of ideas," *Averroès et l'averroïsme* (1852).[20] Although this *"essai historique"* is not an essay in the sense in which we are using the term, it calls for some comment here.

Averroès is certainly one of the most extraordinarily readable theses ever written. Like so much of Renan's work, it represents the realization of a youthful project: it is precisely the kind of critical study he had envisaged in a passage of the *Cahiers de jeunesse* (p. 134), a new type of biography, recounting the life of a great man as it is prolonged in the posthumous influence of his work. Taking the famous Arab commentator on Aristotle, Renan traces his *"vie d'outre-tombe"* through the Europe of the Middle Ages and the Renaissance, through the maze of interpretations given to his work and of the fortunes it experienced. He is at great pains to avoid any involvement in the discussion of doctrine and, of course, any polemical tone; but it is perfectly clear that his sympathies lie with the "rational mysticism" of Averroes, interpreted by him with much personal fervor, and not with scholasticism.

What is of special interest to us about the *Averroès*, from our present perspective, is that here for the first time Renan attempts something like that synthesis of "poetry and religion, science and moral wisdom" of which he had been dreaming since the *Cahiers de jeunesse*. He was less successful in this than in his union of criticism (or scholarship) and artistic form. That Renan had acquired a new kind of esthetic sense is clear not only from the importance he attaches to painting as an embodiment of philosophical ideas,[21] but also from his own manner of presenting very technical and erudite knowledge in prose of great beauty and feeling, and from several striking remarks on the importance of style in philosophical writing. The Italian humanists of the Renaissance, he points out, were right to turn in disgust from the syllogistic jargon of the scholastics and to insist on a new formula, that is, writing well as the means of thinking well. True logic lies in the possession of a supple, penetrating, cultivated mind, sensitive to beauty of form. "Form, in philosophy, is at least as important as content; the turn given to one's thought is the only possible demonstration of its truth."[22] I need hardly emphasize the significance of this idea, not only for Renan's philosophical work, but for his future essays.

Much of the material for *Averroès et l'averroïsme*, and
for many less-known monographs, was drawn from the li-
braries and archives of Italy, where Renan and Charles
Daremberg, author of a dictionary of Greek and Roman
antiquity, had been sent by the French government in 1849–
1850 for the purpose of cataloguing Syrian and Arabic
manuscripts.[23] The discovery of Italy was a profound emotional experience for Renan, producing in him (as he said
it had produced in his fellow Breton, Lamennais) "that
recrudescence of poetry it often brings in harsh northern
natures" (*EMC*, II, 126). He had by no means been totally
lacking in poetic feeling, as his early experiments in lyrical
prose show;[24] at the Sorbonne he had discovered, in the
lessons of the great Catholic scholar and humanitarian,
Frédéric Ozanam, the poetic beauty of his own northern,
Celtic literature (*CJ*, pp. 235–236, 284). But he was still an
extremely cerebral type of philosopher, hardly aware of
painting, sculpture, or architecture; and beginning with his
Italian experience, he was to lend an increasingly attentive
ear to these silent voices of art. Not the least service Thierry
would render him was to introduce him into the milieu of
artists gathered round the painter Ary Scheffer, where he
was to acquire greater social poise and greater feeling for art
—as well as his future wife, the painter's niece, Cornélie
Scheffer.

In Italy he came not only to love religious art with un-
accustomed sensuousness, but also to see in it the expression
of a deeply popular faith which neither rational arguments
nor anticlerical vituperations would ever succeed in destroying. In the face of such overwhelming testimony to
faith, the attitude of "Proudhonian bitterness" (*"âcreté
proudhonienne"* he called it, after the great socialist thinker

—and there had been much of this in himself) seemed child-ish.[25] There is still a certain contempt for priests and prelates in his letters, but he clearly rejects the eighteenth-century tradition of anticlericalism which explained faith itself as a deception imposed upon the people by clerical tyrants.[26] Except for the superstition of the Naples populace, he viewed this deeply rooted faith with sympathy and even with nostalgia (See *Patrice*). It was a consoling discovery, for it allowed him to become a more kindly critic of the Church he had renounced. He could not embrace its dogmas, but he was at least able to shelter himself inside its artistic monuments, to warn himself beside its simple believers, for whom, he thought, dogmas had no meaning anyway. This form of communion with faith by means of historical sympathy and a kind of poetic insight, we recognize as the very cornerstone of Renan's method in religious history. It is not surprising that reminiscences of Italian art make up an intimate part of his first major work as a religious historian, the *Etudes d'histoire religieuse*.

If the illumination provided by the discovery of Italy determined Renan to rid his *Liberté de penser* essays of their harshness, Henriette also played an important role in giving him new perspective. In September 1850 she returned from Poland, where she had been a private teacher, and joined Ernest, still a bachelor, in an apartment in Paris. Henriette was not only a devoted sister who had made many sacrifices to bring her brother from a background of poverty in Brittany to a brilliant career in Paris, she was also a severe proofreader and an exacting critic of his manuscripts. Brother and sister both had written articles on historical subjects for a young people's newspaper.[27] Something of a rationalist herself, Henriette agreed on the whole with her brother's thought, but she found his form abrupt and careless, harsh and disrespectful; she disapproved of his *"sentiment d'ironie"*; she succeeded in convincing him that there was a simple, correct style, formed on *"les bons auteurs,"* which, without exaggerated novelty or violent images, could express exactly what one had in mind. "Therefore from my reunion with her," wrote Renan, "dates a profound change in my manner of writing."[28]

What he admired most in his sister's style, curiously enough, was a certain manly vigor.[29] Not that Renan's own style had already grown soft; he was thinking perhaps of his dangerous tendency toward *sensiblerie*. But vigor was not violence, and Henriette's blue pencil certainly helped eliminate much of the violence from Renan's system: the outbursts of rhetoric, the wild plunges into metaphor, the intemperate irony bordering on sarcasm. Perhaps she also removed along with it the salt and the zest; but her lesson, though a conservative, somewhat negative one, was on the whole necessary and constructive. One has only to read Renan's *Liberté de penser* articles in their entirety to appreciate the value of Henriette's promptings of his literary conscience. Even *L'avenir de la science* seems mild, orderly, and stylistically correct beside them. Phrases like *"indécrottables Allemands," "sottises débitées par des sots," "admirable déchiffrement d'un superstitieux hiéroglyphisme,"* with a faint ring of Léon Bloy about them, abound, and many passages (see, e.g., *LP*, III, 442) seem in fact to be imitations of the worst prose of Victor Hugo. To read this untamed French is of course also an excellent way of cutting through the shell of classical perfection which too many literary historians have foisted on the living, developing, complex organism of Renan's style. The author of the

Vie de Jésus was not born with a silver style in his mouth.

The lesson received from the great historian of the Merovingians and the Norman Conquest, Augustin Thierry, was somewhat more profound. He was, for Renan, "a true spiritual father" (*SEJ*, II, 906).[30] The two men first met in 1852, when Thierry was fifty-seven. He had been blind since 1826, and Renan was one of the young scholars who assisted him in continuing his research. Besides winning Renan's veneration as a saint of scholarship who had given his eyesight in the service of what he called "the passion for history," Thierry made a deep impression on the younger historian with his ideal of history as both art and science, as drama based on materials provided by a sincere and scrupulous scholarly method.[31] Thierry also guided Renan toward a prose style which was greatly to surpass his own in beauty. He taught correctness and vigor, eloquence without false oratory, a sense of the proper economy of colorful details—above all, the value of constant revision. There is even an interesting parallel between his own revision of articles he had written as a young journalist in the *Censeur européen* and the *Courrier français*, fighting for Saint-Simon's socialism, and Renan's revision of his essays for the *Liberté de penser*. He too had had to purge himself of heavy, angry dogmatism and seek calm for his youthful style, marked by feverish ardor, "a superabundance of will which often went far beyond the desired goal." [32]

But most important of all, he confirmed Renan in his growing belief in the seriousness and integrity of literary form. Observing Thierry at work from such a close standpoint must have been an unforgettable experience. Style with this master, as Renan tells us, was much more than the adornment of one's thought: it was the very means of defining thought. "He held to his opinion only when he had given it through the labor of style the utmost degree of measure and clarity" (*EMC*, II, 106). All allowance being made, one seems to hear Maupassant speaking of Flaubert: "That humble part of literary labor, which consists above all of softening and effacing, a task so little understood by persons inexperienced in these matters, who cannot imagine how much it costs art to conceal itself—this was the part he loved most" (*EMC*, II, 103–104). It was the most difficult part of the writer's discipline which Renan learned from Thierry perhaps more than from any other person— the mastery of an expansive and aggressive ego in the interests of that truer expression of self known as art.

Renan's evolution from the undisciplined *verdeur* of the *Liberté de penser* (and of course *L'avenir de la science*) to the balanced, refined prose of *Averroès* and the *Etudes d'histoire religieuse* has one other important aspect, and once again it is the *Cahiers de jeunesse* which provides the clue. A curious debate between two sides of Renan's nature runs through that work, suggesting that his literary development was closely related to the development of his attitude toward eclecticism. This philosophical method, associated with Cousin, consisted of reviewing all the existing systems of philosophy and then composing a synthesis of the positive contributions made by each. It was a method which both attracted and repelled Renan. "There are two ways of judging," he wrote, "absolutely, eclectically: sometimes I use one, sometimes the other, and it would be very hard for me to restrict myself to either" (*CJ*, p. 415). He felt most dissatisfied with the eclectic approach whenever he was compelled to express his thought with strength and vivacity, or, as he put it, to fix theories, "even false theories," in neat, clear-cut compartments and to thrust them out in a blaze of fire (*CJ*, p. 365). He needed to affirm and to deny, to praise and to denounce, more sharply than eclecticism would permit. This was precisely the spirit in which he wrote his first essays. From this perspective, eclecticism appeared to be "an all-absorbing gulf." He formulated against it a complaint which, many years later, worded differently but with the same key verb, "*émousser*," he was to suggest might be directed against his own work (*AS*, preface, III, 718). Of the eclectic approach he wrote in the *Cahiers:*

If we followed the eclectic point of view, we would succeed, for fear of making mistakes, in *blunting the edge* (*émousser*) of all propositions, and in blunting still further what had already been dulled, our pretext being that we must eliminate all exaggeration. What miserable results that would bring, without force, without vivacity, without physiognomy! I prefer the frank and firm manner which grows warm and takes fire. There is much error in it, but also much truth, while in the other there is nothing [*CJ*, p. 342].[33]

Yet, another lobe of Renan's brain persisted in asking certain questions: Is not the world too complex a thing to be sliced into categories? Are not some things simply without well-defined "physiognomies"? Nature, he noted, apropos of Delafosse's lesson in mineralogy, resembles less a set of pigeonholes than a painting in which the colors vary in a thousand ways, with imperceptible nuances (*CJ*, p. 200). The very distinction between truth and error may be a matter of nuances. To register these, Cousin's method alone seemed adequate, and Renan decided to accept it with reservations, not as a definitive philosophy but as a kind of guarantee of the sense of historical relativity, a working principle in the search for truth (*NCJ*, pp. 35–36).

Most critics of Renan have assumed that he himself fell very early into the "all-absorbing gulf" of eclecticism which had caused an earlier, more tragic victim to lament: "When you believe in everything, you believe in nothing" (Gérard de Nerval, in *Aurélia*). Even in the ripest phase of his disillusionment, however, as we shall see, Renan's skepticism may not have been quite as all-absorbing as is often claimed. Actually there were always at least two Renans. There was the Renan who, for the *Liberté de penser*, satisfied his urge to wield the clear-cut opinion, the well-formulated ridicule. This was the absolutist, the dogmatist, the passionate and trenchant idealist, toned down in the revised essays but preserved intact in *L'avenir de la science*. This was the writer who, from first to last, had an incurable fondness for the adjectives "*sot*" and "*niais*." This was the polemicist, little-known but every bit as authentic as the doctor of nuances and the preacher of "gentle vaporous sermons" (as Barrès called them). This aggressive Renan will reappear during the war and postwar years, in many a provoking page of his historical work, in venomously satirical passages of the *Drames philosophiques*, and above all, in a work marked with a resurgence of the anticlericalism of 1848–1850, *La réforme intellectuelle et morale*. The other Renan, not necessarily more characteristic, though certainly better known, is the subtle historian, gifted (or perhaps cursed) with the ability to understand contradictory points of view, never insisting too forcefully on his own, apparently reluctant to define it too sharply.

In the phase of his career under study, Renan had arrived at a kind of compromise between the absolute and the eclectic points of view. He had his own beliefs and they were firm enough; but in discovering a more subtle literary form, he had found the way to express them without the appearance of dogmatism. This seems to me to be the real significance of the revisions of his early essays. "Les historiens critiques de Jésus" furnishes an especially striking example: in that essay, as he reworked it, he presents a delicately organized series of divergent perspectives, namely, the interpretations of Jesus offered by various Biblical critics; in each of these theories he recognizes some merit, but each he judges finally in the light of his own viewpoint, and this viewpoint is not so much explicitly stated as suggested by the very shape and rhythm of his prose.

Of this new art of criticism, now awaiting our closer scrutiny, the first product destined by Renan for a wider public than he had been able to reach through his *Averroès* was to be his first book of essays, the *Etudes d'histoire religieuse.*

Chapter 3

Orpheus in the
Revue des deux mondes

"Once again there will be an Orpheus and a Trismegistus."–
L'avenir de la science

IN OUR age of specialization the *Etudes d'histoire religieuse* is likely to appear old-fashioned in its breadth and sweep: it ranges over the religions of antiquity, the history of Israel, critical works on the life of Jesus, Mohammedanism, the saints' lives, the *Imitation of Christ*, Calvin, Unitarianism, neo-Hegelianism and modern German religious thought, and "The Temptation of Christ," a painting by Ary Scheffer. It would seem that to judge such a volume competently, at least as religious history, would require either a team of specialists or someone with the learning of a Toynbee. However, we general readers should not abdicate our critical duties so easily: to do this would be to misunderstand the very purpose of the book, which was written for us to begin with—or rather, for our nineteenth-century counterparts, the educated but nonspecialist readers of the *Revue des deux mondes* and many other magazines like it, the media of an extraordinary movement of enlightenment. Renan's book bears witness to an immense creative activity in historical scholarship and a widespread dissemination of learning. The nineteenth century was a golden age of scholarship, marked by genius both for precise research of a highly specialized kind and for those vast theories and daring hypotheses which lead to the conquest of whole new realms of knowledge. Little wonder it was often compared to the Renaissance: its great scholars in Germany, France, England, and elsewhere reinterpreted Greek mythology and religion, created Egyptology, discovered Sanskrit literature, revolutionized the study of the Old and the New Testaments. As the Protestant historian Albert Réville proudly and happily observed, Plato was being interpreted in Melbourne, Moses in Canton, and there were Greek statues in New York and at least twenty chairs in European universities devoted to Sanskrit.[1]

Renan was a specialist, as was Taine, whose *Essais de critique et d'histoire* appeared the same year as the *Etudes*. The one felt most at home in Hebrew philology and the other in literary history and the fine arts (already an intolerably broad "area of competence" by modern standards). It was a work of Renan—his translation, with commentary, of the Book of Job (1859)—which served as the springboard for Réville's enthusiastic survey of the renaissance of religious studies in France. But Renan and Taine (and we might add Sainte-Beuve, whose history of Port-Royal had been a magnificent contribution to the renaissance) were also moved by an emotion not very conspicuous in present-day specialists—the eagerness to communicate their knowledge to a wide audience. Specialization was for them only one duty of the scholar; the other was the transmission of knowledge to interested persons, some of whom may have become interested because the scholar himself knew how to win them to his subject. One can understand their eagerness; it seems to have been a widespread virtue of learned men in the last century. The learned world was teeming with exciting ideas about man's spiritual history: theories of the comparison and interrelation of religions, of the supposed origin of European peoples in ancient India, of the nature of Christ and the Sacred Scriptures. A great laboratory for observing newly created religions existed in America. Once we have caught this spirit, we are less likely to accuse Renan and Taine of "dilettantism" or to condemn them when they were superficial—which was seldom. Even in their more foolhardy ventures, such as their essays on Buddhism, it was not dilettantism which inspired them, but a generous will to inform, a sense of the mission to enlighten.

The word which suggests itself for this activity is "vulgarization." The English word, however, often used pejoratively to suggest cheapness and error, is much more misleading than the French "*vulgarisation*," which has been enriched by a long tradition of fine books making technical knowledge accessible to a literate public. French scholars are much less prone than English or American to doubt that a scholar can be readable without being superficial.[2] "Popularization" is not a pleasant word as serious scholars speak it; "despecialization" is ugly and too negative; to find an English term accurately describing the difficult art practiced by Renan, we must turn to Matthew Arnold:

The great men of culture are those who have had a passion for diffusing, for making prevail, for carrying from one end of society to the other, the best knowledge, the best ideas of their time; who have laboured to divest knowledge of all that was harsh, uncouth, difficult, abstract, professional, exclusive; to humanise it, to make it efficient outside the clique of the cultivated and the learned, yet still remaining the *best* knowledge and thought of the time, and a true source, therefore, of sweetness and light.[3]

Light, in Renan's work, alternates with clouds of mist, but with that reservation, he fulfills magnificently Arnold's definition of the humanizer of knowledge. In doing so, he also fulfills one of the traditional and most valuable functions of the essayist.

He was aware of the dangers involved, especially when *vulgarisation* touches on religious problems: one cannot solve the most profound mystery in human experience—the nature of Jesus—in a few pages; readers cannot be inoculated with the critical sense in a single hour. Nevertheless, "to elevate and cultivate the minds of others, to vulgarize the great results of the natural and philological sciences, is the only means of winning understanding and acceptance for the new ideas of criticism" (*EHR*, p. 203; cf. *AS*, III, 965). The true vulgarizer should not be confused with the kind of journalist-middleman between scholar and public, who too often distorts and debases serious learning. The true vulgarizer is the scholar himself.

Renan realized that not all of his colleagues were capable of humanizing knowledge. His attitude toward "scribbling compilers" has changed a bit since the *Nouvelles lettres intimes:* in his reflections on the future of science, he wonders what good a monograph is if its only reader is its author, but in the same work he also calls for monographs on "all the points of science," however limited, as the chief task of the nineteenth century and urges philosophers to draw upon such works as the source of their thought (*AS*, III, 915, 919). Knowledge will be best pursued in an "intellectual community" of scholars, thinkers, and *gens du monde* (*AS*, III, 910; *DFP*, I, 700–701). Even hacks and drudges he generously allows a place in the vast collective enterprise of learning, for theirs are "services rendered to humanity by mediocre minds" (*AS*, III, 1273). Even pedants he paradoxically defends, in Chapter XIII of *L'avenir de la science*, against attacks by such professed enemies of learning as Montaigne, Molière, and Malebranche. But his own ideal was the scholar skilled in both original research and the art of interpreting it to the public (*QC*, I, 124). With all his imperfections, he came closer to realizing this ideal than anyone else of his century.

What were the secrets of the art of humanizing learning as Renan practiced it in the *Etudes d'histoire religieuse?* He furnishes part of the answer in his preface. First of all, one had to read many technical, erudite works, which make up the "*appareil de démonstration,*" the "scaffolding"; then one had to summarize them in a manner both attractive and critical. These essays, consequently, like a great many nineteenth-century essays, took the form of book reviews, but once again the English term is misleading: these were not the mechanically ground out scraps of hybrid matter which fill our periodicals, but small works of art, original essays, using the book to be judged as their point of departure. Renan makes an important distinction between the *compte rendu*, more closely resembling our contemporary book review, though sturdier in quality, and the *article de revue*, at its best a true essay. In two *études* of a more complex character, "Les religions de l'antiquité" and "Les historiens critiques de Jésus," he shows his fundamentally eclectic turn of mind: he surveys a series of books, a whole field, briefly and then seeks to resolve whatever contradictions exist by means of an original compromise. Here the essay became for him, very significantly, the expression of what he believed to be the basic intellectual temperament of France—"a mean between opposing qualities, a compromise between extremes, something clear, simple, temperate" (*EHR*, p. 50).

It took a man of Renan's creative gifts to exploit the literary possibilities hidden in the form of the *article de revue*. In narrating the progress of erudition in a given field, for example, he uses the clash of ideas and his attempted resolution of conflict in order to produce dramatic effects. Creuzer's interpretation of Greek myths was theological and philosophical in nature and traced their source to Oriental mysticism; the counterinterpretation of Lobeck was rationalist and anticlerical, reducing myths to meaningless play devoid of religious substance. Renan, following his principal source, Joseph-Daniel Guigniaut, the highly original interpreter of Creuzer's work in France, proposes that Greek myths, and even more the Greek "mysteries," reveal deeply religious aspirations expressed in spontaneous esthetic forms ("Les religions de l'antiquité"). Through the concise, clear narrative prose there also plays a delightful wit, exercised often at the expense of scholars whose theories, and sometimes whose names, lend themselves to gentle satire. To show how great a pioneer of mythological studies Guigniaut had been in France, Renan remarks that when the translator of the *Symbolik und Mythologie der alten Völker* appeared on the scene, "M. Petit-Radel was still expatiating gravely on the adventures of the cow Io and drawing up synoptic tables of Helen's lovers, with their ages in relation to that of *cette princesse*" (*EHR*, p. 4).

Even sharper strokes of wit are directed at "higher criticism," and this may surprise many readers. We know how much Renan himself owed to this systematic attempt on the part of German scholars to explain miraculous events in Scripture in terms of "simple and natural facts." Witness his suggestion that the raising of Lazarus was a pious fraud or his belief that St. Paul's vision on the road to Damascus was due to sunstroke. However, that Renan felt the rationalist school of Biblical critics (Johann Eichhorn and others) went far beyond the bounds or reason, he makes clear simply by accumulating examples of their so-called explanations: the radiance of Moses on Sinai caused by the heat of "great overexcitement"; the angel seen by Zachary a mere cloud of incense and beams from altar lamps; and their culminating effort—the Ascension explained "by the hypothesis of a mist in which Jesus was able to slip adroitly away and steal down the side of the mountain" (*EHR*, pp. 143–145). Renan also owed much to Strauss, whose *Das Leben Jesu* (1835, translated into French by Emile Littré, 1839), while not exactly denying the historical existence of Jesus, seemed to make him disappear in myth and abstraction. But it would be a serious error to think Renan swallowed Strauss whole.[4] At one point in the essay, by a more subtle form of *reductio ad absurdum* than the ones already mentioned, he twists his French into an amusing pastiche of the famous Biblical scholar's ponderous Hegelian Christology (*EHR*, p. 159).

It is not only by writing of scholarly progress with wit and narrative skill that Renan enlivens his essays in religious history. By arranging them within the book with an eye to thematic structure, he gives them additional beauty. They are held together by what Marcel Proust referred to in Stendhal's work as "the great bone framework of style" (*"la grande ossature du style"*).

Is this not stretching a point? The *études* were written over a period of six years for three different periodicals. Hallowed as the custom may be, are such collected essays ever a "book" in any sense other than pages between a single cover? Renan pondered this question in his preface; it seemed to him that such works sin necessarily against "the rules of composition and the laws of unity" (p. ii). In this case, the collection made a much less artificial ensemble than he feared it might. Each of the *études* can be read independently—one of the essential charms of the book of essays has always been that one may browse in it. Except for the two originating in the *Liberté de penser,* which were thoroughly revised, there is no evidence Renan sought to adapt them to a new pattern. Yet, read from cover to cover, the book presents not a mechanical or superficial unity, but a well-defined ensemble. This ability to give his essays complete autonomy and at the same time the quality of belonging to a larger whole which enriches their meaning is one of the most striking features of Renan's art.

At least three major interrelated themes may be defined in the *Etudes d'histoire religieuse:* the conception of a *sentiment religieux* underlying all religious creeds; the belief that to understand how religions originated is to understand religion; the belief that a form of poetic intuition is the best method for this historical pursuit. I shall first outline these themes and then focus in more detail upon two outstanding and contrasting examples of individual essays.

However genuine Renan's Catholic fervor seems once to

have been, one suspects that he had a hidden predisposition toward a loosely defined notion of religion. The feeling became ingrained in him that well-defined creeds are an obstacle, not a means, to true religious faith. This once privileged Catholic, who had stood on the threshold of the priesthood, lost sight of the experience of centuries of Catholicism, namely, that revelation has the power to nourish piety; precise belief, to fortify prayer; and dogma, to strengthen faith. It had become the fashion in his day to speak of the "death" of dogmas and to write resounding funeral orations for them.[5] Théophile Gautier, in his poem "L'art," published the same year as the *Etudes d'histoire religieuse*, went so far as to proclaim that the gods themselves die. Renan himself later declared in his "Prière sur l'Acropole," that "the gods pass like men, nor would it be good for them to be eternal" (*SEJ*, II, 759).

Renan's mind had been formed in too traditional a religious manner, however, for him to admit Gautier's and Flaubert's parallel discovery, that there is only one truly immortal religion—Art. He was convinced he had found in the history of religion itself a force great enough to survive the death of specific forms of religious belief: this was the universal, age-old aspiration of men toward an unknown, perhaps an unknowable, God. The image of humanity itself at worship became, as humanity in pursuit of the perfect earthly society and perfect knowledge had become for Auguste Comte and the early socialists, the object of his worship. For this rock-bottom, imperishable religious sensibility of mankind, he uses a phrase common enough in French but not easy to translate into English: the *sentiment religieux*. It was the distinction, dear also to Victor Hugo, between *"les religions"* and *"la religion."* Dogmas and creeds, rites and symbols, he thought were at best gropings toward an inexpressible truth, inevitable attempts to represent reality, but condemned to be imperfect representations, vague foreshadowings. "All here below is but symbol and dream" —"Tout n'est ici-bas que symbole et que songe" (*SEJ*, II, 759; *Saint Paul*, p. iii). Definitions of truth would pass; only the search for truth has anything approaching an absolute existence.

The epilogue of Renan's religious thought will show, I think, that his theory of the *sentiment religieux* was little more than a well-meaning rationalization for the absence of positive religious conviction. Nevertheless, in this early work he develops the theme clearly, firmly, hoping thereby not to weaken religious feeling in his time, but to elevate and purify it (*EHR*, p. xviii). Let us not allow the shadow of a later Renan, the ambiguous, irreverent juggler of ideas, to fall across these first essays and trouble their serious and affirmative character. The whole book is intended as proof of the existence of the *sentiment religieux*, from the Greek mystery rites across several thousand years to Boston and William Ellery Channing in his Unitarian pulpit. Not only does Renan affirm the existence of this "integral part of human nature . . . true in its essence . . . the obvious sign of man's superior destiny" (*EHR*, p. xviii); he also, in the best tradition of Rousseau and Kant, affirms its indestructibility, for it bears within its own certitude, which reason can neither fortify nor weaken (*EHR*, p. 37).

This search for a permanent substratum beneath transitory, shifting religious systems is obviously an eclectic approach, inspired in great part by Cousin's approach to philosophical systems. For his second major theme Renan similarly adapts another outstanding motif of romantic scholarship, the exploration of origins. With Renan this becomes a distinct bias in favor of ancient religious forms as against modern. He seems to be saying: Outside the obscure origins of religion, there is no salvation.

A curious fact strikes us about the progression of the *Etudes d'histoire religieuse* when we read it from beginning to end: the passages of deeper conviction, of poetic feeling, are largely in the first three essays, those on the religions of Greek antiquity, the history of Israel, and the life of Christ. Beginning with Mohammed, we detect a down-hill movement. With Mohammedanism, Renan is much too concerned with the "machinery" behind religious creation, the admixture of *politique*, to feel much respect for the content of faith. As for modern Christianity, his "Vie des Saints" suggests that saints of poetic grandeur, of rugged creative force (and not merely good saints), stopped being produced somewhere between Ignatius Loyola and Vincent de Paul. Much delicate humor, much irony work their way into the essays on medieval and modern Christianity, but there is almost no poetic feeling. At the most we find something not quite so specifically religious as his earlier effort to commune historically with powerful and mysterious creative forces in religion: we find a certain vague idealism (*EHR*, p. 423). The fact seems to be that Renan had little enthusiasm for forms of religious life dating much later than early Christianity—with some exceptions, such as St. Francis of Assisi. The risings and fallings of his enthusiasm explain in great part the variations in tone of his prose: it has a poetic quality when he writes of the mysteries of Adonis or the Hebrew prophets, assumes a dry critical air when he discusses the authorship of the *Imitation of Christ*, and turns to ironic humor when he accuses Channing of the grave sin of lacking esthetic sense.

In exalting the so-called *"âges spontanés"* of religious history, the *"homme spontané,"* Renan was carrying on the tradition he had learned from such explorers of origins as Burnouf (ancient Hindu culture), Thierry (the Franks), Fauriel (Provence), and Ozanam (the Celts and the early European church). The *Etudes d'histoire religieuse* touches in essay form on the vast theme of the "embryology of the human spirit" he had sketched out in *L'avenir de la science* and was to make the subject of his major works, the *Histoire des origines du christianisme* and the *Histoire du peuple d'Israël*. His interest in this theme was a scholarly form of romantic primitivism: we should recall that the word "primitive" in Renan's time embraced not only the uncivilized peoples studied by modern anthropologists but also cultures we would consider refined indeed, those of Greek, Hebrew, and Christian antiquity. But primitivism was much more than a bookish theme with him; it was part of his personal and ethnic heritage. Deep in his childhood lay an intimate experience of the mysterious primitive landscape of Brittany, an experience which his later studies and reading were merely to make articulate. "I have seen the primitive world," he declared. Indeed it lay all round him as a child, in the fourteenth- and fifteenth-century towns, the countryside with its traces of fifth- and sixth-century Welsh emigration, the pagan vestiges of the Laplanders; he heard its legends from his mother and treated them with the same mixture of Breton respect and Gascon skepticism which she put into her telling of them (*SEJ*, II, 766–767).

In the obscure origins of its religious experience, then,

lie the clues to the understanding of mankind. The importance of myths and symbols in this light is immense: they are the records of primitive religious experience, the records of man's first dreams of "a world beyond the senses" (*AS*, III, 940). Renan attacked vigorously the popular eighteenth-century thesis (of which Eméric David was a contemporary spokesman) that primitive myths were, at best, allegories with keys to explain every point and, at worst, absurd attempts of irrational men to think according to the rationalist logic of the Abbé de Condillac—which was assumed to be the only logic men had ever used. Symbols, Renan argued, were sometimes created before their precise meaning was realized, and myths were more likely to be the spontaneous expression of deep, perhaps subconscious, spiritual longings (*EHR*, pp. 11–12). But if rationalism is out of its depth in interpreting primitive myths and symbolism, how *can* we understand them? "Full of life, meaning, and truth for the peoples who breathed a soul into them, they have become for us little more than dead letters, sealed hieroglyphs; created by the simultaneous effort of all the faculties acting in perfect harmony, they are no more for us than curious objects of analysis" (*EHR*, p. 6).

Renan's solution to this enigma leads us to the third major theme of his book, and here again his debt to romanticism was great. "The essence of criticism," he once wrote, in a memorable definition, "is to know how to understand states very different from that in which we live" (*SEJ*, II, 766). He made this remark, appropriately enough, about the strange Breton environment which had awakened his historical sense to the sights and sounds of worlds long dead. The historian will acquire this penetrating sympathy only by virtue of a kind of intuition, of divination, familiar enough to the poet and the artist. Renan was all the more convinced of this since he believed that at the core of religion itself is poetry, even though it may be what Matthew Arnold called "unconscious poetry." [6] Had not the author of *Le génie du christianisme* supplied overwhelming proof that the strongest part of religion is its poetry? For all the severity with which he treated Chateaubriand's faulty erudition, naïve interpretation of Scriptures, and "immodest" style,[7] Renan never questioned the Chateaubriand equation: religion equals the most sublime form of poetry.

Scholarly and critical abilities are not enough for the historian who seeks to understand the childhood of humanity, to reach the remote source of its religious experience. With such abilities, he may establish accurate texts, evaluate inscriptions, determine chronology, and the like. But to understand the poetic spirit of irrational or prerational religions, one must be part poet; one must be able to feel oneself into them (*"einfühlen,"* to use Herder's term); one must possess what Renan calls "an understanding of the naïve" (*"une intelligence du naïf"*).[8] All that appears absurd in Greek myths or even in the visions of Hebrew prophets; all their "angles, contradictions, and harshnesses," will take on meaning when the historian has added unto himself the poet. This is probably what Renan had in mind when he declared, in his essay on Scheffer's "La tentation du Christ," that "art appears to be the highest degree of criticism" (*EHR*, p. 431). Artistic intuition is the highest step on the ladder of historical scholarship and criticism.

To turn now from general themes to particular essays, two *études* reveal especially well the richly interwoven patterns of Renan's scholarly and poetic thought, as it is applied to two completely different types of *sentiment religieux.* These essays are "Les religions de l'antiquité" and "L'histoire du peuple d'Israël." They have the further interest of illustrating some fundamental points about Renan's esthetics in general.

The first, which deals above all with ancient Greek religions, opens, as do most of his essays, with an introductory section placing the subject on a large background; in this case it is mythology in general and the value of studying it. The prose is in the restrained "grand manner" characteristic of his introductions, soberly eloquent, a bit vague. Certain concrete associations may arise from the Biblical "Man does not live by bread alone," but most of the abstract phrases— "the commonplace nature of life," "a world of superior intuitions and disinterested pleasures," "the portion of the ideal," phrases which make up the backbone of Renan's vocabulary—have lost much of the forcefulness they may have had for his nineteenth-century readers, living in the midst of growing industrialism. We feel less than they did, in the vague refinement and idealism of the style itself, an expression of reaction against an increasingly materialistic and utilitarian society.

This overture is followed by a brief tribute to the pioneer work of Creuzer and Guigniaut: the prose is now concise and witty, scholarly yet engaging. Then, in the course of some critical remarks on the excessively rationalistic tendencies of Creuzer as an interpreter of myths, the style changes once again, this time more significantly and in a very subtle fashion, perhaps beginning with the sentence: "One would need a soul filled with poetry in order to grasp the intense joy which the man of these races [the first Indo-Hellenic peoples] felt initially in the presence of nature and of himself" (*EHR*, p. 14). Renan will shortly resume his narrative thread of the discoveries, theories, and disputes of various Hellenic scholars, his critical control of the historical picture; but for the moment he has taken up another thread, the task of understanding the "*aperçus délicats*," the "*impressions fugitives*" of myths, some of which even ancient Greek scholars themselves had found unintelligible. A new accent appears, suggested gradually by an increase in visual elements, by the brief evocations of Venus and the sea and Bacchus in his flowing robe and Oriental mitre. What follows is not intended as a purple passage but as an application of a valid historical method, the intuitive approach to the poetic content of the myths themselves.

The climax of this movement is reached in a striking page on the myth, or rather the complexity of myths, of Glaucus, the melancholy puckered-up old god of the mariners. It seems like a purely personal bit of poetic meditation; actually, the essayist, drawing for scholarly substance upon a very technical article by one of Guigniaut's collaborators in the *Annales de l'Institut archéologique*, has created a passage of literary beauty as well as historical insight.[9] He has, first, attempted to recapture some of the wonder and awe of a humble Greek fisherman before the spectacle of the sea. He alludes discreetly to his own childhood—"*ceux qui ont passé leur enfance sur les bords de la mer*"—and we may recall that his father, a merchant sea captain, probably disappeared at sea when Renan was a boy.

However, what is uppermost in his mind is the imagined experience of an ancient Greek mariner, and from this point of view the outstanding effect of the passage is the delicate blending of two things: on the one hand, colors and forms, sensuous qualities, "*impressions*," and on the other, moral or spiritual states and beliefs, in words like "*désespoir*," "*malheur*," "*immortalité.*" This total effect corresponds perfectly with his view of Greek religion as a mixture of sensuality and spirituality, of esthetic play and moral strivings; the same effect is achieved in a later passage describing the cult of Adonis (*EHR*, p. 55). Stylistically, the "humble myth" of Glaucus calls for, and receives from Renan's hands, a deliberately simple type of eloquence: humble colloquial phrases such as "*pauvres gens*" and "*gens de mer,*" foreshortened rhythm rather than an oratorical period. In the last two sentences the loose rambling structure is well adapted to the impression Renan wishes to leave with us, that of the curious amalgamation of different branches making up the central myth. One might reasonably object to one phrase, "the long ennui of a certainty exhausting itself in its struggle with sophism" (striking in itself as an unconscious foreshadowing of Renan's later work), as too sophisticated a form of disillusionment for a primitive Greek sailor. On the whole, however, he has taken care to respect the historical content, limited though it may be, of the myth of Glaucus; he has given us not a somewhat arbitrary Gothic prayer over Greece, as will be the case with his "Prière sur l'Acropole," but a small, genuine enough vision.

One aspect of this essay calls for more extensive comment, its sensuous nature. Except for a long, wildly imaginative, lavishly colorful description of the miraculous birth of Çakya-Mouni (the Buddha) in the essay on Mohammedanism, recalling Flaubert's *Tentation de Saint-Antoine*, there is more of a feast for the mind's eye in "Les religions de l'antiquité" than anywhere else in the book. And when we view Renan's essays as a whole, these and a few other pieces appear as rare islands of color in an atmosphere which, despite Renan's reputation for bewitchingly sensuous prose rhythms, is predominantly moral and spiritual in nature.

The reason for this seeming contradiction is worth developing. Renan's historical work in general did not provide anything like the generous role allotted to colorful detail, to *coloris*, by Michelet, Chateaubriand, or Flaubert. The most famous, the most romantic, but in many ways the least characteristic of his historical books, the *Vie de Jésus*, of course makes use of "local color" in a manner nothing less than revolutionary in the writing of Biblical history. Yet even that work he spent a year simply toning down and chastening, to rid it of glittering pendants and tinsel (*"pendeloques"* and *"clinquants"*—*SEJ*, II, 898). Color as he uses it in *Les apôtres*, in *Saint Paul*, and in other less-known volumes of his Judeo-Christian panorama assumes a clearly subordinate role; it becomes instrumental in the achievement of the principal effect he seeks to create—the sense of spiritual life in great moral heroes, whether they be individual or collective. In much the same manner as Henriette when she contemplated famous Near-Eastern sites, he tried to extract from historical documents not mere local color but "the soul, the idea, the general impression." [10]

The year in which the *Etudes d'histoire religieuse* appeared—1857—is an unforgettable date in the development of that search for beauty and truth in the documented, tangible material world to which we refer as realism, but which was also once known as *"sensualisme."* It is the year of *Madame Bovary*, the continuing controversy over Courbet's paintings, the first essays of Taine, the first projects of Claude Bernard in a field literary artists were increasingly exploiting, the field of experimental medicine. Yet to approach Renan from the angle of realism is to make little progress in understanding him. Like Baudelaire, whose *Fleurs du mal* also appeared in 1857, he had little sympathy for realism. He was a nineteenth-century Platonist, a spiritualist, trained to the Catholic priesthood and to the end a lay priest of idealism. It is hardly a surprise to find many objections against realism scattered throughout his work, the most incisive of which are concentrated in his essay on Thierry and directed against realism in history. The artificial application of local color he calls the novice's way of making up for his lack of the *"art savant"* which knows how to arrange facts in the most vivid way (*EMC*, II, 103). He perceived very astutely that realism, by seeking to share the power acquired by the new art of photography, would only condemn itself to all the limitations of photography. The so-called "scientific" presentation of facts in history is like photography and can show us nothing but inanimate lines; the true historical imagination is like engraving, which can reveal the most intimate spiritual reality (*EMC*, II, 102).

Renan's objection to materialism in any form of art, whether painting, architecture, or prose, will remain a firm, consistent stand with him. It will be expressed in his essay on Counter Reformation Italian art, especially Jesuit art, which he calls *"réalisme dévot,"* contrasting its misguided attempt to honor God by the sheer weight of material detail with the moral symbolism of Gothic art.[11] It will be the subject of many a lively discussion with Flaubert and Sainte-Beuve during the famous dinners at the Restaurant Magny, Renan maintaining against Flaubert that color is only an accessory serving to throw into relief a "principal fact" which ordinarily must be of a moral nature.[12] Although too polite a critic to say so, there is no doubt he felt that both these authors abused concrete details. For him, the primary aim of prose was not to reproduce the object so that it can almost be touched and smelled on the printed page, but to introduce the soul of his reader into a moral atmosphere and to acquaint him with certain moral facts.

In this light, the last of the *Etudes d'histoire religieuse*, "La Tentation du Christ par Ary Scheffer," [13] has special importance: through his analysis of this painting, Renan presents us indirectly with a credo of his own spiritualist esthetics. He first admits that he cannot speak for the technical aspects of the work and that some viewers may regret that the execution is not more vigorous and the coloring more brilliant; but he goes on to defend Scheffer by saying that since his intention is to render idea and feeling, "too much body," too sharp a delineation or too brilliant a coloring, would have been out of place. Such artifices, in any case, are for those who "speak to the eyes when they cannot speak to the soul" (*EHR*, p. 432). Renan exaggerates the stature of this painter,[14] for much the same reason that he exaggerates the greatness of George Sand as a novelist: his artistic taste and judgment were easily carried away by his idealistic bias. His essay on Scheffer remains, nevertheless, extremely significant, not only as a quiet manifesto against materialism and sensualism in art, against realism, but because it reveals a seldom-mentioned pictorial source of his own ideal of vague spirituality in art.

Perhaps the most successful attempt in the *Etudes d'histoire religieuse* to "speak to the soul" is "L'histoire du peuple d'Israël." In this essay, as in so many others, much of our pleasure is of a simple kind and derives from Renan's skill as a master *vulgarisateur:* from the provocative wit with which he brings Old Testament figures closer to the modern world (David the *condottiere*, the prophets as forerunners of political journalists, the Book of Daniel as the first essay in the philosophy of history) or from the colloquial vigor of parts of the narrative (e.g., the harem intrigues of Bathsheba). There is a strikingly human, dramatic touch in the conclusion, where we glimpse Israel for the last time through the eyes of an old Jew in the archives of the Bibliothèque Nationale. But more subtle pleasures are to be found in the curiously poetic quality of the essay, by which I mean not so much the long passage from Isaiah woven into the text (*EHR*, pp. 117–118) or the rhythm of individual paragraphs as the rhythm of the whole essay, the extraordinary sense it gives the reader of irresistible forward movement.

Taking Heinrich von Ewald's *Geschichte des Volkes Israel* (1854) as his point of departure, Renan encompasses in sixty pages the major events in the history of the Jewish people. The engine spark that sets and keeps his essay moving is the theme of the "great dominant law of Jewish history," the law of struggle between liberal and conservative tendencies (*EHR*, pp. 128–129), the law of conflict between desire for political existence and political glory, and fidelity to a unique mission, the conservation of monotheism. Here we recognize in Renan a contemporary of Thierry and Taine and other formulators of "laws" intended to explain the evolution of peoples and literatures. With remarkable concision, he sketches the growth, the *devenir*, of the Jewish monotheistic mission; and just as he believes that Israel's chances of becoming a true political kingdom with a great profane literature were sacrificed to this spiritual mission, so he sacrifices personal reveries, odd facts, digressions, even metaphors,[15] in order to keep this mission clearly and constantly before our eyes. When we have reached the last page, we suddenly realize that we have been carried forward in one supreme direction by this obstinate, triumphant movement. As of Israel's history, so we may say of the essay itself that "the direction of its movement belonged by right to the prophets" (*EHR*, p. 106).

To the prophets also belong the most memorable poetic passages. The austere moral beauty of these spiritual giants, "blind according to the flesh, clairvoyant according to the spirit" (which is precisely what the essayist has tried to make himself), lends an unusual kind of spiritual color to the whole essay. One of the strongest tendencies of nineteenth-century French prose, as Lanson has pointed out, was to make the abstract term "productive of color and vision." [16] Victor Hugo had a special gift for this magic, and Renan knew many of its secrets.

Much of the beauty, for example, of an unusual passage of his essay, his evocation of the prophets standing on the ruins of Jerusalem,[17] may be explained in this light. Using hardly a single concrete detail, he has succeeded in creating the impression of life and vigor. He has done this partly by joining abstract words to words having some fleshliness: thus the object of "*battre en brèche*" is not "*murs*" or "*remparts*" as we might have expected, but "*la royauté*"; the verb "*exciter*" has two objects, the abstract noun "*puritanisme*" coupled with the concrete noun "*menaces.*" Israel's fate was that of all peoples consecrated to a single idea: they must "*promener leur martyre*" not "*à travers le monde,*" but (something more abstract) "*à travers les dédains du monde.*" In describing the prophets atop the remains of the city, Renan stimulates our retina up to a certain point—"On les vit sur les ruines de Jérusalem. . ."—but then he presents us with a picture in reality quite moral and invisible; we see these ghostly victors "maintenir leur obstination et tri-

Orpheus in the Revue des deux mondes

ompher presque des désastres qui réalisaient leurs prédictions."

This passage shows in concentrated, dramatic form the profoundly spiritualizing tendency of Renan's prose. The whole essay in this respect is more significant than the sensuous tribute to Greek religions: it points ahead to the *Essais de morale et de critique*. Before we turn to that work, some critical remarks on Renan's first book of essays will be appropriate.

A second edition before the year 1857 was out, others in the years following, translations into English, Spanish, Russian—all this attests to the success of the *Etudes d'histoire religieuse*. Lest we think this success was all due retroactively to the fame Renan acquired in 1863 with his *Vie de Jésus*, we should take note of a review in the *Journal des débats* by a fellow essayist, Prévost-Paradol. Common sense, of which he had a great fund, told Prévost-Paradol that Renan's reduction of the United States in the essay on Channing to a society of vegetarians and Unitarians was absurd, as was his willingness to exchange the whole country for one Italian town like Pisa. But once he had noted these flaws in critical perspective (and there are others he failed to note), he warmly admired "the clarity and force of the reasoning, the virile grace of the language"—a description worth remembering, since it reminds us once again that in this early stage there are few traces of effeminacy in Renan's style.

Prévost-Paradol, with fine discernment, singled out for special praise the unusual combination in Renan of scholar with artist and poet. Speaking for the nonspecialist in religious history, he welcomed this "happy art of interesting all cultivated minds in questions that seem to be the exclusive territory of scholars, questions of which scholars—though they are busy solving them—seem too often to overlook the greatness." [18] Half a century later a distinguished enemy of Renan will pay substantially the same tribute, declaring on behalf of his own generation (Barrès, Bourget, Faguet, Péguy, and others) that a single article by Renan on Mohammed or Buddhism taught them more than a whole laborious volume by the "venerable Barthélemy Saint-Hilaire." [19] What Brunetière took great pains to point out in fairness to the arch apostate—his originality in opening up to literature a whole new field, the field of scholarly religious history—has now become a commonplace of literary manuals.

A more interesting question is this: Almost a hundred years after its appearance, how does Renan's first work in religious history stand up under critical appraisal? To begin with, one thing should be clear, especially if we read the *Etudes d'histoire religieuse* on the background of developments in nineteenth-century historiography: when Renan urges the historian to cultivate a power of intuition and divination akin to the poet's and the artist's, he is not resorting to emotionalism or unwarranted subjectivity. We have to do here with a widespread nineteenth-century conception of historical method, according to which history is as much an art as a science. Far from being a matter of personal vagary, his view was partly derived from Thierry and Michelet and was related to views of Taine, of Macaulay and Carlyle in England, of Burckhardt in Switzerland, of Prescott in America. [20] Roughly since the turn of the century, this older view has been supplanted by the Rankean notion of history as factual, "objective," impersonal science; but recently it has been rehabilitated with great vigor by some outstanding contemporary historians.[21] However, would Renan's work have the right to share in any revival of history as both art and science? Granted he was a great artist, with the imaginative and literary qualities George Macaulay Trevelyan considers essential to the true historian. But was his scholarship trustworthy? This question has been raised by many of Renan's critics and has even gnawed at the consciences of some of his devout admirers. Is unreliable scholarship really his Achilles heel?

That such a question should ever have been raised ought to, but apparently does not, seem strange. Renan was one of the most learned men of the nineteenth century and one of the most learned men France has ever produced. But he was also a magnificent writer, and therein lies the difficulty. It must be admitted that the charge of many Catholic critics that he was a "prestidigitator of erudition," a "Houdini of religious polemics," is not too wide of the mark if we limit ourselves to the *Vie de Jésus.* The very real defects of that work—his unashamed projection of personal dreams into the interpretation, his apparent suppression of evidence running counter to his portrait of Jesus as a tender, charming idealist, his abuse of hypothesis—have created the impression that he was not really interested in accuracy and truth and have cast a shadow of doubt over all his historical work. Nevertheless, the testimony in favor of his competence as a scholar remains clearly preponderant. French and non-French historians alike, while pointing out in his work occasional errors of detail, theses no longer tenable, interpretations needing retouching by specialists, also recognize the firm foundation of his learning in many fields, his historian's instinct, his rare combination of scientific and artistic gifts, and, above all, his unusual powers of synthesis.[22]

Perhaps the most valuable testimony of all, because it comes from a methodologist one might have supposed contemptuous of all that Renan's "literary" history stood for, is the judgment of Charles Seignobos, who represented in France at the turn of the century the German-born "scientific" school of history. Seignobos reminds us that Renan came to the writing of history by way of one of the most highly specialized and exacting fields of scholarship, the Semitic branch of Oriental studies. "Linguist, archeologist, epigraphist, he had practiced all the highly technical callings which prepare the materials of the historian." And then Seignobos quotes the remark of the pioneer German historian of Rome, Theodor Mommsen, that "in spite of his beautiful style, Renan was a true scholar." [23] Lanson, with wonderful irony, has suggested that had Renan written badly no one would have raised any objections against his scholarship.[24]

We need not, then, be overly suspicious of Renan either as a historian or as a *vulgarisateur*. Nor should we read into the *Etudes d'histoire religieuse* any of the disturbing irreverence, the equivocations about religion, we find in the last phase of his writing. We need to distinguish very carefully between this book and the one masquerading as its sequel, the *Nouvelles études d'histoire religieuse* of 1884. Here there is no lightness of heart in regard to sacred things, but, on the contrary, an admirable moral intensity. To be sure, real undercurrents of skepticism flow through the work and will widen and push upward as the years go by. It will seem to many that in removing the supernatural from religion Renan removes the vital organs. But the *Etudes d'histoire religieuse* is in any case not the work of a true skeptic, much less the work of a nihilist. However sharply one may quarrel with the author's denial of the supernatural, one should recognize his conviction, here given "firm and frank expression" (*EHR*, p. xxvii), that man is an essentially religious animal and his serious purpose of defining the common religious experience underlying systems of worship throughout the ages.

The real weaknesses of the book lie elsewhere. Some of them may be put down to its relative immaturity, and they would include rash generalizations such as the astounding footnote (*EHR*, p. 200) dismissing Chinese culture as infantile or the facile paradoxes about Christian sensuousness and pagan Greek purity in the essay on Feuerbach. The generalization about the inherent monotheism of desert peoples was more of a fixed idea and was to engage Renan in lively controversy with his colleagues. A more serious weakness is the error in perspective which Renan owed to his bias in favor of the study of "origins." This scholarly primitivism satisfied his own very revealing taste for the ill-defined, the unintellectual in religion; it freed him as a historian from certain rationalistic preconceptions and helped him to understand ages in which religion was "the element in which all lived and moved" (Herder). But it also prevented him from doing justice to several centuries of more sophisticated religious experience. There seemed to him to be more poetry in the "*âges spontanés*," but the tendency to insist on poetic content as the criterion for judging religious movements blinded him to the virtues of religious "men of action" like Mohammed, Calvin, or Channing, none sensitive enough to beauty to please him. What further distorts his prejudiced portraits of Mohammed and many Protestant religious gen-

iuses, we might add, is his unproved assumption—which
even Catholics ought not to accept as such—that Catholicism is "the most religious of religions" (*EHR*, p. xxix).

The Catholic imprint may still seem strong in remarks
like this, but judging from the central thesis of the book, it
has faded almost completely, for what we have is neither
Catholicism nor any other recognizable form of supernatural
religion, nor indeed any established form of natural religion.
What we have is the new nineteenth-century religion of
humanity, which had come to life with Comte and Michelet, the socialists, and George Sand. A vaguely poetic *"sentiment religieux"* has replaced God as the object of Renan's
worship; or, rather, humanity in search of God has replaced
God. For who, Renan asks, made Christianity and theology
itself and everything of value, if not humanity? (*EHR*, p.
416). Even Jesus himself is but one of the sublime symbols
"humanity has chosen in order to remind itself of what it
is and to become intoxicated with its own image. There is
the living God, there is the one we must adore" (*EHR*,
p. 215). Is this not, we might ask, the basic flaw of Renan's
thought in the *Etudes d'histoire religieuse?* Has he really
fulfilled his avowed and sincere purpose of "purifying" religion, or has he tried to purify his wine by adding water
to it?

In judging the thought of this book, however, we should
remind ourselves that it is not a systematic exposition of religious philosophy, but a collection of essays in religious
history. I have tried to show how closely linked historical
interpretation and literary form are in two of the most successful essays, "Les religions de l'antiquité" and "L'histoire
du peuple d'Israël." On the whole, in this first book of
essays, Renan shows that his command of his art is as yet

quite uneven. In "Mahomet et les origines de l'Islamisme" he has made a striking attempt to suggest by the very structure of the essay his conception of Mohammedanism as a religion of "average humanity" (*"humanité moyenne"*); by alternating moments of sordid buffoonery and moments of true spirituality, he hoped to convey the spirit of a religion made up of "dissonances and consonances of earthly and divine instincts" (*EHR*, p. 295). But the essay, one of the earliest in date of composition, dissolves into a series of anecdotes much too strongly seasoned with the profane to allow us to taste anything very sacred.

"Les historiens critiques de Jésus," also an early essay, falls short, even in its revised form, of being a composition of movement, force, and clear outline; sharp and astute in its negative criticism of Strauss and the other *mythologues*, its final synthesis is vague and arbitrary, a troubled mixture of Catholic orthodoxy and Cousinian spiritualism. Vagueness of style, in fact, that demon which Renan will never manage or perhaps never care to shake loose completely, spoils several passages of the *Etudes d'histoire religieuse*. At such moments, one has the impression that the moorings to which Renan's thought is tied are no more substantial than pleasant-sounding words, airy phrases repeated like incantations, as in the conclusion of "Les historiens critiques de Jésus" (*EHR*, pp. 213–215): *"belle incarnation de Dieu," "la plus belle des formes," "Les poèmes homériques seraient-ils plus beaux . . . ," "L'Evangile serait-il plus beau . . . ," "Sa beauté est éternelle . . . ," "la beauté morale," "l'éternelle beauté."*

Such patches of nebulous prose, however, are not as frequent in the *Etudes d'histoire religieuse* as in some of the later works and do not seriously harm it. For all its weaknesses in thought and style, it remains a work from which we may learn much about the history of religion. Many of the questions it raises are beyond the competence of the general reader to decide, for example, the authorship of the Psalms, the authorship of the *Imitation of Christ*, the authenticity of passages relating to Jesus in the Jewish historian Josephus. But Renan at least arouses our interest in these questions and in addition provides keen insights into many of them. One of the most valuable of his insights is his distinction between spontaneous, symbolical ritualistic expression in religion and the intelligent, practical, logical use of language in other domains of life.[25]

But I think it is precisely as an essayist that Renan is most original in this work. Other Second Empire essayists in the history of religion, Edmond Schérer, Ernest Havet, Albert Réville, to name but a few, had worthy enough ideas and readable enough styles. What they lacked, and what accounts for the fact that the interest we take in them today is largely academic, while Renan can still be read for pleasure, is not only the superior quality of his style and his ability to make the essay more than a mere article, but also his vision of the book of essays as an artistic whole. Renan's essays have that attractive quality which John Middleton Murry defined, in Baudelaire's prose poems, as "the complex solidity of an attitude." The attitude admits of a rich variety of manners: graceful reporting of scholarly events and achievements, concise, dramatic historical narrative, poetic intuition, lightness of touch, wit, irony. Not all the successful essays resemble the first two, those miniature histories, small but compact and ambitious syntheses bearing the triple insight of scholar, critic, and poet. If I have stressed these, it is because in them (as in the famous

"Poésie des races celtiques") Renan strives to be a new Orpheus, a new Trismegistus, singing the ancient mysteries of religion in terms intelligible to an era of positivism. This, we know, had been his dream ever since he left the Catholic Church. It was his *raison d'être* as a historian. It was in fact the fundamental role he assumed throughout his life.

The *Etudes d'histoire religieuse* alone might have sufficed to establish this brilliant young scholar as a leading essayist of his time, a vulgarizer not unworthy of the great national tradition of Descartes, Pascal, Fontenelle, Montesquieu, Voltaire, Sainte-Beuve. Already, however, he was busy perfecting his mastery of the genre in new articles for the *Revue des deux mondes* and the *Journal des débats*. Only two years later, he was to raise these articles to the full dignity of formal essays in a much more mature work. It was to be perhaps his greatest book of essays and certainly one of the wisest of his books.

Chapter 4

An Idealist in the
Age of Lead and Tin

"In a time like ours, when every personality of distinction has so little room to move around in, dreaming of an ideal past has become a necessary diversion." – *Essais de morale et de critique*

~~~~~~

THE first impression we are likely to have when we take up the *Essais de morale et de critique* and read through the preface is one of disconcerting vagueness. The word *"morale"* (moral philosophy, ethics) is frequently repeated, but never defined. We are told about *"la foi,"* but not what we must have faith in; about *"l'amour,"* but not what the object of our love should be; about *"esprits honnêtes,"* but not what their *honnêteté* consists of. We are reassured that good is still good and evil still evil ("Le bien, c'est le bien; le mal, c'est le mal"), but at this point it seems hardly more than a tautology, and a particularly bad one, since its terms are not defined. What is good? What is evil? We may begin to suspect that these phrases are all so many verbal cushions against the shock of reality, like the fuzzier passages of the *Etudes d'histoire religieuse.*

Then, gradually, the brush strokes become a little firmer, the picture a little clearer, and we recognize a kinship between these vague affirmations, this "moral tradition" which the author seems to take for granted, and the neo-Kantism of Cousin, as well as the Rousseau–George Sand tradition of reliance on moral instinct. With them, Renan seems to believe that ethics is a matter of the intuition of self-evident "moral certitude," a dictate of the individual conscience and the individual *"sentiment moral,"* free of uncertainty, infinitely above opinions or hypotheses, "sheltered from all discussion." Even Christian ethics, he goes on to say in the first essay, has been given a firmer foundation now that it has left the sphere of disputes and taken refuge in "the calm region of feeling." The preface ends with a prayer to his Breton ancestors—"Oh fathers of the obscure tribe at whose hearth I received my faith in the invisible . . ."—and an evocation of the "splendid Eden of the soul's joys, the very one our saints beheld in their dreams."

A most unusual overture for a book which would grapple with critical and moral problems! We seem to be pointed toward a kind of morality which begs the question, toward sentimentalism and beautiful day-dreaming. And yet in the essays which follow, there is hardly a single moral abstraction of the preface which does not assume precise meaning. We are drawn by magic into the circle of Renan's *morale* and see its circumference with greater and greater clarity. Specific attributes of good and evil emerge distinctly enough from the moralist's reflections on diabolical forces in Italian political history, from his portrait of the cynical poet-beggar Abou-Zeid de Saroudj, or from his analysis of the fifteenth-century success story as told in the *Farce de Pathelin*. Real qualities of *honnêteté*, that indefinable gentlemanliness raised to a moral virtue and so esteemed by the French, catch hold of our imagination in the portrait of Sacy, Renan's friend and literary adviser, who somehow succeeded in combining the piety of a devout layman reciting his daily breviary with the editorship of the *Journal des débats* and the exercise of political responsibility as spokesman of the Ecole libérale.

"Liberty," hackneyed word that it had become less than a century after the Revolution, assumes real meaning when we are asked to imagine what would have happened to the free speculative spirit of Immanuel Kant had he been a *"professeur de faculté"* toward 1858, ordered to the ministry, called on the carpet by any number of *"inspecteurs"* and *"chefs de cabinet."* The "world of the spirit," of the "soul," the "devotion to truth" are no pious phrases when Renan describes the blind Thierry, no longer able to read books, being led about by Fauriel and other friends among the ruined monuments of southern France, still eagerly seeking, through these vaguely perceived architectural outlines, to know the truth of the past.

It is a method which yields very little of what Emile Faguet liked to call "doctrine," but which is extraordinarily rich in observation, in perception, in concrete meaning. It is, we recognize by now, the traditional method of the essayist. Renan's authentic literary ancestors here are not systematic philosophers like Aristotle, St. Thomas Aquinas, Descartes, or Hegel (among the philosophers, Plato and Malebranche with their poetry and their use of dialogue impressed him most): his real ancestors are the literary thinkers for whom the French language reserves the honored name of *"moralistes"*—Montaigne, La Rochefoucauld, Saint-Evremond, La Bruyère, and others—and also their kinsmen beyond the Channel, from Bacon on down the long, vigorous line of English essayists. It would be disastrous to read the *Essais de morale et de critique* as if it were an orderly exposition of Renan's moral and critical beliefs. Although it lacks the aphoristic form, the penetrating observation of conduct, the cynical wit associated with many of the *moralistes* and the whimsy of so many English essayists, this work should be read like theirs, as an empirical approach to moral problems, an intricate pattern of anecdote, imaginative detail, and meditation, offering no final solution, suggesting its truth in the most subtle manner. There is a greater amount of precision and traditional wisdom than Renan has been given credit for in his frequent, deliberate coupling of the words *"morale"* and *"poétique."*

But in his artistic approach to moral questions and to the broad literary, political, and social questions he enveloped under the term *"critique,"* Renan is also very much a man of the Second Empire. For the moralist of his time, especially when he touched on political questions, this approach was the most practical and the most effective one. The tyranny of Napoleon III has no doubt been exaggerated,[1] but from the point of view of many liberal spirits who suffered oppression, who lost jobs or were exiled, the period from the *coup d'état* of 1851 down to the liberalizing reforms of the 1860's was a harsh one for freedom of thought. Renan, as we shall see, was hardly in the category of the liberal opposition; he already possessed a fine style and had not been forced by censorship, as the *rallié* Sainte-Beuve claimed Prévost-Paradol had been forced, to polish his style into ironic literary form in order to express political dissent safely. But Renan was a critic of the spiritual climate of the Second Empire and as such, of course, often touched on sensitive political questions. The peculiar interplay of moral, artistic, and political motifs we find in the *Essais de morale et de critique* will therefore become more intelligible if we consider briefly the Second Empire background of the work.

First, the very preoccupation with moral problems which we find in the work was a distinguishing feature of Renan's time. This of course contradicts the accepted picture of the Second Empire as a world of vaudeville and lavish court life, *boulevardiers* and gossip columns, gay immorality and innocent materialism—the Offenbach, Meilhac, and Halévy Second Empire. It also contradicts Zola's evocation of a somber world of lust and greed. There existed, most certainly, a real and widespread materialism, and Renan was one of its most stubborn critics. But beneath the patina of frivolity lay another Second Empire of strangely persistent, at times even profound, moral feeling.[2] The emphasis on moral questions in the literature of the time is proof enough, even though it may have been the protest of thinking men against the diminishing moral sense of the populace. There was an extraordinary variety of approaches, ranging all the way from the misunderstood poetry of that tormented searcher after purity, Baudelaire, or the grave moral tones of Taine and other philosophers (positivists like Littré, Cournot; spiritualists like Caro, Ravaisson, Vacherot, Renouvier), to the didactic moral poetry of Sully Prudhomme or the *pièces à thèse* of the bourgeois lay preachers Dumas fils and Augier.

Among the most interesting manifestations of moral sensitivity are other essay works, for Renan was by no means alone in this field. One notes, for example, a revival of interest in earlier French moralists. *Les moralistes du XVIe et du XVIIe siècle*, by an influential spokesman of an older generation, the Swiss Protestant moralist Vinet, appeared posthumously in 1859. There were also Schérer, whose career as a "liberated Protestant" paralleled to some extent that of Renan, Montégut, for whom criticism seemed to have chiefly a moral function, Prévost-Paradol (*Etudes sur les moralistes français*, 1864), and Ernest Bersot, whose essays, written during the Second Empire, were collected and published after his death by Schérer in 1882 under the title *Un moraliste*. Nor should we forget Sainte-Beuve, who renewed and prolonged his career through the Second Empire with his *Lundis*. "Literary study," he wrote, and he could have been speaking on behalf of these younger critics as well, "leads me quite naturally to moral study." [3]

The reasons for this moral preoccupation may be found, I think, in deep disturbances of a philosophical, economic, and political nature. It is a well-known fact that Catholicism, despite a vigorous revival of thought on the part of Catholic writers earlier in the century, had lost its hold on many thinking men. Renan himself is a striking example. The bitter disputes between liberal and reactionary Catholics, the example of the defrocked and excommunicated Lamennais, who died in 1854, in the eyes of many the symbol of the futility of attempting to modernize the Catholic Church—all this had a further demoralizing effect. The disputes were no less bitter between positivists and spiritualists, with their rival claims to philosophical truth. The crucial problem, which would lead to the well-known moral crisis of the 1880's, was actually an old one, familiar to the eighteenth-century *philosophes:* How could the experimental method of science (wrongly equated by numerous thinkers with materialism) be made the basis for a sound system of moral beliefs? Were the spiritualists right in insisting on the validity of the concepts of God and the immortal soul, or were these outmoded ideas, watered-down Christian dogmas? Far from the academic scene where these questions were being debated, the great mass of Frenchmen, shopkeepers, merchants, farmers, politicians, were demonstrating their own *esprit positif*, their practical positivism, in one of the greatest periods of material prosperity France had ever known. The Industrial Revolution was at last fully under way; vast quantities of wealth and credit were being amassed; new ideals of luxury, comfort, leisure, stability, safety, order were forcing themselves on the attention of moral inquirers.

If Napoleon III had been able to exploit the theme of "order" with such success in the campaign of 1849 and again in 1851 and 1852, it was because recurrent political upheavals had put the fear of anarchy into the hearts of many Frenchmen. Renan was only thirty-six when he published the *Essais de morale et de critique* in 1859 and even a little younger when he wrote most of them. But as a child he had heard vivid tales of 1789; he was seven when the Revolution of 1830 broke out; he had witnessed the Revolution of 1848 and the *coup d'état* of 1851, which were indeed part of his own coming to manhood. It was probably this education by history to which he was referring when he implied that he, like Lamennais (of whom he uses the phrase), possessed a "maturity rich in experience and in disillusion" (*EMC*, II, 136). These recurrent paroxysms of the French state must surely be counted as one of the principal causes of moral anxiety in Renan's time. Faguet's maxim, that "all political questions are at bottom a moral question," [4] seems to apply with special force to France. Without over-stating the tyranny of Napoleon III (his seems hardly a dictatorship beside Hitler and Stalin), one might add that he himself contributed to moral anxiety, in one very terrible form, especially in the critical year 1852, by the repressive measures intended to strengthen his hand. For many men, such as Bersot, a professor who refused to take the oath of fidelity to the Emperor, this repression posed the question —no abstract one, it will be agreed—of duty and conscience and called for great moral courage.[5]

On this background of the Second Empire, with its ma-terialism and moral sensitivity, its frivolity and vigorous thought, its political repression and prosperity, its vulgarity and artistry, Renan's *Essais de morale et de critique* takes its place. With one exception, "Dom Luigi Tosti," pub-lished in *La politique nouvelle* in August 1851, the essays were written (the majority for the *Journal des débats*, a few for the *Revue des deux mondes*) between 1853 and 1859, that is, during the so-called "authoritarian" phase of the imperial regime (1852–1860). This book is Renan's very personal attempt to know and to judge his society, whose strangeness and complexity still puzzle historians. How does he view it? What meaning can his scholarly, artistic soul discern in the contradictions surrounding him, the contra-dictions of a world where department stores and boule-vards, credit banks and ironclad warships were springing up and overgrowing figures from the past like Sacy, who wrote in seventeenth-century prose with purity of heart?

Renan's response to this world is a kind of traditionalism counterbalanced by strongly liberal beliefs. But it is not yet extreme political traditionalism. Many of his ideas will, of course, later provide nourishment for the *traditionalistes*, for Charles Maurras and the *Action Française*—arguments against the French Revolution, pleas for the revival of monarchy and for the organization of a hierarchical society with an intellectual aristocracy leading from on high.[6] These ideas will not receive explicit form until 1871 when, in *La réforme intellectuelle et morale*, they blaze out against the somber background of invasion, war, and potential anarchy. Only the first of them (the critique of the Revolution) is to be found in the *Essais de morale et de critique*. But they had all long been germinating in his mind.

In *L'avenir de la science*, which contains some of Renan's most sympathetic insights into democracy and even into socialism, there are passages of deeply antidemocratic instinct, as, for example, the argument that the good of humanity calls for the sacrifice of the ignorant masses to the comfort of an elite oligarchy (ch. xviii), or the suspicious theory that these same masses need a benevolent despot to tide them over until they are ready for democracy (*AS*, III, 1007–1009). In the *Essais de morale et de critique*, there is no such extreme antidemocratic spirit, but nostalgia for the *ancien régime* hovers over the reverent essay (indeed slightly superstitious, in Sainte-Beuve's opinion) on the French Academy and whispers distinctly from such passages as the one in which Renan states his belief that "the only sheet anchors on which independence of spirit may still find safety today are pieces of wreckage of what is called in France the *ancien régime*" (*EMC*, II, 228).

The point I wish to make about these essays, however, is that they represent a remarkably balanced view of French society. Whatever confusion there may later be in Renan's political thought, this work testifies to great equilibrium:

his respect for the past is held in check by a strong pull toward liberalism and what he calls the "modern spirit." Let his own paradox in the form of an aphorism express it more precisely: "Liberty is assured only when it is founded on institutions of long duration" (*EMC*, II, 228). It was in great part because Renan feared for the survival of liberty in France that he developed his critique of the French Revolution. Like so many of his generation, he had become increasingly disillusioned with the whole *mystique républicaine*, especially after December 2, 1851, the ironic epilogue of the practice of democratic suffrage. "Would you believe," he wrote to Bersot, just a month after the *coup d'état*, "that in the fever of these first days, I almost became a legitimist, and that I am still tempted to become one if it can be proved that the hereditary transmission of power is the only means of escaping caesarism, the fatal consequence of democracy as it is understood in France." [7] In a little-known article of May 1851, when his faith in republicanism was still warm, he had accepted the Revolution uncritically as an instrument of "rational progress"; he had condemned political medievalism; he had venerated the state, according to the rubric of Hegelian liturgy, as "the most enlightened part of the nation, alone capable of judging what is most useful in forming the citizen." [8] In the *Essais de morale et de critique*, he examines, as a severe historical judge, the credentials of the Revolution; he attempts to rehabilitate certain liberal political traditions of the Middle Ages and the *ancien régime;* above all, he laments and decries the tyranny of centralized state bureaucracy. It is true that the early article on the Benedictine monk Tosti, a great visionary of Italian nationalism and republicanism, is naïve in its praise of the Revolution, as Renan admitted (*EMC*, II, 16–18, 154–155). But he included it because he still believed in "*l'esprit moderne*," and hated, like André Gide, to disown the little core of truth present in even the most naïve of his past errors.

Seen through Renan's eyes, the crimes committed in the name of liberty by the French Revolution might have been excused, but not the harm he claims it did to the cause of individual liberty by its highly abstract, rationalistic conception of the state. That is the first count on which he condemns it. He also blames it for imposing with more massive weight than ever the centralized administrative bureaucracy of the monarchy; Tocqueville had shown only a few years before, in *L'ancien régime et la révolution* (1856), that this was one of the unbroken links between the old and the new states. He condemns it furthermore (and here again his arguments recall Tocqueville) for having made a fetish of equality, which, under the all-powerful state, becomes in fact "equality in servitude" (*EMC*, II, 197), the leveling down of all citizens to the same mediocre model, the standardization of their intellectual lives.

None of this criticism is especially original; it can be found in Maistre, Tocqueville, and many others. What is interesting is that Renan applies it indirectly to the Second Empire: his prudently veiled message seems to be that the faults of the Second Empire—its repressive bureaucracy, its distortion of the ideal of equality, its materialism—were logical consequences of the Revolution, part of a muddy wash which had not yet receded. But Renan does not condemn *en bloc*. Many of his contemporaries shared his distaste for what they considered the cult of vulgarity and mediocrity on the part of the modern state. Renan, however, never goes as far as the pessimistic disdain of Leconte de Lisle in his ivory tower, or Flaubert's morbid fascination, in his, with the *"marée de merde"* beating on the walls outside. A truer historian than either of these men, he offers a much saner and better-balanced critique of his times.

Renan's guide for the critic in a harsh political world may be outlined as follows: He will not allow himself to be drawn, like so many of the generation of 1848, into complete political disillusionment, even though events since 1848 had understandably sickened the heart. Instead, he will qualify his distrust of the common man by a kind of ironic detachment, which does not exclude a certain sympathy. He will not reject the impassioned sense of *engagement* found in those who still continued to believe in the republican dream; he will simply try to temper it with a greater critical awareness, in order to protect it against the repetition of another cruel disappointment like the failure of 1848. Finally, he will not deny the "modern spirit"—in his historicism and scientism, was he not part and parcel of it? —but will attempt to correct its naïve faith in technology and progress by reminding it of what he calls "the useful prejudices" of the past (*EMC*, II, 233).

Enthusiasm tempered by critical sense, political responsibility guided by a spirit of detachment and contemplation, the measurement of true progress in the light of enduring values of the past—these make up the positive side of the *Essais de morale et de critique;* the negative side is the criticism of the Second Empire as the unfortunate heir of the Revolution. Let us look more closely at these themes and at the manner in which they are arranged.

A legend which Renan himself had a hand in launching has made him a kind of Gallic Buddha, smiling ironically at existence, not really very interested in how things turn out. The real principle of his life was actually profound enthusiasm chastened by critical sense. Like the romantic generation, which he admired in so many respects, he knew how to "seize life ardently like a desirable prey" (*EMC*, II, 57). The only act ever to bore him, so far as I can determine, was writing letters, and then it was not so much boredom as mild torture. In living, in planning his career, in teaching and writing, he took great zest, not the outward zest of a Hugo or a Balzac, but the hidden gusto of the scholar. Even in later years, when poor health, political discouragement, and notorious skepticism seemed to undermine his existence, he never really lost his profound inner enthusiasm.

This enthusiasm was, of course, in great part his precious inheritance from the romantics. Renan, here showing himself an astute critic, did not believe that their melancholy was very deep; these Werthers, he pointed out, were ready for lucid and realistic action when the occasion demanded (*EMC*, II, 57). It was to shame his own generation—the truly disgusted, the real doubters in the human spirit, "without taste for the contemplation of things, without passion for the study of the universe"—that he summoned up a great generation of enthusiasts. The first part of his book is devoted to a few carefully selected examples of intellectual ardor among the romantics, the philosopher Cousin, the historian Thierry, the politico-religious prophets Lamennais and Tosti. The first essay, on the editor of the *Journal des débats*, reproduces a gentler form of enthusiasm, the quieter, milder flame of *honnêteté*. But from the opening of "M. Cousin" on page 55 to the conclusion of the "Révolutions d'Italie" on page 187, the dominant note is Renan's appeal to his own generation to embrace some cause, some ideal, with enthusiasm.

But he warns that his own generation must put on a stronger protective armor of criticism than had been worn by these romantic thinkers. This is the motif of his analysis of Cousin's achievement, one of the fairest judgments we have of this much-abused writer, whom Hugo called, among other things, an "empty goatskin bottle." [9] The whole essay is a masterpiece of delicate, probing irony. The key to Cousin's character, Renan feels, was his enthusiasm for the study of philosophy and his gift for communicating it. Thus far he is worthy of emulation. But insufficient critical spirit made a *chef d'école* out of him and eventually the semimilitary leader and administrator of spiritualism, for many years the official government philosophy. We should imitate his fervor, his sense of political responsibility and his legitimate desire for authority, but control them with greater scholarship and greater disinterestedness. We should preserve Thierry's passionate love for history while broadening his conception of it beyond mere lively narrative and by making its scholarly base even firmer. We might well admire Lamennais' ardor for truth but avoid the heavy impetuosity with which he rushed upon it, like a wild boar, causing it to turn and flee (*EMC*, II, 139). Let us admire his eloquence, like Cousin's, but let us learn from the negative examples of both that there is danger in being eloquent merely for the sake of eloquence.

As for enthusiasm in Italian political history, Renan wrote of the Italian city-states, in a sentence which Stendhal would have eagerly subscribed to: "Nowhere has man enjoyed so profoundly the happiness of living and dying for something great" (*EMC*, II, 182). Reading his description of Tosti's mystical love of his country as it struggled to make itself a nation, one feels that Renan is pointing out to his fellow citizens of the Second Empire, to disheartened idealists and selfish exploiters alike, a sublime lesson in patriotism. Yet his critical sense continues to function even in this emotional tribute: he knew that the intense factional rivalries of the city-states had done much to prevent the unification of Italy, and he also knew that Tosti's lyrical prose, his "*amour démesuré*" for his country, admirable as they were, were not enough to achieve that goal.

To keep the vital fire of the romantics alive, to control it without destroying it, Renan felt his generation must also strive for a greater balance between political action and contemplation. In the years of disillusionment following on 1848, when political interest and political intelligence were drying up on the part of the artist and contempt for art was beginning to flourish in the hearts of politicians, Renan avoided a one-sided position. It was his conviction that quiet, peaceful, disinterested contemplation (of the kind Gautier and Leconte de Lisle urged on the poet) and commitment to the political and social struggle of one's time can and ought to go hand in hand.

Nowhere has he better demonstrated this point than in his beautiful essay on Augustin Thierry, which teaches the possibility, in fact the necessity, of uniting a sense of political *engagement* (Renan calls it "*enjeu*") with the spirit of scholarly detachment. "The wide comprehension of human affairs," he writes, "can be obtained only by understanding of the present, and the present gives up its secret to us only in proportion to the stake we have in it" (*EMC*, II, 94). Thierry's *engagement*, in the form of ardent republicanism, inspired in him the desire to reveal the neglected role played by the common people, the *"roture,"* in French history, and this, in Renan's opinion, made him not only a more compelling writer but also a better scholar, for it led him to read neglected documents in a new light and to acquire new historical perspectives. Literature must never let itself become a form of political ambition, but neither must it become a game of wit without bearing on contemporary social problems, for that, as Renan warned in his essay on Sacy, is a petty conception, degrading for both politics and literature, a falling back to the grammarians of antiquity (*EMC*, II, 27). This first essay concludes, in fact, with a parallel between Renan's own time and that of the Stoics and Boethius: there was a similar political disillusionment, a similar feeling of being smothered under an all-powerful administrative machine. But Renan, very significantly, avoids offering any "Consolation of Philosophy" to his contemporaries; the true scholar, the contemplative spirit, will not be indifferent to or remote from political realities.

Renan's effort to understand and to guide his own generation by comparing it with those immediately preceding—a very original, fecund critical method, to which later works such as Bourget's *Essais de psychologie contemporaine* and Faguet's *Politiques et moralistes du dix-neuvième siècle* owe much—occupies roughly the first half of the *Essais de morale et de critique*. Then, beginning with "L'histoire secrète de Procope," he brings his criticism more directly to bear on the foibles of the Second Empire; his grievances become more sharply defined. This essay in its outer garb seems nonpolitical enough: it is a discussion of a famous historical problem, the authenticity and historical validity of Procopius' memoirs, a violent diatribe against the Emperor Justinian and the Empress Theodora. But under this harmless academic guise, Renan is actually warning against the dangers of Napoleonic caesarism. When he suggests that Justinian might never have provoked the diatribe had he not surrounded himself with corrupt, mercenary administrators shutting him off from men of virtue and honor and from his own subjects, he is presenting Napoleon III himself with a historical lesson. In the closing paragraph the allusion to the Emperor is quite striking: "Repressed truth will avenge itself by calumny. . . . But who is to blame? Those who, by suppressing liberty, have confessed they have something to hide; those who, by falsifying opinion, have rendered approbation of what they do suspect and calumny alone credible" (*EMC*, II, 198).

But the atmosphere of repression, which had in fact abated since the early years of the régime and was soon to disappear altogether, is by no means the most serious defect Renan finds in the society of his time. He was more concerned with its moral decadence, its materialism. His picture of it is a gray panorama, relieved only by faith in obscured promises of a saner world and by transfigured memories of the past. The *Essais de morale et de critique* represents a kind of underground moral resistance movement against reigning bourgeois materialism. The words *"résister"* and *"résistance"* occur frequently in the text and are key words. "The essential thing, in our time, is not to create, but to endure and to resist" (*EMC*, II, 236–237).

How is moral resistance to be fed and kept alive? In great part by historical traditions. Here much of Renan's critique seems chimerical; to be more exact, he is often sound in the values he wishes to restore but cloudy in the manner suggested for restoring them. Thus it is true that too much centralization of power may undermine liberties; but one wonders exactly what he is trying to prove by contrasting the overpowering bureaucracy of bourgeois officials with the feudal balance of powers and the guarantee of liberties given by the Capetian monarchs. Are we to go back to feudalism? In his essay, "La farce de Pathelin," he makes out a pretty vigorous case for the harmful effects of the *esprit gaulois*, "insipid, practical, base, terribly shrewd about the things of the world, moralistic in its own way, providing we mean by morality the art of succeeding here below" (*EMC*, II, 2 1 1–2 1 2). But even if we grant some truth to the theory that the spirit of individualism, of moral grandeur and poetic imagination (which, by the way, Renan claims was born in the "forests of Germania") [10] faded in proportion as the bourgeoisie grew to power in the fifteenth century, what is the conclusion we are to draw? Are we to return to the age of chivalry? Granted the Papacy may have lost some of the "Catholicity" of Gregory VII and Innocent III, has it really been reduced to nothing but a petty, narrow-minded Italian institution (*EMC*, II, 1 6 6–1 6 7)?

Renan seems to be on firmer ground when he turns for spiritual sustenance to a remoter past, "La poésie des races celtiques," in the sixth to eighth centuries. Here the motif of resistance is especially strong, for he believed that the Celtic peoples, including the nineteenth-century Bretons, had inherited from their ancestors a tradition of resistance (*EMC*, II, 2 5 6–2 5 7) against false progress, and therefore remained one of the last strongholds of idealism and indi-vidualism in a world of materialism and bureaucracy. "L'art de réussir ici-bas," the art of Pathelin and of the Pathelins of the Second Empire, seems mean indeed beside the heroic

Breton devotion to an idealistic cause, an antiquated, perhaps even a lost cause, simply because it is a matter of moral integrity.

One begins to suspect by now that the most serious defect of the Second Empire, indeed of modern society in general, in Renan's eyes, is its deficiency of poetic spirit. This criticism of course also has a moral significance with Renan, not only because he considered serious moral purpose and highly developed artistic form inseparable, but also because he felt great poetry can be produced only where there are idealism and moral greatness. That he looked on his own era as an unpoetic "age of lead or tin" (*"âge de plomb ou d'étain"*—*EMC*, II, 250) becomes clearer and clearer as the book progresses. This theme in fact culminates in the contrast, drawn in the last two essays, between the counterfeit "Poésie de l'Exposition" [11] and the genuine "Poésie des races celtiques."

"Our century," he wrote, reaching out to include the whole nascent modern world in his dark prognosis, "is moving neither toward good nor toward evil; it is moving toward mediocrity" (*EMC*, II, 251). *"Médiocrité"* and *"vulgarité,"* like *"résistance"* and *"idéalisme,"* are key words of the book. What frightened Renan was not so much the widespread existence of mediocrity as the fact that it was the surest path to success (*EMC*, II, 251). Like Flaubert (he even uses the verb Flaubert liked to apply to bourgeois ineptitude, the verb *"épanouir"*), he predicted the triumph of "stupidity, self-contented, flowering unhindered in the sunlight and proceeding without regret to the burial services of genius" (*EMC*, II, 250). A thought haunted him: would the immense industrialization of the modern world bring with it techniques for the industrialization of souls, the mass production of human personalities? The utopia toward which humanity was moving might turn out to be like the *"Pays des Intérêts-Unis"* in the year 3000, as described by a fellow regionalist from Brittany, Emile Souvestre: [12] a country where citizens were first reduced to idiocy and then artificially "moralized" in "moralization hothouses" (*"serres à moralisation"*). Here Renan is not so chimerical; had he lived he would have seen much of this nightmare turned into reality far ahead of schedule, in modern methods of publicity and advertising, assembly-line universities, advanced techniques of propaganda, and even "brainwashing," to which the *"serres à moralisation"* bear an uncanny resemblance.

Some of his worst fears were justified, but in predicting the "imminent end of poetry in the human race" (*EMC*, II, 40), he may have erred in understanding his own times. We can appreciate his contrasting, with stinging humor, the Olympic games and tournaments, the pilgrimages and jubilees of the past with the industrial fairs of his century (here again, he is close to Flaubert, mock epic poet of the *"comices agricoles"*). There is delightfully mocking humor also in his recalling Charles Fourier's prediction that the rival portions of humanity, having lost all their greatness of soul, would one day gather not for great battles or ecumenical councils but to dispute their excellence in the making of pastry (*EMC*, II, 241)—a prediction which unfortunately has not come true. But Renan lacked the insight of Baudelaire and Balzac, and even of lesser men like Maxime Du Camp, into the hidden "heroism of modern life," as Baudelaire called it, the promise of a new kind of moral courage and poetry stirring in the vulgar modern world. He in fact mentions Balzac, but only to compare his *Comédie hu-*

maine unfavorably with the series of twelfth-century Arabic stories known as the *Séances de Hariri* (*EMC*, II, 203). Curiously enough, he paraphrases, probably unknowingly, the story of one of Balzac's greatest creations when he implies that the only way for a man to achieve heroic proportions in this age of mediocrity is to become a criminal (*EMC*, II, 213, 248).

But men were not really yet as mechanized as he thought. The "world of unlimited individualities" which he admired in Italy of the Renaissance and the nineteenth century (*EMC*, II, 212) had its counterpart in modern French society, the dynamic world which had provided Balzac with his materials. There were even strange forms of poetic beauty concealed in what Renan probably looked upon as mere disfigurements of the French landscape, in railroad and factory, in mine and department store; and it would be a moralist every bit as severe as Renan in his critique of the Second Empire who would discover this poetry, that is, Zola. "Banks and tariffs, the newspaper and caucus, Methodism and Unitarianism," wrote Emerson, "are flat and dull to dull people, but rest on the same foundations of wonder as the town of Troy and the temple of Delphi, and are as swiftly passing away." [13]

However, if Renan erred in declaring that contemporary society was not a "favorable milieu" for the development of poetry and art (*EMC*, II, 87), it was a fruitful error. It led him, happily, to conceive of the critic, the historian, and the essayist as the preservers of the poetic spirit in his century. This was, as we have seen, an idea he had long cherished, beginning with the speculations and projects of the *Cahiers de jeunesse*. He formulates it anew in the *Essais de morale et de critique* when he declares that since "poetry is no longer to be found except in the past . . . the true poets of our time are the critic and the historian who search for it there" (*EMC*, II, 251).

Renan's own moral and critical reflections on his society are expressed in terms of a true work of art, having many of the qualities of poetry. In analyzing the main themes of the work, I have suggested something of the beautiful structural pattern in which these essays are arranged. The arguments they present derive much of their appeal from this artistic setting and, it is even clearer, from his style. In turning to his style, we arrive not at an afterthought but at the heart of the matter. For if his book is a protest against moral decadence, a plea for idealism and for an intelligent traditionalism, it is through his style that he communicates this point of view most strikingly.

I shall take a somewhat indirect approach to this aspect of the *Essais de morale et de critique* by first indicating the type of style Renan was trying to avoid and the reasons for his stand. The many remarks on style scattered throughout the book provide an insight into this question; far from being interesting *hors d'oeuvre*, they make up an essential part of his moral message. The essay on Thierry is especially significant from this point of view. After stating his belief that in history, an art as much as a science, perfection of form is essential (a remark which should not surprise us after the *Etudes d'histoire religieuse*), he goes on to declare: "As soon as it is a question of moral or political subjects, thought becomes complete only when it has been given an irreproachable form, even with regard to harmony, and it is no exaggeration to say that a badly arranged sentence always means an inexact thought" (*EMC*, II, 103).

Like most of the sensitive writers of his generation, like

Baudelaire and Flaubert, for example, though without their somewhat ambiguous attitude toward romanticism, Renan considered the great romantic sin to be love of the declamatory. In a broader sense, he rebelled against an older tradition of which romantic rhetoric was a recent product— the tradition of rhetoric in the schools. These days, needing all the eloquence we can get, we can hardly afford to condemn romantic eloquence, or rhetoric when it produces great writing. But for Renan in the 1840's, *la rhétorique* had been a "diabolical invention . . . a fracas of round, square, cornered, two-cornered periods, an assortment of words baroque enough to split one's head open!"—not to mention a dangerous application of professional legal trickery to what should be the honest art of literature.[14] More soberly, Prévost-Paradol, another voice speaking for this generation of the victims of rhetoric, had defined it as the labor of "looking in a dictionary for ways of not calling things by their names." [15] This was in connection with the practice of *vers latins*, and it is perhaps no exaggeration to see in the empty virtuosity of Cousin and Lamennais at their worst, or even Lamartine and Hugo at theirs, the end result of that form of humanism dear to the French, which consists in making small boys write Latin themes on subjects of no interest to them whatever.

Romantic eloquence, as Renan appraised it, bordered on the immoral—certainly on the untruthful. He implies that Cousin's defection from the path toward truth was largely a matter of style, when he points out that Cousin ended up rejecting ideas which could not be beautifully expressed: "All doctrines are not equally eloquent" (II, 67). The "powerful orator" Lamennais succumbed in the end to the unworthy trick of collecting antitheses and other "brilliant bursts of eloquence" and putting them away in his drawer (*EMC*, II, 143). Could it have been the same *"tiroir"* Claudel had in mind when he called it the scourge of romantic verse? Lamennais came to adore the turn of his own sentences, not a serious failing perhaps in a poet, but suspicious in a prose poet whose mission was to lead humanity to truth and redemption. In saying this, Renan put his finger on one of the reasons that the prose of Lamennais has not worn well, and even the passages he quotes from the *Paroles d'un croyant* as among the best (*EMC*, II, 130–132) are likely to seem to readers today stilted and hollow.

Writing well, *"le soin du beau langage,"* is not, then, for Renan, the same as romantic eloquence. Paradoxically, this "care for fine language" is an austere discipline and the best guarantee of *sérieux* (*EMC*, II, 143), that untranslatable word meaning moral seriousness or seriousness of purpose, that *sérieux* which, standing at the center of Renan's artistic code in the *Essais de morale et de critique*, was responsible for all that is finest in his early and middle periods.

His cautious attitude toward romantic eloquence, the care he took that his own eloquence be sober and muted, are related to still another aspect of his stylistic code, his conservatism. This might be defined as the desire to give his thought, often romantic in content as we have seen,[16] a guarantee of sobriety by casting it in a traditional classical mold. "A man has reached full maturity of mind," he wrote in his essay on the French Academy, "only when he has come to see that . . . the Dictionary of the Academy contains all he needs to express any thought, however delicate, novel, or refined it may be" (*EMC*, II, 232). The proof that for Renan, at least, this conservatism made sense is to be found in the quiet tour de force by means of which he holds our interest in these essays, using words that ought to seem worn and syntax that ought to seem undistinguished (the infinitely subtle, barely perceptible variations of rhythm give it much of its real distinction). Stylistic conservatism was also, of course, intimately related to his general message upholding the "useful prejudices of the past" (*EMC*, II, 233).

Henriette, Thierry, Sacy had taught him their lesson extremely well. So also had his favorites among the good old models of classical prose, especially Fénelon and the writers of Port-Royal. From the author of *Télémaque*, he learned something of the evocative power of abstract moral language—"the art of depicting nature through moral traits" (*SEJ*, II, 847)—and also the art of insinuating moral lessons by way of pleasurable prose cadences. As for Port-Royal, it seems to have been less the original Jansenist authors who impressed him than Sainte-Beuve's description of their style and, above all, the example of their descendant Sacy, whose ideal of self-concealment, correctness, and respect for the *"vieux modèles"* impressed itself upon Renan as "the best lesson in style I have ever received." [17]

Henri Bremond, it is true, has questioned the accuracy both of Sainte-Beuve's and of Renan's conceptions of Jansenist style ("alleged Jansenist style" he calls it), objecting especially to their notion that it was an austere, self-effacing, "unliterary" form of literary expression.[18] Yet if his own description of the common features of many different Jansenist styles is accurate, it would, curiously enough, tend to bring out a resemblance to the style of the *Essais de morale et de critique*. Though infinitely superior to Arnauld or Nicole as a stylist (we leave aside Pascal, whose prose is unique and who in any case had little influence on Renan's style), Renan aims at a similar combination of moral intensity with an appeal not to the eye—like theirs, his style in this respect lacks striking, colorful qualities and often borders on the banal—but to the ear.

But what, more precisely, are the outstanding stylistic features of the *Essais de morale et de critique?* I would say that two general impressions predominate: great regularity and harmony, beneath which one can detect a certain *inquiétude;* and an intense, indeed rarefied, atmosphere of moral idealism.

The drive toward order and regularity in Renan's prose, as in his philosophy, takes the form of an attempt to blend contradictory, sometimes violently contradictory, elements into a harmonious pattern. The key words here are *"fondre"* ("to blend"), *"contexture,"* and *"ensemble."* In "Les Révolutions d'Italie," Renan praises the "delicate truths," the "bold insights," the "strong, lively colors" of the Italian historian Giuseppe Ferrari (who wrote in French); but he adds, in a very revealing phrase, that Ferrari has failed to blend all this into a harmonious structure (*"harmonieuse contexture"*) defying minute analysis (*EMC,* II, 174). And again, in the essay on Thierry, he points out that historian's skill in blending different tones and balancing different parts so as to construct *"un ensemble harmonieux"* (*EMC,* II, 103).

This preoccupation with *"contexture"* is a deeper matter, I think, than the concern of every good stylist with composition. It reveals a characteristic trait of Renan's mind—his strong will to arrange his thought in equipoise, to give it the appearance of a calm, well-ordered structure, to mute whatever traces of disquietude might be present in it. In one of the few enlightening analyses we have of

Renan's style, Gabriel Brunet asks us to observe how his thoughts pass by, with their bewitching, graceful movements, their "pensive regularity," signifying his "belief in the seriousness of life and his scorn for the vulgar." And yet Brunet asks us to detect the "slight smile" which "seems to betray their attitude of recollection," and also a certain trembling of unrest (*"frissons d'inquiétude"*).[19]

Many examples of this *"régularité"* with its underlying *"inquiétude"* might be chosen from the *Essais de morale et de critique*, but an especially striking one may be found in the essay "M. de Lamennais." In the opening paragraph Renan describes the confusion which follows when a pagan tribe of Saxons, converted to Christianity, is asked to destroy its idols: only a man who had himself been a pagan priest dares commit this act.

On raconte que, quand les missionnaires de Rome, après avoir converti au christianisme les Saxons de Northumbrie, les engagèrent à renverser eux-mêmes les idoles que jusque-là ils avaient adorées, nul n'osa porter la main sur ces images longtemps consacrées par la foi et la prière. Au milieu de l'hésitation générale, un prêtre se leva et abattit d'un coup de hache le dieu dont il connaissait mieux que personne la vanité. L'attaque du prêtre a toujours ainsi un caractère particulier de froideur et d'assurance: on sent dans les coups qu'il porte une sûreté de main que le laïque n'atteint jamais. Celui-ci, habitué à regarder de loin le sanctuaire, ne s'en approche qu'avec respect, même quand la divinité l'a quitté; mais le prêtre, qui en connait les secrets, l'ouvre et le livre aux regards avec l'audace d'un familier [*EMC*, II, 109].*

* Renan, *Essais de morale et de critique*, II, 109, quoted by permission of Calmann-Lévy, publishers.

These are balanced, harmonious sentences, calmly describing an act of violence, though what appears to be a justifiable act of violence. There is a sureness and firmness of grasp which implies that the critic will now proceed to throw light on the mystery of a modern apostate's personality and perhaps give us eventually a calm rational explanation of the supposed mystery of the Christian Divinity Himself. Whatever *"sourire"* is present (the *"sourire"* seems to me to be much more characteristic of Renan's last phase) takes the form of irony: the whole paragraph is ironic in its theme of the apostate priest who attacks his former faith with *"une sûreté de main que le laïque n'atteint jamais."* Yet the tone is far from being all *"froideur et assurance."* There are emotional overtones, a suggestion of regret, in the phrase *"ces images longtemps consacrées par la foi et la prière."* The author is well aware of the pathos, the cruelty, of what he is describing. The harmony of the first sentence is somewhat upset by the broken-up rhythmical effect of the subordinate clauses (*"On raconte que, quand . . . après avoir . . ."*). The slightly disagreeable repetition of hard *c* sounds in the first three words continues throughout the paragraph, and is especially obvious in the last sentence. There also, the alliteration of the *r*'s in various consonantal combinations—*"prêtre,"* *"secrets,"* and especially the *l*'s and *vr*'s of the striking alliteration *"l'ouvre et le livre"*—gives a somewhat harsh effect. A shudder runs through the whole paragraph, with its picture of the laymen waiting in fearful anticipation, the sudden blow of the axe by the apostate priest, the violated sanctuary.

A no less remarkable feature than the striving after order and harmony is the sustained idealism. The *Essais de morale et de critique* in this respect may be said to have grown out of a hope expressed in the *Etudes d'histoire religieuse,* namely, the hope that idealists of all kinds, believers and nonbelievers alike, might find a "common language" (*EHR,* p. 423) in which to express their opposition to the increasing materialism of nineteenth-century life. Here Renan calls it *"la riche synonomie de la langue que parlent les belles âmes"* (*EMC,* II, 150). In some of his other works this basic vocabulary of sensitive souls, so to speak, is unfortunately too genteel, too sentimental, too intangible for the taste of many modern readers. This is especially true of *Ma soeur Henriette,* written on the whole in the glossy manner of the *style Saint-Sulpice.* But the *Essais de morale et de critique,* on the contrary, is a remarkably successful example of that *"idéalisation et poésie"* with which nineteenth-century neo-Platonists sought to beat back the rising tide of materialism.[20] Its spiritual atmosphere is not only bearable and believable, but congenial.

How has Renan achieved this effect? By the tour de force of excluding all "coarse precision," even the legitimate precision poets seek through imagery and metaphor. There are few metaphors and most of them have a vaguely Platonic character, or are drawn from the Bible or from Dante and are therefore rich in spiritual associations. One of Renan's favorites, that of *"parfum,"* carries a similarly spiritual meaning, and often a vaguely Platonic one, whether he tells of the aroma of poetry and morality he retains from the lost faith of his youth or describes the sweet odors greeting ships approaching the islands of the Erythraean sea, like "the augur of an unknown land, the messenger of the infinite," or whether he refers to the perfumes which clung for forty days to the clothing of privileged souls who had visited the *terre de promission.*[21]

Even concrete images are rare. The few which appear take on a beauty all the more striking for the austerity of the background. Among the most memorable are the brief view of Lamennais being lowered into a common unconsecrated grave on a misty day, the gravedigger asking "Il n'y a pas de croix?"; Dom Luigi Tosti rejected by the Papacy, exiled in his cell of St.-Paul-Without-the-Walls, listening to the rustling of the reeds along the banks of the Tiber; and of course the islands glimpsed by St. Brendan in his voyage to the land of promise, "the green islands crowned with tall grass bending over into the water"—the French is so much more musical: *"les îles vertes couronnées d'herbes qui retombent dans les flots"*).

And this last image leads us into the last essay in the book, the famous "Poésie des races celtiques," which deserves special attention for several reasons. Not only does it explain the essays that precede it, as Renan points out in the preface (*EMC*, II, 22); it also sums up his whole protest against materialism and his dream of a harmonious blending of old and new. Its message is the underlying message of the whole work: faith in a future union of moral idealism with the critical, scientific, technological skills of modern society; hope that *"poésie"* and *"morale"* will join *"critique"* not in a death struggle, but in a fruitful alliance.

"La poésie des races celtiques" has sometimes been abused by critics who judge it as though it were an article in a learned journal rather than an essay. But Renan very carefully lets it be known that the value he attributed to it was not so much scholarly as moral and esthetic (*EMC*, II, 22).

Its moral purpose, like that of Matthew Arnold's *On the Study of Celtic Literature*, which it helped inspire, is to counteract modern materialism and rationalism with virtues drawn from the Celtic cultural heritage. There is little original research in it; it relies heavily on the work of various French, Irish, and Welsh translators and editors of Celtic texts, the most frequently cited of whom is the not altogether reliable popularizer of Celtic legends and songs, Théodore de La Villemarqué. The substructure of learning is therefore perhaps less sound than in the *Etudes d'histoire religieuse*. But fortunately the thesis is less rigid than Arnold's program for correcting "Saxon" philistinism with "Celtic" romanticism; it also depends much less on racist jargon. In fact, the word "race" as Renan employs it seems to be synonymous with "people" or "ethnic group": what he is attempting to define are the common traits of several such groups united by a linguistic bond. The resulting generalizations may be debatable from a scientific point of view, but there is little doubt that this is one of Renan's most fertile essays, for much of the revival of interest in Celtic studies stemmed from it.

It is far from being his greatest essay, however. There is something fundamentally disjointed about it, which explains its weakness both as a study of Celtic poetry and as an essay structure. Renan generalizes on two different planes, jumping from one to the other quite arbitrarily. First he speaks, from his own intimate ethnic experience as a Celt, of certain characteristics of the Breton people: fidelity to a cause once adopted; resignation; reserve; gentleness of customs (*"douceur de moeurs"*); a certain sadness; a highly spiritual, idealistic, visionary nature. The first and second of these traits seem contradictory merely as attitudes, and one could object that there was hardly much *"résignation"* or much *"douceur de moeurs"* in the royalist insurrections of the late eighteenth century. Renan, forgetting for a moment the hidden stubbornness and tough fiber of his own nature, has idealized and poeticized the Breton people and exaggerated their *douceur*.[22]

However, this character analysis might not have been so objectionable had he not tried to make it fit the Welsh and Irish peoples as well as the Bretons. Here, as the Irish Celticist Robin Flower has pointed out, Renan makes the same mistake as Arnold, although not because, as Flower implies, he knew no Celtic language (he certainly knew Breton): his error is in overlooking the characteristic sharpness, vigor, and color of the original texts in their own setting. But although Flower rightly objects to the "twilight mysticism" bias of the neo-Celtic school, with Arnold and Renan at their head, he quite sensibly places poets in a separate category, for "it is the poet's business to take his good where he finds it and to make the best of it, and he is under no obligation to adopt a strictly historical attitude toward his borrowings." [23]

If he had added "the essayist's business also" (within reasonable limits), he would have absolved Renan from some of his guilt. His texts are, to be sure, chosen with prejudice; the impression they give of the Celtic peoples may well be distorted in many respects. But what matters is that the whole essay is beautifully suited to the central argument of his book. Once we realize that he never intended to write a learned monograph and that he would hardly have denied the very personal quality of his interpretation, we are more likely to enter into the spirit of his "Celtic races" and to recognize in them a splendid symbol of his most intimate moral beliefs and aspirations.[24]

For it was here, in the world of Celtic legends, that Renan found an ideal place of refuge from the mechanized society surrounding him, a source of refreshment and sanity in a society growing increasingly indifferent to poetry and imagination and to the "joys of the soul." Here was an "ideal fatherland," *"une idéale patrie"* (*EMC*, II, 22). Once again Renan shows a certain affinity with the romantic primitivists. Mérimée, we know, liked to confront the bourgeois world (and the bourgeois in himself) with specimens of passionate, cruel humanity he had unearthed in remote semi-primitive corners of Europe. I use Mérimée as a convenient foil to bring out the much softer and more idealistic tone of Renan's primitivism. Unlike Mérimée, Renan seeks to root the gentle and the kind, the joyful and the humorous, as deeply as he can in human nature and in that "life hidden in nature" (*EMC*, II, 22) which is one of the great themes of Celtic folklore. This, to give but one example, is the effect he achieves in presenting a long selection from the Welsh romance, the *Mabinogion*. It is a passage telling of the long search for the lost child Mabon throughout the animal kingdom. In reading it, one feels for a moment the enduring beauty of this naïve poetry, the wry wisdom of folklore, and the activities of the industrial age assume, by contrast with this awful ancient presence of nature and animal life, a rather absurd and futile appearance.

Renan works a similar magic in his handling of the legends of St. Patrick's Purgatory and St. Brendan's voyages, this last being an incomparable source of poetic beauty and spiritual symbolism. To understand what Brunet meant by calling Renan's essential trait *"charme"* (in the etymological sense of magic, enchantment) one should read carefully his retelling of how the bard of bards, Ossian, complained to his Christian conqueror, Patrick, that his arm had grown too feeble to manage the sword; one should savor the humor of the tale of the Dutch canon who, in 1494, descended into one of these Irish "purgatories," only to come up with the report that he had seen "nothing at all"—this being merely one of the many humorous touches which relieve the *sérieux* of the *Essais de morale et de critique*. Sometimes humor is combined with the most delicate spirituality, as in the description of the last hours of the scholarly St. Columba who, "secretly warned that his end was approaching, finished the page of the Psalter he was working on, wrote at the bottom that he bequeathed its continuation to his successor, and went off to the church to die." This is perhaps not so much humor as an indefinable lightness of touch which seems to belong to another world.

In his retelling of the various legends of St. Brendan, Renan provides the key, I believe, to the deepest meaning of this final essay. In a remarkable passage surprisingly close in spirit to the *"voyage métaphysique"* of Baudelaire and Rimbaud, Renan makes use of the legend of St. Brendan's promised land as a symbol of that intermingling of illusion and truth, dream and reality, which so impressed him in Celtic literature, and which he also believed to be a fundamental condition of human thought. In an exceptionally colorful and precise paragraph (*EMC*, II, 295), he describes the mixture of poetic reverie and accurate geographical observation which characterizes the vision of the polar regions as we find it in the writings of these ancient explorers who were in search of the land of promise. It is a strange topography, Renan points out, "at once dazzling like fiction and speaking to us of reality," and it makes the poem of St. Brendan "one of the most astonishing creations of the human spirit and perhaps the most complete expression of the Celtic ideal" (*EMC*, II, 295).

This passage is far from being mere escapism, mere literary play on the part of an antiquarian too soft-minded to face the problems of his own day. I hope I have shown in my analysis of the *Essais de morale et de crtique* that "dreaming of an ideal past" could be for Renan a means of gaining a fresh perspective on his own time and bringing constructive criticism to bear on it. Renan, in this respect a faithful heir to the age-old contemplative tradition of Catholicism, is one of the most skillful defenders of the so-called "dreamer" in the so-called "practical" world. "Who knows," he asks of his Celtic ancestors and of all idealists, "if our dreams are not truer than reality?" (*EMC*, II, 22–23) —and the word "*réalité*" here has some of the overtones of the "real world" of the positivists, the closed world of matter. This is but one illustration of Renan's refusal to accept the closed world of positivism, his striving to blend mysticism and positivism in a new synthesis. The Irish monks, he shows us, were not mystics alone, but courageous explorers; they may have reached Iceland, perhaps even, before the Vikings, America; their "vision" served the very realistic end of drawing men on toward the full discovery of the New World.[25]

Renan could hardly have chosen a more vivid and suggestive way of closing the *Essais de morale et de critique* than by symbolizing in this manner his hope that moral idealism and poetic imagination might work in collaboration with the critical and scientific spirit. Did Renan really believe this possible? Throughout his critique of the industrial age, there is a certain sadness, a certain pessimism; but it is what he calls *"tristesse féconde"* (*EMC*, II, 34); it is a creative pessimism. This seems to me to be the dominant note of the *Essais de morale et de critique*. We are still a long way from the frivolous *badinage* of the last years.

"Tristesse féconde" seems also to be the dominant note of Renan's political thought as a whole. In his opinion, France, for all its material prosperity and superficial gaiety, was suffering from concealed moral and political disease. But he did not despair, for "in a country gifted with such inexhaustible resources as is France, one must never despair" (*EMC*, II, 60). If, in his next two books of essays, he turned more directly to political questions, one reason was of course that they were becoming more and more urgent in his mind. He was also, however, anxious to show that as an idealist he was not, as Prévost-Paradol had implied a few years earlier, negligent of "the laborious, practical improvement of human affairs." [26] He would now pursue in greater detail what he had called in the *Essais de morale et de critique* "the essential work of our time, the establishment of liberty through the regeneration of the individual conscience" (*EMC*, II, 17). His style would be much less poetic, but it would be admirably suited to a very different type of essay.

Chapter 5

The Political Essays

"Each of us, to the extent of his ability, has the duty to think of the public good and to work for it with all his strength."– *Questions contemporaines*

"We shall speak frankly."–*La réforme intellectuelle et morale*

ACTUALLY, almost ten years went by before Renan published his third book of essays, the *Questions contemporaines* (1868). There was no slackening up of his contributions to various periodicals during this time, but his essays were overshadowed by the most momentous event of his entire career, the publication in June 1863 of his *Vie de Jésus*. The trip to the Near East which made this book possible was the central strand in a whole fabric of dramatic events in Renan's life during the 1860's. Indirectly, it was even related to the *Questions contemporaines* and his political thought.

Renan had gone to Syria in 1860–1861 to direct the first large-scale archeological expedition ever carried out in that country. He had gone as a scientist, and was to reveal, in this pioneer archeological undertaking, for which he is still given far too little credit, a new facet of his scholarly genius.[1] But it was during this scientific mission that he also conceived one of his least scientific and most personal works. Treading the same ground Jesus had walked on, breathing the same air, he was deeply moved. Contrary to his generally more austere artistic principles, he knelt briefly to worship at the shrine of local color. He devoted himself to making the Saviour more real historically, and he seems at first, in the finished work, to have succeeded. But for all the wonderful precision of *race, milieu,* and *moment* in the *Vie de Jésus,* the total effect is to rob Jesus of historical substance and spiritual depth, to make him in the end a mirror of Renan's own mind, a nineteenth-century humanitarian eclectic, preaching to the poor what looks suspiciously like the idealism of Victor Cousin and George Sand.[2]

There were poignant memories associated with the *Vie de Jésus,* for Henriette Renan, to whom it is dedicated, had accompanied her brother on this rugged journey and, devoted to the end, had died of fever at Amschmit in September 1861. Only narrowly did Renan himself escape a death which would, curiously enough, have left French letters with the work of a highly idealistic, thoroughly serious scholar-artist, without scandal and without *renanisme.*

But Renan had consolations for the tragic death of his sister. In January 1862, a few months after his return to France, he realized the ambition of which they had often dreamed together: he succeeded his former professor, Etienne Quatremère, in the chair of Hebrew, Chaldaic, and Syriac languages at the Collège de France. This was indeed his life's ambition; he was thirty-nine. The consolation soon turned, however, into trouble. Less than a month after his appointment, in the course of his inaugural lecture, speaking a bit in the manner of a bishop *in partibus infidelium*,³ he made clear his philosophical position, which involved a firm denial of the supernatural. He described Jesus as *"un homme incomparable,"* and thereby, with some help from rival student factions, proclerical and anticlerical, who created a noisy disturbance (Taine claimed even to have seen a little bloodshed), was plunged into the waters of controversy. Soon afterward, in 1863, after two years of extremely scrupulous toning down, his *Vie de Jésus* came off the press. When the full impact of his disturbingly sweet and tender denial of Christ's divinity hit the public, fame swept around him in huge waves. He was committed to the serious historical work which would be his *magnum opus* and at the same time tempted along that most dangerous of paths for a writer, the path of flirtation with an admiring public.

Renan's name was now controversial; he had become himself a *question contemporaine*. He was deprived of his professorship, which he did not regain until the advent of the Third Republic; he served out in the meanwhile a form of interior exile, comfortable but vexing to the cause of freedom of thought, as assistant director of manuscripts in the Bibliothèque Impériale. But he had been shaken very abruptly from his "dream of an ideal past," the main theme of the *Essais de morale et de critique*. He had become a central figure in the moral and political issue of academic freedom, an issue on which, in fact, he writes at length and with special eloquence, in the *Questions contemporaines*.⁴

Even without this personal incentive, however, Renan would surely have given expression to his thought on political problems, for they had always interested him deeply. The time was ripe for such expression. The political climate had changed markedly since his last essay work. Toward

1860 the Emperor, seeking to offset loss of support from Catholics, who resented his failure to re-establish the temporal power of the Pope, and from businessmen, who were offended by his free-trade policies, reached out for the support of the liberal opposition. He granted political amnesty and relaxed restrictions on the press. His parliamentary government, until then largely a hoax, became more of a reality; as Renan described this transformation in *La réforme intellectuelle et morale:* "Roman caesarism was also originally a despotism surrounded by the fictions of a republic; the despotism killed off the fictions; with us, on the contrary, the fictions of representative government have killed off the despotism" (*RIM*, I, 500–501). Renan welcomed as much as anyone else this chance to breathe some of the air out of his lungs, to talk politics more frankly than he had done since his days on the *Liberté de penser*. He reworked, in fact, his "Du libéralisme clérical" and "L'état des esprits en 1849," as we have seen. It was an opportune moment to publish them, with more recent essays, in a new book.

Renan's two volumes of political essays, the *Questions contemporaines* and *La réforme intellectuelle et morale*, despite the great historical gap between their dates of publication—between 1869 and 1871 the whole Second Empire collapsed—have much in common. To define first their general themes and arguments, and then the sharp differences between them, and, finally, to bring out the special qualities of Renan as a political essayist—such is the order I propose to follow.

When we call these essays "political," we include not only questions of the correct principles, structure, and conduct of government, in the accepted Anglo-Saxon use of the term "politics." We go beyond these to others involving education, cultural life, and even religion, for it is well to remind ourselves that we are in France, where the sphere of governmental influence has always been extraordinarily wide. "Political" means also to a great extent historical. Renan exemplifies the peculiar emphasis of a people which for generations had tended to consider its present political problems in the light of its greatest historical experience in recent times, the Revolution of 1789. This was especially true in the nineteenth century, when the Revolution seemed to many to be an unfinished event—either a blessed promise to be completely fulfilled or a demoniacal force to be once and for all exorcised.

There are, in the *Questions contemporaines*, four general themes of this broadly political character: "*politique géné-rale*," or the question of the interpretation of recent political events, especially revolutionary upheavals; the question of education; the question of the "civil organization of religious cults"; and finally, the question of the "moral and religious state of our country" (*QC*, I, 12). These issues are of course all interrelated, and all part of the great question which haunts political thinkers of nineteenth-century France, how to attain true liberty while at the same time achieving an orderly and stable form of government. In *La réforme intellectuelle et morale*, these same general questions are pursued, but with increasing emphasis on the diagnosis of France's moral condition.

Underlying all these themes, however, is another: if we except the two *Liberté de penser* essays, we find that through all the others, from 1849 to 1871, one theme runs like an ominous undercurrent—the rivalry of France and Prussia.

In the *Essais de morale et de critique*, "the forests of Germania" had been for Renan the cradle of liberty and individualism, as against Roman centralization and bureaucracy, and also the cradle of the free philosophical spirit—an illusion held by many nineteenth-century thinkers, including Carlyle, Arnold, and Emerson. In 1866 came Sadowa, Bismarck's defeat of Austria, the identification of the cause of German nationalism with the cause of Prussia: out of the cradle arose a powerful economic and military machine, a powerful moral organization. This "sudden, triumphant appearance of Germany on the great European battlefield" (*QC*, I, 23) caused Renan to push his ideas not toward a recognition of the potential military menace of Germany (few Frenchmen felt the groundswell of war in the making) but toward a more precise program of French imitation of supposed German virtues. Renan pleaded for the French to imitate not the fruits of the Prussian system, not its military institutions, but the tree and the roots: "German schools, German universities, German moral education, the German method of handling religious questions" (*QC*, I, 23). The *débâcle*, far from destroying the validity of this thesis in Renan's mind, simply altered its purpose. The rallying cry of *La réforme intellectuelle et morale* will be: Let the vanquished learn from the victor how to rise up again with renewed strength!

The *Questions contemporaines* is a much less complex book than its successor. In educational matters its argument is a simple one: in primary and secondary schools, less regimentation, a greater recognition of the family as a moral teacher; in higher education, and here the emulation of Germany is especially apparent, greater academic freedom, the strengthening of scholarly research, particularly scientific research, and the organization of large universities throughout France endowed by the state but independent of it.

Renan believed that the tendency to turn the living idea into an institution, organized according to very abstract notions, was a dangerous defect of the *esprit français* in politics as well as in education: "The error of France is, in general, to believe that one can replace the free spontaneity of souls with well-contrived institutions" (*QC*, I, 259). In calling for higher standards of scholarship, he hoped to correct what he considered another serious national fault, the penchant for superficial rhetoric, or at best brilliance of form, at the expense of sound intellectual content. "The danger for France in the intellectual order," he wrote, "is to become a nation of talkers and *rédacteurs*, without concern for content and the real progress of knowledge" (*QC*, I, 84). He even goes so far as to call it *"le mal français,"* the national disease, "the need to perorate, the tendency to reduce everything to declamation," and accuses the University of Paris itself (at least in part) of fostering the disease contentedly (*QC*, I, 13–14). Such criticisms, which Renan was not alone in making, were to bear fruit in many educational reforms beginning in the 1860's.

As for the form of government he believed best suited to guarantee both freedom and stability, his position has to be defined indirectly from remarks on the Revolutions of 1789, 1830, and 1848, remarks found largely in the preface and in the first essay, "Philosophie de l'histoire contemporaine." The Revolution of 1789, the object of some severe criticism in the *Essais de morale et de critique*, is still "an infinitely honorable experiment," but "an abortive experiment" (*QC*, I, 12). The July Revolution, which he believed might have been prevented, produced the monstrosity of the Citizen-King, and it might seem that this illegitimate government, in Renan's eyes, would excuse in advance the Revolution of

1848. But if we compare what Renan now writes of that Revolution with what he had written years ago in the *Liberté de penser*, when that event was almost sacred, he now damns with faint praise indeed: it is "that good, irreproachable, improvident, superficial Revolution of 1848," whose lack of foresight led to the most ponderous and obstinate conservatism (*QC*, I, 20). Scarcely a year later, in "La monarchie constitutionnelle en France,"⁵ the February Revolution has lost even the mild virtue of irreproachable honesty and has become a crime, equal in heinousness to the *coup d'état* which shortly followed (*RIM*, I, 496–497). The *républicains* by then have become the party which is fit to make revolutions but incapable of lasting more than two months in power (*RIM*, I, 509). But by the time we have reached that essay, Renan's declaration in favor of constitutional monarchy, the form toward which he had been moving for several years, is only too plain.

And what of religion? What, in particular, of the position of the Roman Catholic Church in France? In the 1860's the Church and the state were coming to grips in a terribly bitter struggle. The Pope had condemned liberalism (1864) and was soon to define papal infallibility as a dogma (1870). The French state was moving toward the complete secularization of government and education, a movement which would gain momentum under the Third Republic and culminate, after Renan's death, in the Separation Law of 1905.

What was Renan's position on these questions? There is no doubt that he felt that political liberty is intimately related to freedom of worship. There is no doubt that he too wanted the secularization of French life, believing it to be the best guarantee of both these freedoms. But his anticlericalism, mild in the *Questions contemporaines*, virulent in *La*

réforme intellectuelle et morale, is of such a highly indi-
vidualistic nature that only by distorting his thought can
we make him, as Anatole France and many politicians of
the Third Republic tried to do, the patron saint of anticlericalism. Secularization meant for him "higher moral and
intellectual education, a pure cult, *not separated violently
from religion, but independent of religion*" (*QC*, I, 23, my
italics). Anticlerical politicians like Jules Ferry, René
Waldeck-Rousseau, or Emile Combes could make capital
out of such remarks as "Supernatural beliefs are like a poison
which kills if one take it in too strong a dose" (*RIM*, I, 393)
or such essays as "Du libéralisme clérical," but on the whole
Renan's attitude toward the Church is such an ambiguous
personal one that it is difficult to imagine what they really
made of it. In one of the rare lyrical passages of the *Questions contemporaines,* in an extraordinary tribute to the
Catholic Church which even contains an echo of Bossuet's
Sermon sur l'unité de l'Eglise, Renan writes:

How many excellent souls among her faithful who draw only
milk and honey from her breasts, leaving to others the wormwood and gall! How tempted one is, at the sight of her tents
drawn up on the plain, Jehovah still walking in their midst,
to bless, like the infidel prophet, what one had come to curse,
and to cry out: "How beautiful thy pavilions! how delightful
thy dwellings!" [*QC*, I, 271].

But Renan himself had left these dwellings for good and
had set up his own tents on the plain—the pavilions of "*le
culte pur.*" In the long defense of his religious position and
his right to teach, "La chaire d'hébreu au Collège de France,"
in "L'avenir religieux des sociétés modernes," and in the
last essay, "La théologie de Béranger," he attempts to dem-

onstrate that the effort to separate the religious from the supernatural is not necessarily irreligious. In the last-named essay, after demolishing with brilliant wit the poet and song writer Pierre-Jean de Béranger's bourgeois "theology," Renan goes on to preach his own gospel of the God France should believe in. Taking as his text a skeptical verse "prayer" of Musset, he outlines a vague deism composed of moral delicacy, the murmur of distant church bells, the "perfumes of ancient days," and the assurance that one's works will survive one's death (*QC*, I, 313–315)—a religion undoubtedly more refined, but hardly much more substantial, than Béranger's theology for "good folk" (*"Dieu des bonnes gens"*) or his *"Dieu gaulois"* of grisettes and tavern drinkers.

Nor does the long ambitious essay on "L'avenir religieux des sociétés modernes" put much more flesh on the bones of Renan's *"vraie religion,"* his *"religion épurée."* Berthelot pointed out the basic inconsistency of this essay in a letter to his friend: Renan seems to be predicting a great future for Christianity as the only truly creative religion (needless to say he cavalierly dismisses Mohammedanism and Far Eastern religions) and yet he argues as fervently as ever for his own "individual religion." [6] Or does he favor Protestantism? One thing is clear: if he does, it is not because of any personal attraction to Protestantism; he praises it, in fact, less as a religion than as a guarantee of spiritual liberty, an environment favorable to free thought,[7] just as in *La réforme intellectuelle et morale* he urges Catholic France to shake off stultifying clerical influences and learn from Protestant Prussia how to produce superior citizens and soldiers.

The *Questions contemporaines* is a collection of fifteen essays which present their arguments, outlined above, in an atmosphere of calm and with a certain amount of objectivity. *La réforme intellectuelle et morale,* with its seven essays, is one of the most violently provocative of all Renan's works. But it is not unique among his books; it is in fact characteristic of much of his writing in the 1870's. One can correctly apply to it Henriette Psichari's observation about the fourth book of *Les origines du christianisme, L'Antéchrist* (1873): "The whole volume is written in a harsh, incisive style which contrasts with the supple, refined manner of so many of his other works." [8] The *Questions contemporaines* is a prewar work. *La réforme intellectuelle et morale* was, except for two essays,[9] composed in the midst of the convulsions which almost destroyed France in the early 1870's—invasion, crushing military defeat, civil war, profound demoralization, and disunity. Much of its violence is the violence of *l'année terrible.*

The style is well suited to the thesis (actually, as we shall see, there are several theses and they are contradictory), for Renan's harsh program for the salvation of France contains great coarse seeds of fascism. Little wonder that Georges Sorel, one of the spiritual fathers of Mussolini, called this Renan's masterpiece and the only "sincere" work he ever wrote—on the principle, it would seem, that an author is sincere when he writes what you agree with.[10] For Sorel, who could not accept, any more than Maurras and his disciples, the genuinely democratic ideas Renan expresses elsewhere (and to some extent in this very book), could revel with the other pre-fascists in what seems to be a total and irrevocable indictment of the baseness and stupidity of democracy.

But that is hardly the worst of Renan's thesis. The leading essay, from which the book derives its title, provides a manual on how to despise the people and keep them in a state of productive ignorance and suffering; how to organize for a war not only as a means of revenge but also as a means of moral progress; how to realize the manifest destiny of Frenchmen (which also happens to be a good means of preventing the growth of socialism at home), namely, the conquest and colonization of "inferior races" (*RIM*, I, 356–357, 373, 390–391). The new France, the future Utopia here outlined, would be a hierarchy: at the top, the aristocracy, the elite (blood nobility, military men, and of course the intellectual nobility, or scholars), controlling the bourgeoisie and the masses, those masses who would naturally be at the bottom, maintained in a state of willful superstition by innocuous *bons curés* who ease their suffering with doses of the opium of faith (*RIM*, I, 485–487). Such, hardly overstated, are the leading ideas of this cornerstone essay, innocently entitled "La réforme intellectuelle et morale de la France." No overstatement is called for, so clearly and vigorously, so brutally do these ideas strike us. One is tempted to fly from them into the arms of Karl Marx, or at least to give up trying to fit the undeniably liberal elements of so much of Renan's thought into the same picture with this vision of an oligarchy of supermen. For the moment, the very title of Marcel Jaspar's *Renan, le génie libéral de la France* seems like a hollow joke.

Nevertheless, the denigrators of democracy, the forerunners of fascism, the *traditionalistes*, have erred in making this one of their sacred texts. It has a saving grace they have overlooked: it is much less doctrinaire, much more confused and self-contradictory than they have been willing to admit. There are a number of flagrant contradictions which alone would tend to alert us to the fact that the book is not a carefully thought out, definitive system of political philosophy. "It has not," wrote Matthew Arnold, who reproached the author for his lack of patient faith in democracy, "the usual consummate roundness of M. Renan's composition, the appearance of having been thoroughly prepared in mind, and of now coming forth in perfect ripeness; there are, or we seem to see, marks here and there of haste, excitement, and chagrin." [11]

There are, for example, vigorously militaristic pages, where the flags rustle and the trumpets blare with the call to *revanche* and war appears as the path to glory and honor, virtues the vile democratic soul cannot understand (*RIM*, I, 513, and the first essay generally). But there are also pacifist pages where war is denounced as a "web of sins, an unnatural state," and the desire for revenge is branded as *"funeste"* (*RIM*, I, 432, 447, 514, and in general "La guerre entre la France et l'Allemagne" and the letters to Strauss). The initial essay calls for a program of brutalization of the masses which it would be hard to surpass for cynicism; and yet the last essay, "La part de la famille et de l'état dans l'éducation," a prewar electoral campaign speech of 1869, condemns this same *"abrutissement d'une partie de l'espèce humaine"* as bad ethics and bad politics and makes an eloquent plea for the development in each man of the sense of his duty to cultivate soul and mind (*RIM*, I, 524–525).

Obviously, these contradictions have much to do with the circumstances in which the essays were written; they were, as Arnold suggests, perhaps inevitable. Unlike the contradictions inherent in Renan's philosophical thought or those he tossed about as part of the intellectual play, the mystification, of later years, these are the uncertainties of a mind struggling to keep up with events, to understand them, to offer a constructive plan for sane action before it is too late. What resulted was much less a reasoned manifesto for monarchy (the relatively calm essay on constitutional monarchy is the closest the author comes to that) or a political treatise than a kind of intimate journal, the dramatic account of Renan's mind under the impact of a series of national calamities—a year by year, almost month by month, record of his reactions to national tragedy.

But it was not as a one-man Greek chorus that Renan looked on. He was too sincerely patriotic for that. Besides, he had been an active participant. To understand his shifting viewpoints, his unusual pessimism and cynicism in *La réforme intellectuelle et morale*, one has to recall the background of these essays, the political experiences their author went through from 1869 to 1871.

In 1869, as a candidate for the Corps législatif in the rural districts of the Seine-et-Marne, Renan had faced the electorate. His party was that of the leader of the liberal *ralliés à l'Empire*, the *Tiers parti* of Emile Ollivier, and their platform a conditional endorsement of Napoleon III. Renan was defeated. He came away, however, not with hurt pride, but with disgust at the prosperous peasants of the Seine-et-Marne, a perfect example of *"l'esprit démocratique,"* here used of course pejoratively—lacking in civic responsibility, athirst for equality at all costs, indifferent to all but selfish material interests, content with keeping the government uncostly and powerless so long as things were prospering (*RIM*, I, 347, 504). This was indeed, to use Henriette Psichari's phrase, a "sad political apprenticeship," and she is perfectly right in saying that it left her grandfather for many years afterward "disillusioned and full of regret." [12] It accounts for much of the antidemocratic spirit of his book.

But more bitter wormwood than this was in store for him. The war with Germany was "the poignant sorrow which left a permanent mark on his mature years." [13] "Germany," he wrote, "had been my teacher; I was conscious of owing her all that was best in me. Judge, then, what I have suffered, on seeing the nation which taught me idealism make a mockery of every ideal" (*RIM*, preface, I, 327). The "intimate political journal" aspect of *La réforme intellectuelle et morale* is nowhere more strikingly apparent than in the evolution we can trace therein of Renan's attitude toward Germany—his gradual discovery of the import of Prussian militarism, his clinging to the hope that an older, more liberal, more enlightened and peaceful Germany would absorb Prussia as the dough absorbs the leaven which has caused it to rise (*RIM*, I, 439), his disillusionment, his abandonment of all hope of postwar co-operation, his extraordinarily prophetic denunciation of German "racial politics" in the second letter to Strauss. [14]

Finally, there was the culmination of this whole series of bitter disappointments, the apocalyptic horror of the Commune uprising, the "Bloody Week" of May 22–28, 1871, Frenchmen destroying themselves as the enemy looked on. It seemed to Renan the crime of a populace driven to madness by the madness surrounding it, and what he saw of this horror from Versailles—the flames rising in the distance above Paris—left him with memories which never faded, "bruises," he confided to a friend, "which do not heal." [15]

Was not this traumatic experience, this wound of disillusionment, sufficient reason for the pessimism of *La réforme intellectuelle et morale*, not to mention the pessimism of the *Dialogues et fragments philosophiques*, begun at Versailles in May 1871? Small wonder that Renan, in desperate concern for the survival of his country, was haunted by the necessity of restoring order to France at any cost, even at the cost of the liberty we know he prized so highly. A political void seemed a more intolerable evil to him than rule by an elite intellectual oligarchy armed with absolute military power. In retrospect, his vision of a reconstructed France seems to us like a nightmare, but the historical moment from which it sprang was perhaps an even greater nightmare.

It would be unfair to Renan to end a survey of his political essays on such a somber note. This unbalanced stance was far from being his definitive political position, if we may use such a phrase for a thinker of his elusiveness. He was a vigorous and constructive political essayist, with a gift for penetrating observation and wise comment, a gift for provoking our thought even, perhaps especially, when we disagree with him.

Much of the attraction of these two books lies in the fact that Renan has communicated to us through them two of the most admirable traits of his character: his sense of political responsibility and his capacity for intelligent action. One could hardly have blamed him if, in the face of the frustrating political developments of his day, he had laid down the burden of thinking about his country's problems and withdrawn into the convenient shelter bounded by the card files and erudite monographs of his scholarly trade. But the record shows he took a far worthier course. From the time he cast his vote thoughtfully for Lamartine in 1848 and, one eye open for what was going on, picked his way through the barricades of the *journées de juin,* bound for a library to determine whether Abélard knew Greek; from his youth down to the *Discours et conférences* and beyond, Renan combined scholarship most admirably with a vivid concern for the "public good." His political essays run parallel with his supervision of a collection of Phoenician inscriptions and his contributions to a literary history of France begun by Benedictine monks in the eighteenth century. He was under no illusion as to the influence a philosopher-scholar is likely to exert on public affairs; but he insisted on the profound duty in conscience of every citizen to help improve the health of the body politic (*RIM*, I, 325, 478; *QC*, I, 11). In fact, in the 1870's, the less likely he was to be heard, the less popular his conception of the public welfare, the more vigorously he spoke out.

He was, furthermore, willing and indeed eager to act. Despite his often expressed contempt for *"hommes d'action,"* despite his implication that to be a successful "man of action" one must stop thinking, above all stop thinking critically, and become a fanatic,[16] Renan himself, within modest limits but more than most of us, was a man of action. Even though he once defined politics as "the way of governing humanity as though it were a machine or a herd" (*QC*, I, 231), he was eager to show that this much-maligned activity need not exclude intelligence and critical sense. His motto—"A legislative mandate ought neither to be sought nor refused"[17]—revealed not indifference toward political responsibility, as has sometimes been alleged, but a spirit of generous sacrifice on the part of a man whose vocation was not politics but scholarship.

Twice Renan ran the electoral gauntlet: in the campaign of 1869, to which we have alluded, and again in 1878 in the Bouches-du-Rhône as a candidate for the Sénat. He did not, it is true, rush into these contests like a ward politician, and he was defeated both times; but these are hardly reasons for claiming that he had no real aptitude for political action. Eugène Meyer, distorting Renan's portrait by too insistent a *rapprochement* with Vigny (also an unsuccessful political candidate), has even gone so far as to congratulate the voters for their wisdom in rejecting Renan, who, in his opinion, was a "political philosopher," not a "positive theorist," and least of all a "man of action," and who, in any case, could not have prevented the war of 1870 or helped win victory! [18] This is grossly unfair. Not only does it distort Renan's vigorous political journalism into some sort of speculative treatise written from calm Platonic heights and overlook the many examples of precise, constructive programs for practical action, such as the essay entitled "De la convocation d'une assemblée pendant le siège" (*RIM*, I, 463–475). It also denies his great potentiality. There is no reason whatever to believe that he would not have brought to the French Parliament the same energy and skill with which he directed complicated scientific expeditions in the Near East or administered the Collège de France,[19] not to mention his insight into political history and his exceptional talent as an orator.

But the myth purveyed with such ironically loving care by Barrès, in his *Jardin de Bérénice*, his *Huit jours chez M. Renan*, and elsewhere, the myth of Renan the indifferent, impractical dreamer, persists. The best way to refute it is to rediscover for oneself, as Bourget did, the essentially vigorous and active nature of this descendant of seamen and peasants. Bourget, too, had once believed him an impractical dreamer, but in an invaluable appendix to his essay on Renan, he courageously rectifies his error and points out how this man who may have been embarrassed about taking his seat in a bus had nevertheless the "physical and moral robustness" of a man of action.[20]

Bourget made this discovery on reading the correspondence with Berthelot, but the same spirit of vigor and responsibility animates the political essays. Nothing could be further than these essays, in their very existence and preoccupation with contemporary issues, from the *"charmante promenade"* Renan liked us to think he took *"à travers la réalité*—to quote the all too famous last words of the *Souvenirs d'enfance et de jeunesse.* No style could be further from the soft delicate poetry of so much of his other work, an incomparably beautiful style at its best, but hopelessly woolly at its worst. Here, with the exception of a few passages on his religious belief where his thought seems inevitably to become vague,[21] all is simplicity, concision, energy, frankness. The frankness should be stressed, for here Renan is playing no game of intellectual hide-and-seek with his public. We owe it to our country, he declared, "to say exactly, and without the sacrifice of a nuance, what we believe to be the truth" (*RIM*, I, 478). Truth sometimes meant *"vérités importunes,"* hard truths, which the cautious, conciliatory François Buloz feared might endanger the reputation of the *Revue des deux mondes* for political middle-of-the-roadism and patriotism.[22]

In moving from the *Essais de morale et de critique* to his political essays, Renan followed a well-defined esthetic of what one might call his political prose style. He by no means renounces his literary skill or his sense of nuances. But he seeks to reach a wider audience, even *"le peuple"* if possible, and therefore he is anxious above all not to be misunderstood (*QC*, I, 71). This meant, as he saw it, avoiding all suggestion of *"arrière-pensée littéraire,"* especially since one of his main theses was the attack on superficial rhetoric in higher education. Here, if he had a model, it was not the great prose stylists Chateaubriand or Michelet, but Guizot, the architect of the July monarchy, the Protestant historian, a man of action now reduced to writing his memoirs. His *"diction,"* not too polished but sober, strong, and measured, seemed best suited to writing on great affairs of state (*QC*, I, 31). Even his lapses from impartiality, his occasional polemical verve (it will be more than occasional with Renan) seemed appropriate for political writing. In politics, remarks the author of the *Questions contemporaines* dryly, one must not try to be impartial, like a historian; above all, one must be careful not to admit errors, for if a man dared challenge those of his detractors who are without sin to cast the first stone, "a mob of madmen would advance boldly and stone him to death" (*QC*, I, 30).

Renan by no means abandoned his historical sense, his broad, calm philosophical perspective, in his political essays. He still believed that the fanatical party man was very poorly situated for "judging the whole picture, comparing different times and countries, grasping long-range movements and foreseeing the future" (*QC*, I, 11). Only the historian could do that, and it is as much the long-range philosophical view as the vigorous style which has prevented these essays on ephemeral political questions from dating, whether the vital thread their author is tracing in recent history is higher education, the evolution of the monarchy, or relations between France and Germany. There is a fascinating meditative pattern in these reflections on four or five great political problems, to which the essayist keeps returning, in search of their deeper meaning. But although not exactly partisan, the prose has the virtues of hard-hitting partisan prose, that is, clarity, energy, incisiveness, polemical wit.

The reader will find in an appendix to this book some samples of this forceful prose which, unfortunately, hardly ever finds its way into anthologies. The passage quoted in Appendix 3 is typical, in its realism, firmness, and clarity, of the way in which Renan defines a scholar's responsibility in political affairs. A second passage (Appendix 4), much less solemn, shows his great flair for controversy and the wit that demolishes an opponent: it is an excerpt from the second of his letters to Strauss, part of the public debate (which would be unthinkable in today's climate of cold war and propaganda) between two distinguished scholars whose countries were at war. With that energetic anger which crackles all through *La réforme intellectuelle et morale*, and sometimes burns with moral indignation, Renan argues that if the German racial, ethnographical, or "archeological" approach to the question of rights over disputed territories (in this case, Alsace-Lorraine) is correct, French claims might be pushed back further until we reach prehistory, and the orangutans, dispossessed by civilized men, appear as the rightful owners of the earth. (Only Louis Veuillot would have tried to improve on this, probably by calling Strauss himself an orangutan.)

Elsewhere in the same letter (Appendix 4) Renan achieves an extraordinary combination of down-to-earth prose, familiar and unlearned in its phrasing, with the classical wisdom and irony that are resources of a learned man. Throughout *La réforme intellectuelle et morale*, which is much more interesting stylistically than the *Questions contemporaines*, solemn Latin quotations, from Michel de l'Hôpital, Cicero, Juvenal, Virgil, the Bible, and other sources, go hand in hand with the vocabulary of finance and gambling. Although lyricism had little place in this political style, Renan on rare occasions employs that gift to advantage, as in the passage on the mystique of the French monarchy (see Appendix 5, a good example of the range of his political prose), where historical facts are mixed with elements of the monarchist, nationalist mythology to make a nostalgic paean in honor of France's "eighth sacrament," an effusive patriotic poem which seems to have a solid historical basis but which ends on a note of bald counterrevolutionary invective.

It will be noted from some of these illustrative passages that Renan's prose tends to take the form of aphorisms ("L'orgueil est le seul vice qui soit puni en ce monde," "Triompher est toujours une faute"). This gift for concise, witty formulas, many of them aphorisms—a neglected virtue of this great prose stylist—is especially striking in his political writing, which differs in this respect from the critical or historical works with their patient instillment of ideas expressed in language dilated to catch the most subtle shade of thought. In Appendix 6 will be found some of the most memorable of these pithy sayings. Their provocative character accounts for much of the continuing life and readability of the essays.

As essential an element as style is in the durability of the *Questions contemporaines* and *La réforme intellectuelle et morale*, we must in the end judge Renan's program for the reform of his country on its own merits, as he undoubtedly intended us to. Looking back on his ideas, we find that some were valid and deserving of wide influence, some were extraordinarily prophetic, while others were contradictory or blind. Few, however, are the essays without great interest, and few those not marked by their author's extraordinary critical intelligence.

The reforms Renan urged in the educational system, beginning with his earliest articles, later reprinted in *Questions contemporaines*,[23] were partly responsible for the renovations undertaken in the 1860's by the Emperor's Minister of Education, Victor Duruy, with the chief purpose (dear to Renan) of promoting a more serious scholarly and intellectual life in France.[24] His observations on religious life in France were much less penetrating. His celebrated quip, "France is the most orthodox country in the world, because it is the least religious," seems to me palpably untrue in both of its clauses, but it unfortunately governed much of his thinking about religious questions. His vision obscured by events which were truly disturbing (the beginnings of modernism, the struggle over infallibility, the papal loss of temporal power) but which have not led to the deep rent in the Roman Catholic Church, the great schism that he predicted, he was unable to see the promise of a liberalized Catholic social, economic, and political thought.

But in another area, that of the political future of Europe in general, his prophecies and warnings were remarkably sound. The passages of *La réforme intellectuelle et morale* clearly foreboding Hitlerism, race politics, the German use of a Fifth Column, the emergence of Russia as a "Muscovite Ghenghiskhan" unifying the Slavic peoples and becoming the nemesis of Germany, are among the most remarkable in his whole work [25] and should destroy once and for all the legend that he never stripped himself of his illusions about Germany. But he was also a prophet in a less spectacular sense. With admirable courage and stubbornness, he preached to his fellow Frenchmen fasting and abstinence, expiation and penance; in other words, hard intellectual work and self-discipline, the Prussian hair shirt France must wear like "a sharp-pointed steel sunk into her flesh to keep her awake" (*RIM*, I, 370). And yet he did this in a spirit of genuine patriotism. Some critics have accused him of defeatism and moral treason—which has usually meant that they did not agree with the remedies he proposed for moral reform.[26] There are indeed passages of *La réforme intellectuelle et morale* (especially of "La guerre entre la France et l'Allemagne") which, insinuating that the French were unjust aggressors in the war of 1870, must have looked suspect in 1939. But to read Renan carefully is to discover that in reality he practiced an authentic form of patriotism, perhaps the only true form (it has never been very popular), which consists of "telling the truth at the risk of displeasing." [27]

The greatest weakness of Renan's political essays, in my opinion, is the contradictory or at best confused nature of his philosophy of government, and *La réforme intellectuelle et morale* sins especially grievously in this respect. The fundamental contradiction is this: Renan stressed liberty, education, and constitutional government and yet could never seem to make up his mind whether he trusted the broad mass of people who must form the base of such a liberal state. It is not his belief in constitutional monarchy which is in question here, for such a belief was perfectly consonant with liberalism, as Benjamin Constant, Madame de Staël, Victor Hugo, and many others had shown; indeed the most brilliant liberal spokesman of Renan's day, Prévost-Paradol, was a constitutional monarchist. The question is one of distrust in the people or trust in them. Hesitation on this point runs throughout Renan's work, from

L'avenir de la science to the *Souvenirs d'enfance et de jeunesse* and the *Drames philosophiques.*

It is difficult to believe that the most harsh and brutal expression of his distrust, "La réforme intellectuelle et morale," an almost unforgivable outburst of contempt for the miserable, the humble, and the oppressed, sprang from anything more than the momentary bitterness of the war years, perhaps also from panic at the thought of anarchy. It seems to me very significant (we know the importance of structure in Renan's essay books) that he places last in *La réforme intellectuelle et morale* the two most sober and reasonable essays, "La monarchie constitutionnelle en France" and "La part de la famille et de l'état dans l'éducation," although they were the earliest in date. It is also significant that he ends the book with an expression of faith in a democratically conceived educational system, in fact with the reiteration of the word "faith" (*RIM*, I, 542). Elsewhere, it is true, in another very restrained essay, he seems to exclude the people once again and to limit his faith by placing it only in "true aristocrats," "the elite in mind and heart," those "few citizens" upon whose intelligence and virtue the salvation of a country rests (*RIM*, I, 470).

It is tempting to try to resolve the contradiction simply by saying that Renan was profoundly antidemocratic in spirit. But we know of his subsequent adjustment to the Third Republic. Was he moved by mere expediency or mere gratitude for comforts and honors extended to him? He had, certainly, great facility in adjusting to different regimes, while retaining the right to be critical of them— an attitude some will call spineless lack of principle and others good political sense. But, knowing that his political thought is much more complicated than a survey of his essays can show, I hazard the guess that his belief in constitutional monarchy was not irrevocable and that he did not entirely give up faith in the possibility of a working democracy for France.

If Roger Soltau is right in calling the true test of political liberalism one's attitude toward the French Revolution.[28] Renan stands up pretty well under such a test. In 1875 he wrote to Berthelot from Brittany that in the hours of relief from rheumatism he had been reading Thiers's *History of the Revolution;* it was, he said, a "strange, grandiose, unheard of" event, comparable to the origins of Christianity or Islam, all "facts of the first order" but all inimitable events which can never be reproduced again.[29] Of *Les origines de la France contemporaine,* which Taine had been reading aloud to him, he wrote to Berthelot in 1879 a most revealing criticism: Taine, he declared, shows only the sad, horrible, shameful aspects of the revolution and hides its grandiose, heroic, sublime side.[30] This remark to Berthelot bears out the confession he makes in his autobiography of an "invincible taste" for the Revolution (inherited, he claimed, from his mother), which made him love it in spite of his reason and in spite of all the evil he had spoken of it (*SEJ*, II, 775). "The task," he wrote in "La monarchie constitutionnelle en France," "'is less to continue the Revolution than to evaluate it critically and repair its mistakes" (*RIM*, I, 514).

Unlike practically all the other great nineteenth-century French historians, Renan never wrote a history of the Revolution. Midway in his career it was too late for him to undertake such a task. Not only was he deeply immersed in his own history of Christianity and Judaism, but to do the subject justice, as he remarked to Berthelot, one must begin at twenty-five and treat it with the combined powers of critic, artist, and philosopher. But the Revolution haunted him, as it has haunted most Frenchmen down to our own day. His two books of political essays are fragmentary attempts to write its history, or rather its postscript, and therefore they are essays in the original sense of the word. Artistically they are not as great as the *Essais de morale et de critique*, and they are less profound. But they bring to bear on the great problem of the Revolution's legacy to modern France a vigor and frankness, a passion for reform, which, unusual in Renan, give to this part of his work a special vitality.

Chapter 6

The Metaphysician
despite Himself

"We must be mystics with a sense for facts and with the scientific method."–*Cahiers de jeunesse*

RENAN wrote only four philosophical essays: three are *"fragments"* composed in the 1860's and published in the *Dialogues et fragments philosophiques* of 1876 ("Les sciences de la nature et les sciences historiques," "Lettre à M. Adolphe Guéroult," and "La métaphysique et son avenir"), and the fourth, "Examen de conscience philosophique," is the final essay in his last book of essays, the *Feuilles détachées* of 1892. They form a small but very significant part of his total philosophical writing. To come to them from his political essays is to leave clear, forceful, practical prose for an extremely tenuous verbal music, bearing the imprint of its author's belief that philosophy is essentially a form of poetry. This transition also takes us from an atmosphere of firm, even at times dogmatic, convictions into one of uncertainty and dream and illusion. The ground seems to slip out from under us. Here we find, for the first time in Renan's work, a compelling reason for his reputation as one of the most fluctuating, wavering thinkers ever to set pen to paper. Yet even here there is more firmness than he has been credited with; there is even a curious tenacity about a number of fundamental points. What other philosopher has ever shown the complaisance with which Renan demarcates for his readers areas of doubt, certainty, and fancy, either by chapter headings, as in the *Dialogues philosophiques* (*"Certitudes," "Probabilités," "Rêves"*), or by the structure of the essay, as in the "Examen de conscience philosophique"?

Renan was a philosopher-poet, a philosopher-artist, a modern descendant of Plato and Malebranche, a forerunner of Santayana. But he was much less a "professional philosopher" than these; he was what the French, with greater esteem than they often give to a mere philosopher, like to call a *penseur*. His whole work is based on the concealed philosophy of the artist (less concealed, however, than he thought), the hidden paradise of which his readers see the emerging streams but not the source; the music which they hear without seeing the instruments (*DFP*, I, 690).

In order not to underestimate the weightiness of Renan's philosophical essays, however, we should also clearly recognize his importance in the history of philosophy. In adapting some of the key ideas of German philosophy into French thought—Herder's comparativism and sense of evolutionary growth, Hegel's "becoming" and notion of the relativity of truth, Kant's categorical imperative, Fichte's sense of stoic resignation to the hidden trickery of nature —Renan, like Cousin before him, exerted a widespread influence. Though not a professional philosopher himself, he was often closely related in purpose and spirit to those who were, especially to Cousin and his successors, such as Vacherot, Ravaisson, and Renouvier; his real kinship was with these spiritualists and idealists rather than with the positivists, under whose banner (or banners, for there were several dissident sects) a leading historian of philosophy has placed him.[1] Finally, in his insistence on the concept of a dynamic, spiritually grounded universe, discoverable by intuition, he was, like Ravaisson, a critic of positivism and a precursor of Bergson.[2]

But although Renan made these significant contributions to modern philosophy, and many others besides, he gives us the impression that philosophy, as traditionally conceived, is a luxury the serious, busy thinker can ill afford, and that metaphysics is a game of words. Skepticism toward metaphysics, toward philosophical systems, which Renan compared on several occasions to epic poems (*AS*, III, 773; *DFP*, I, 693–695), was nothing new in the nineteenth century: the *philosophes*, especially Voltaire, had already sounded this note. But in the second half of the nineteenth century philosophy passed through a crisis which brought it, at least in its traditional form of the search for first principles, close to extinction. "Faith in philosophical truth," wrote the positivist Cournot in 1861, "has grown so cold that the public and the Academies hardly receive, or hardly welcome, anything more in this genre than works of erudition and historical curiosity."[3] Renan's essays show a significant preoccupation with redefining the function of philosophy and with settling the future of metaphysics. Great and original metaphysical thought, he wrote in "La métaphysique et son avenir," had come to an end in 1831 with the death of Hegel (*DFP*, I, 681). He was inclined, like the positivists, to deny the validity of metaphysics on principle, but, as we shall see, there was much ambiguity in his denial. Cousin, he pointed out, was still "dissecting the soul into faculties" (*DFP*, I, 683), still spinning verbal cobwebs. The most original of his successors, in Renan's opinion, Etienne Vacherot, whose work he discussed in the aforementioned essay, had made a valiant effort to revive metaphysics, but was forced to devote two huge volumes to prove that it exists (*DFP*, I, 690–691).

If metaphysics had reached an impasse, science and history, on the other hand, were exulting in growth and progress. What treatise on Being and Essence could hope to be as meaningful as contemporary discoveries in archeology and history, in chemistry, biology, medicine, natural history, psychology? What proof of its validity could metaphysics offer as striking as those inventions (occurring either during or shortly after Renan's lifetime) which proved the validity of the scientific method: steamboat, railroad, telegraph, photography, electricity, X-ray, submarine cable? We must bear this nineteenth-century pentecost of worldly knowledge in mind in order to have the correct perspective on Renan's cult of history and science, his half-derisive, half-patronizing attitude toward philosophy.

Renan had not always believed that philosophy was the handmaiden of science and history. He had passed through an individual crisis of belief in philosophy comparable to the collective crisis of the 1860's described by Cournot. Formed in scholastic, Cartesian traditions in the seminary, he had continued his intense interest in philosophy throughout the *Cahiers de jeunesse*, thinking along traditional speculative lines, absorbed in such problems as free will, Leibnitz' monadology, the definition of substance and matter. He had drawn diagrams of God's nature. Such speculation was all part of his intense struggle in 1845–1846 to retain his belief in God and in the spirituality of the soul, after losing his belief in the Catholic faith. His philosophy professor at the Sorbonne, Adolphe Garnier, stimulated his interest in epistemology. For his *agrégation*, after all, he had written a brilliant examination on the "Common Sense" school of contemporary Scottish philosophers, and his *Averroès* showed no lack of competence in handling ancient metaphysical problems. So far, philosophy had a traditional aura with him.

But gradually, his study of philology and history led him to revise this more or less traditional notion of philosophy. He became convinced that philosophy as a *"science particulière"* was doomed to die, but that there would be new life for it as the co-ordinator of the discoveries of the true sciences, the formulator of "general truths" based on "specialized scientific disciplines" (*DFP*, I, 695, 700–701). This is one of the dominant themes of *L'avenir de la science* and also of the *Dialogues et fragments philosophiques*. His conception of the philosopher as the thinker who draws general conclusions for the guidance of mankind from the data furnished to him by specialists is the most affirmative definition of philosophy Renan manages to give us. Comte and the positivists also favored this conception, and it is a far from ignoble one. But it leaves a shrunken mantle indeed around the shoulders of anyone who might fancy himself the successor of Plato or Aquinas, Descartes, Locke, or Hegel, bold explorers of the realms of being. In lighter, more skeptical moments, Renan seems to undermine even this dignified definition by suggesting that philosophy is "the seasoning without which all meats are tasteless, but which in itself is hardly a form of nourishment" (*DFP*, I, 693), or a highly subjective, very unsubstantial form of poetry: "the sound, the light, the vibration from the divine ether which each of us carries within himself" (*DFP*, I, 695). Sometimes he ridicules philosophy: as Pascal pointed out long ago, however, "Se moquer de la philosophie, c'est vraiment philosopher." As for metaphysics, it seems he would have it resign itself to being the sad demonstration of how we form abstractions having little if any correspondence with reality.

The ironic truth is, nevertheless, that Renan pursued to the end the very questions which philosophers, especially metaphysicians, had been turning over in their minds for centuries, the ancient, venerable questions of the existence and nature of God, the origins and destiny of the universe and of man. What is more, he pursued these questions, despite his highly original form and the *grain de sel* which flavors his work, for the most part in conventional terms. It was not for nothing that Lucien Lévy-Bruhl called him the "Malebranche of the nineteenth century." [4] He was a metaphysician in spite of himself, an incorrigible lay theologian. The explanation of this inconsistency lies, I believe, in the deep-rooted, stubbornly dual nature of his thought —the key to so much that is difficult and contradictory in his work.

Renan once called himself "a tissue of contradictions," and compared himself to the *hircocerf*, "the stag-goat of scholastic philosophy, which had two natures" (*SEJ*, II, 760). This was in the course of a self-portrait intended to gloss over any serious conflict in his mind and leave the public with the picture of an untroubled epicurean. But the division within him was much more serious than he let on; it may, in fact, have been his most serious handicap as a thinker. What were his two natures? In a general way, through the drama of his loss of faith, they are well enough known: the side of him which turned toward scientific and historical truth, and the other side oriented toward religious truth. Could they be reconciled? Without any of the "anguish" and "*inquiétude*" which some best-selling novelists wear on their sleeves today as the fashionable signs of profundity, Renan was deeply troubled by this problem throughout his life—and this fact is less well known. It is the crux of his philosophical thought and determined his whole manner of handling philosophical problems.

We need to put this dualistic problem in more precise terms than "Science versus Religion." Renan was divided between the two dominant French philosophical schools of his time, which was far from being the monolithic age of positivism it is often supposed to have been: positivism, or the attempt to build up a logical, coherent interpretation of reality based entirely on experimental science; and spiritualism or idealism, the attempt to prove the existence of God, of the soul, and of transcendent moral and spiritual reality without recourse to revelation or supernatural religion. Renan was by no means the only thinker to attempt the impossible task of reconciling these two general positions, although his was the most ambitious and most persistent effort. With him, however, the search for a compromise between them came dangerously close to being a *parti pris.* I mean by this that he held to certain consoling truths of spiritualism with suspicious willfulness. He was far from being the disengaged searcher after truth he fancied himself to be. His freedom of movement was seriously hampered.

The philosopher Lévy-Bruhl has made a penetrating observation which is very much to the point here:

In what terms was the philosophical problem to present itself to him? In terms, no doubt, quite different from those which occurred to such men as Maine de Biran, Cousin, or even Auguste Comte. His situation is unique. He wanted a doctrine which would restore to him all that he had lost in losing faith, which would, without having recourse to the supernatural, supply him with an acceptable interpretation of the universe, and at the same time with a certain rule of conduct. Had he examined the whole of the problem—had he begun, as Descartes did, by temporarily considering as false all that he had hitherto thought and believed—he would have entered upon an undertaking unsuited to his character and perhaps beyond his power. He adopted a less radical solution. Instead of developing his doubt logically, he set limits to it.[5]

The "limits to doubt" referred to by Lévy-Bruhl are certain fixed, though not always well-defined, spiritual beliefs which, following his loss of faith, he set up as a boundary to protect himself from the nihilism or the atheism that lay beyond. God (referred to usually as *"le divin,"* or, sometimes mockingly, as *"l'Eternel"*), Providence, the soul, a transcendent world of beauty and truth reflected in our moral consciences—whatever disguises Renan may have dressed these concepts in (with no insincerity), there was no hiding their metaphysical nature. "I hold tight to morality and truth, even when I am a skeptic"—so he wrote at twenty-two (*CJ*, p. 372), and many years later, a little sensitive about his reputation as a skeptic, he said essentially the same thing in a famous paradox: "I have made everything the object of my criticism, and, whatever people say, I have upheld everything" (*DP*, III, 529)—meaning by "everything," most likely, the fundamental moral values by which he lived. Refusal to accept thoroughgoing skepticism is one of the constants in his allegedly inconstant thought.

It was the failure of positivism to meet his moral, spiritual, and also esthetic needs ("I don't find it *beautiful enough*") that caused his dissatisfaction with it and led him to note that he had already progressed beyond its narrow, "experimental science" point of view (*NCJ*, p. 84); he would be a *"mystique avec le positif et la méthode scientifique"*(*CJ*, p. 268). Unlike the strict positivists, he recognized the value of "intuition" and the existence of significant, unsolvable mysteries in human experience—an attitude which kept him well-disposed toward metaphysics. Our moral sense, he wrote in his examination for the *agrégation*, directly intuits principles which experience has not given us, principles *"qui font immédiatement partie de l'esprit humain"* (a striking, but by no means unique, anticipation of Bergson's *"données immédiates de la conscience"*). The elaborate metaphysical systems of the Germans, he goes on to remark, are in great part fantasies; but one precious thing they have which young Renan refused to give up—a sense of mystery, of *das Jenseits*, the beyond. The worst error of positivism was to forbid man's intelligence and imagination "to pass beyond the heavens, and to fly toward the infinite." [6]

These rapturous thoughts, it is true, date from his youth. But there is a striking continuity throughout his work, so far as his favorable disposition toward metaphysical concepts is concerned. We have only to recall the *Etudes d'histoire religieuse* and the *Essais de morale et de critique*, even the *Questions contemporaines*. The existence of the soul and of a divinity (his lack of precision is beside the point here) are, he writes in the *Dialogues et fragments philosophiques*, self-evident truths, "dogmas" of a kind (*DFP*, I, 686–687). "*La sainte morale*," which he had vowed as a youth that his heart would never surrender, whatever his head told him (*CJ*, p. 128), remains for him a matter of "previously established laws" ("*lois préalables*") —laws, it should be noted, which are not a legitimate matter of inquiry and which he, a conservative moralist like Descartes whose authority he cites, has no intention of subjecting to the *doute méthodique* (DFP, I, 555–556).

As for his sense of mystery, he continued to balance it off against his admiration for the scientific method. In the face of the unknown, man feels a dual emotion: respect for the mysterious and a bold desire to tear aside the veil (again the curious motif of the *voile déchiré* in his work) and discover what lies beyond (*AS*, III, 742). Over twenty years after writing this he felt the same *double sentiment* before one of the boldest attempts of the nineteenth century to dispel the mysteries of the soul by reducing its activities to physiological terms. Commenting on Taine's *De l'intelligence*,[7] he gave his general approval to the experimental method but added what seems to me a significant qualification. There are, he pointed out, "two totally mysterious questions . . . the origin of human consciousness and the final purpose of the universe." The first of these questions he believed the more likely to be solved, and solved by Taine's method, but before the second, before this mystery of our "primordial and final cause," human reason must perhaps remain "struck with eternal dizziness." Despite the *"peut-être,"* this remark, as well as the general tenor of the brief article in which it occurs, seems to place less emphasis on the need for extending the realm of the knowable than on preserving respect for the mysterious.

But the strongest proof that Renan remained fixed until the end in his role of mediator between positivism and spiritualism is the extraordinary last will and testament of his thought, his "Examen de conscience philosophique." One of his finest essays, it occupies a place in his work similar to that of "De l'expérience" in the *Essais* of Montaigne or "Des esprits forts" in the *Caractères* of La Bruyère. It is the nearest thing to a definitive expression of his philosophy.

Like most of his philosophical writing, he considered this essay an occasion for a diverting pause in his foremost occupation, the exacting labor of completing his history of the Jewish people.[8] It was in the summer of 1888, at his country home in Rosmapamon on the Armorican peninsula, at the age of sixty-five, that he composed this summing up of his deepest beliefs. Although it was a diversion, although it found its way eventually into the frivolous and occasionally trivial *Feuilles détachées*, there should be no mistaking its importance and, despite a touch or two of irreverence, its utmost seriousness. To its thought he devoted great care, among other things by sending the manuscript to Berthelot to make sure that the scientific passages were accurate and up to date.[9] For one of his last essays, the style is unusually polished. The title alone shows that he conceived of this essay as a quasi-religious duty. Here his resilient, ingenious mind made the last of a life-long series of attempts to bring the contradictory philosophical ideas of his time into some kind of orderly, integrated picture. What that picture is, a detailed analysis of the essay will reveal.

If we take as the "double basis" of positivism the two principles enunciated by its most thoroughgoing French representative, Emile Littré, namely, "the immutability of natural laws" and "the renunciation of any knowledge of the infinite and the absolute," [10] we find that Renan adheres firmly enough to the first principle and professes but does not practice the second. His position is clearly expressed in the very structure of the essay. In Part I, the realm of "objective certainty," in precise, scientific language, with a rigidity bordering on the geometrical, he upholds Littré's first principle, the concept of "immutable laws" governing the universe. In Part II, the realm of possibility, he veers off in a direction unacceptable to strict positivists: he opens a door onto the mysterious and bids us enter, covering with pseudo-scientific garments our naked, shivering illusions, the *"quatre grandes folies"* of mankind, Love, Poetry, Virtue, and Religion. In the last and third Part, the realm of practical action, far now from Littré and closer to Kant and even to Pascal's "wager," he calls upon us to exercise our practical reason and to act *as if* God and the immortal soul were true.

The opening paragraph (see Appendix 7) is rich in meaning. Generally, it conveys the idea that men should be as objective as possible in their philosophical views, even at the cost of personal sacrifice. The personal note, the *apologia pro vita sua*, is obvious, even though the first person pronoun is avoided: this is Renan looking back serenely on his religious crisis, reaffirming the rightness of his apostasy and the basic principles of his life. In comparing the whole process of thinking to a form of sacrifice, he speaks from experience: had he not given up his dream of a useful life as a scholarly priest, his rightful place in the great family of the Roman Catholic Church? [11] The objections against the divine inspiration of the Bible which drew him away from the Church may not seem to us today as commanding, as inexorable, as he thought—his contemporary, Newman, for example, was able to surmount them—but one can hardly deny that they appeared inexorable to *him*, or that the metaphor he used to describe his struggle against such arguments ("interior battles" in which the thinker is bound and dragged away by the truth) [12] is an accurate one.

But although the process of reasoning may entail personal sacrifice, it is essentially an impersonal operation. Such, with the help of phrases like "our intellectual retina," "the dark room of the photographer," and "chemical precipitate," is the more specifically positivist notion that Renan introduces also in this first paragraph. We are detached spectators of our own minds, no more able to influence what goes on in them than we are able to influence a scientific experiment—as questionable a description of the process of thinking as it is of a laboratory experiment. But from the very beginning there are clear signs that Renan himself cannot fully accept this comparison of human reasoning to a scientific experiment which he describes in such rigid terms. Certain phrases—"depths of consciousness" (or of "conscience," for the French *"conscience"* has this double meaning), "spontaneous operation," "unconscious evolution," perhaps even the metaphor of the *"chambre noire"*—point ahead to the author's defense of obscure, mysterious intuitions of a moral order, "categorical im-

peratives," which speak to us in as commanding a voice
as experimentally verifiable facts and reveal far more important truths about our human nature.

For the moment, however, positivism advances. In clear,
insistent tones, Renan develops one of the dominant themes
of his philosophical thought, his denial of the miracle. There
may, he argued, be signs of apparent finalism in the "general constitution of the universe," but the concept of "immutable natural laws"—a dogma with nineteenth-century
positivists—prohibits absolutely the occurrence of any
event revealing the presence or intervention of a being
superior to man. Here endeth Renan's gospel of the anti-
miracle, his dogmatic affirmation (ironic in the man who
professed hatred for all dogmas), of the a priori impossibility, not to mention the historical nonexistence, of the
miraculous event.[13] "God," he repeated, with something
of the absurdity of a phonograph whose needle is caught in
the groove, "never acts by miracles."

But *was* this his last word on the subject? Here the testimony of the "Examen de conscience philosophique" is of
special interest. For on this question of miracles, which he
rightly recognized as a crucial one for the positivist philosophy, Renan now hedges. He at least relaxes the rigidity
of his denial. "In the universe *accessible to our experience*,"
he has said, there are no events unexplainable by natural
laws. This clearly implies that there may be a reality which
transcends our field of observation. The question, he asks,
"is to know if this universe is the totality of existence. Here
doubt begins. An active God is absent from this universe;
may He not exist beyond it?" (*FD*, II, 1164–1165). The
doubt insinuating itself here is doubt in the positivist creed,
in the completeness and finality of the positivist world view.

At this point in the essay, we pass from *positif* to *mystique*, from the patronage of Comte and Littré to that of a far greater scientist than either of these men, and a mystic as well, whose identity becomes clear, even though his name is not mentioned, from these words reminiscent of his own: "Our reality . . . is made with infinites of a lower order; it serves itself to make infinites of a higher order. It is an infinitely great for what is below it, an infinitely small for what is above it, a middle term between two infinites" (*FD*, II, 1165–1166).

The presence of Pascal in Renan's work should not surprise us. As a seminarian, he had read the *Pensées* with fervor. To their example of a bold, free-spirited Catholicism, he owed, in fact, an extended lease on his own faith; but to their supposed skepticism (that dubious image of a Pascal clinging desperately to the pillar of faith, dear to Cousin and Sainte-Beuve), he also, ironically, owed some of the growing doubt which led to his loss of faith.[14] For many years, except for occasional reminiscences, Renan seemed to have forgotten Pascal—insofar as any serious reader of Pascal can ever forget him. And then, in his old age, Renan looked back once again on the great disturber of our complacency.

His renewed awareness of Pascal may, I think, be explained in this way: although he nowhere explicitly declares it to be so, it seems clear from the "Examen de conscience philosophique" that he looked upon his role among nineteenth-century freethinkers as analogous to Pascal's mission among seventeenth-century *libertins*. He adapted to his defense of spiritualism some key arguments in Pascal's apology for the Christian religion. They lived at comparable moments of great discovery in the history of the mathematical and natural sciences. Just as Pascal sought in his "Disproportion de l'homme" to touch a spiritual chord in atheists by evoking the vision of an infinite reality, so Renan in this part of his "Examen de conscience philosophique" calls on atheists to acknowledge at least the possibility of God. Drawing on the discoveries of Berthelot in organic chemistry, Claude Bernard, Louis Pasteur, and Paul Bert in biology, Jean-Henri Fabre in entomology, he insinuates, like Pascal, the humbling thought of the *deux infinis*.

Like Pascal also, Renan uses mathematics for metaphysical purposes: "The two great postulates of human life, God and the immortality of the soul, gratuitous though they may be from our finite point of view, are perhaps true from the point of view of the infinite" (*FD*, II, 1170). Even the *pari*, the metaphysical gamble, echoes clearly in such exhortations as the following: "The most logical attitude of the thinker in regard to religion is to act as if it were true. We must act as if God and the soul existed" (*FD*, II, 1177); "We must make our decision" ("Il faut donc en prendre notre parti"—*FD*, II, 1179). This argument rests not only on the "practical reason" of Kant, but also on the mathematics of chance and probability as developed by such contemporaries of Renan as Marie-Ennemond Jordan, Antoine Cournot, and Henri Poincaré.

Again he reaches out to join hands with Pascal, but of course, for all their curious affinity,[15] an abyss nevertheless separates them—belief in Christ as the Son of the Living God. Renan is the "honest pagan" whose life, one of great personal probity, is proof that he himself consistently acted "as if God and the immortality of the soul existed." However ill-defined his spiritual beliefs may appear to many readers, he argued for them because they were deeply rooted in his character and in his will, even more than in his intelligence and his reason. With all his respect for Littré, the saintly atheist, the paragon of positivist virtue, he confesses his suspicion that "men are atheists perhaps because they do not see far enough" (*FD*, II, 1166).

But in his pursuit of the idea of God, across microbe and evolving universe, solar system and infinitesimal calculus, what conclusion does Renan reach? What does he offer in the place of atheism? The answer is—his "rich jewel case of synonyms" for the Divinity ("Nous avons trouvé à Dieu un riche écrin de synonymes"—*DP*, III, 529).

By his remarks on the mysterious universe and the "point of view of the infinite," Renan has carefully prepared the background for the hypothesis of God's existence. He finally expresses the possibility in what seems like a mere *boutade*—"A God will be revealed some day. . . . Everything is possible, even God" (*FD*, II, 1169)— but actually this quip occurs in a context of the greatest seriousness. Parts II and III of the "Examen de conscience philosophique" are devoted to an elaboration of this great possibility. The definition of God's nature is the apex of Renan's philosophy, the summit to which all the roads of his philosophical work eventually ascend. Yet it was precisely this type of metaphysical speculation, this natural theology, which strict positivists dismissed as meaningless.

What, in brief, was his conception of God? It is a difficult question to answer. Negatively, we might first note that nowhere does he seriously defend theism, the belief in a God who loves and is loved, knows and is known, who hears and saves men, made in His own image. Renan resembled the Benedictine hero of a turgid novel (a novel in name only) by George Sand, *Spiridion*, which he once declared to be "an essential image of my religious dreams." [16] The God of theism is open to communication, but like Père Alexis, carrying on a tradition of rationalism in a monastery whose spiritual atmosphere he could not bear to leave, even though he had lost his faith, Renan might have said: "I no longer dared communicate with God." [17] But —and this is a little surprising—Renan also rejects deism, God the remote First Cause and Supreme Engineer of the universe. Both these concepts he condemns, in "La métaphysique et son avenir," as too anthropomorphic (*DFP*, I, 710)—and too precise. They both run counter to his view that God's nature is not only mysterious (which even Christian theologians would grant), but so enshrouded in obscurity that even the language of the French Academy, adequate to all other purposes, can formulate no meaningful proposition about God other than, "He is."

Renan, however, leaped ahead of his own precautions and attempted to define God's nature. His error, in fact, was overfertility in definitions. Let us approach the problem as he does, in terms of one of the most ancient dilemmas of philosophy, which he tried to solve in his essay on the future of metaphysics and in his "Examen de conscience philosophique." If God is perfect, can He be real? If He is real, can He be perfect? Renan quotes approvingly the alternative which Vacherot presented to theologians: "Un Dieu parfait ou un Dieu réel: il faut que la théologie choisisse" (*DFP*, I, 706). To attempt to have them both, thought Vacherot, is to involve oneself in intolerable contradictions. His own solution, essentially Renan's also, is that the perfect God is an ideal, while the real God "is living and developing in the immensity of space and the eternity of time, manifested under an infinite variety of forms: He is the cosmos" (*DFP*, I, 706). It is with Vacherot's *"métaphysique positive"* rather than Hegel's "developing God" or Absolute Idea that Renan's natural theology has its closest affinity. Both their philosophical structures are half-way houses between positivism and spiritualism.

The synonyms for God which this verbal jeweler scattered throughout his work can, accordingly, be classified under two principal headings. On the one hand, as the loftiest ideal ever conceived by human minds, the summation of all man's noble and beautiful aspirations, God is "the place of the ideal" (*"le lieu de l'idéal"*—*DFP*, I, 647), the "transcendent résumé" of humanity's "suprasensible needs," *"la catégorie de l'idéal"* (*AS*, III, 1108). But Renan also wanted a truly existing God, even if he had to take an imperfect one. On this side of the diptych are inscribed the names of a divinity who is not exactly the cosmos, as Vacherot had said, but the mysterious striving (the "nisus," to use a favorite term of Renan) of man and nature toward perfection; the universal creative force, "the universal becoming" (*devenir*), *"l'éternel fieri"* (*AS*, III, 873); a force which, "acting upon the totality of the universe, will some day perhaps become conscious, omniscient, omnipotent" (*FD*, II, 1176). Then God will exist; but not until He has fulfilled all the laws of His special *"évolution déifique"* and the ideal has become an absolute reality.

The evolutionary theories of Lyell and Darwin, both of whom are mentioned by name in the "Lettre à M. Marcellin Berthelot" (*DFP*, I, 637–638), provided Renan with a springboard for this pseudo-scientific, pseudo-mystical pantheism, which seems to be the final resting place of his thoughts about God, as expressed in the "Examen de conscience philosophique." Progressive evolution seemed to confirm his belief in a *"nisus profond,"* a mysterious final cause, and he even found in it, contrary to many of his contemporaries who took it to be an invitation to cynicism and the cult of brute force, a support for his idealism, for what he calls the "sacred illusions" of mankind (*FD*, II, 1174). If nature herself moves, through love and sacrifice and suffering, toward perfection, man can do no more than add his conscious exercise of love and duty to the unconscious striving. Of doubtful philosophical, of doubtful scientific, validity, this concept contained much moral consolation and, besides, a strange poetic beauty. On such a note, Renan concludes his "Examen de conscience philosophique." The first paragraph had described truth in terms of two scientific metaphors: recording itself objectively in the dark room of our minds, emerging like the result of a chemical experiment. The last paragraph (see Appendix 7) translates the profound universal striving into an image which has become famous, that of the *huître à perles*, the pearl oyster, secreting beauty out of painful growth—a vision of nature which owes much less to science than to religious and poetic sensibility. Such is the extraordinary range of Renan's essay in positivist mysticism.

As a philosophical essayist, Renan leaves much to be desired. There are fine moments in his essay-letter to Berthelot on the natural and historical sciences; the evocation of vast prehistorical events as imagined by contemporary astronomers, geologists, and chemists approaches a true poetry of positivism. The pages in "La métaphysique et son avenir" outlining the purpose and spirit of a truly enlightened scholarship are among the soundest and most inspiring Renan ever wrote. But on the whole neither these essays nor the letter to Adolphe Guéroult have quite the interest of the "Examen de conscience philosophique." Of course it would be unfair to make our criticism of Renan's philosophy depend on our judgment of his success with the essay form alone. He reserved much that is most suggestive in his thought for the somber *Dialogues philosophiques*, with its foreshadowing of atomic power and atomic tyranny, and the kaleidoscopic, sometimes exasperating but on the whole fascinating armchair theater, the *Drames philosophiques*. All essays are in a sense philosophical, but the essay served Renan less well in "pure philosophy" than in other areas of his thought. It was but one form among several with which he experimented, and it seemed to satisfy less well than the philosophical dialogue or drama the needs of that debate between different "lobes of his brain" which profound philosophical questions touched off within him.

What is it about his philosophical thought which fails to satisfy critical minds? It is not, in my opinion, his skepticism. Renan is really a pseudo-skeptic. He comes dangerously close, it is true, especially in his last works, to that most terrible of all forms of skepticism, which consists in denying everything by being willing to affirm everything. But in practical, moral questions we have seen how little skepticism there is in him. And even in speculative philosophical questions, where there is a great deal, his real fault was not skepticism, but, on the contrary, the tenacity with which he anchored himself to certain unproved assumptions, certain fixed ideas: the immutability of natural laws, the absolute impossibility of miracles (a true skeptic would have expressed doubt or perhaps suspended judgment), the *nisus profond* supposedly producing a mysterious spiritual work which transcends mankind.[18]

An even more serious fault than this is the vagueness of his language. This is a grave charge to make, but I believe it is justified. Renan was a great critical mind in much of what he wrote, in his moral observations, in his reflections on society and politics and history. But his attempt to integrate positivism and spiritualism, admirable though it was, fell far short of satisfying critics in his own day and is even less capable of withstanding critical analysis today. A contemporary of Renan, the philosopher Paul Janet, has, I think, given a critique of his philosophical thought which is still valid. Agreeing with Renan that abstract speculation must reckon with the sciences and draw upon them —ethics upon history, logic upon linguistics, psychology upon ethnology, metaphysics upon physics—he nevertheless warned:

By mingling philosophy in this way with all things, by failing to take it in itself as an object of study, and a very difficult and complex object, one succeeds in effacing and confusing most of the questions; one proposes principles without proofs; one no longer discusses, one affirms; and these rapid affirmations, which swallow up real difficulties and objections, are unfortunately accepted by superficial readers as acquired and demonstrated truths.[19]

Renan's philosophical thought, so often suggestive and, in a good sense, disturbing, is without disciplined, forceful, logical argumentation. It seldom comes to grips in a precise manner with the profound questions it raises. The blame must be laid on his stubborn effort to reconcile contradictory points of view, for it led him in this case onto dangerously marshy, mist-covered verbal ground. Without imputing bad faith to him, Sainte-Beuve revealed some of the tricks of verbal legerdemain by means of which he gave himself the illusion of being a thoroughgoing rationalist: his replacement of the word "Providence" with the word "finalism," for example, or his substitution of "divine" for "supernatural." [20] Language is the crux of the matter here. Janet's generalization, "He stands in horror of too well determined a fact," [21] is a bit too sweeping. Renan the historian, the scholar, the artist, loved as devoutly as Flaubert or the Parnassian poets the beauty and strength of precise facts. Renan the philosopher, the religious thinker, has the tendency to becloud whatever he touches. Precision seemed almost contrary to the synthesis he had undertaken; to reveal some of these warring ideas in a clearer light might have destroyed their ability to dwell together harmoniously in the hospitable mansion he had constructed for them; for he had come to bring peace, not a sword. "I was afraid," he had written many years before, noting a curious trait of his mind, "to push my ideas too far, for fear of seeing my castle crumble" (*CJ*, p. 46).

Let me illustrate by one example this characteristic and highly objectionable vagueness of Renan's philosophical language. Writing of theism and deism in "La métaphysique et son avenir," he says:

Neither one is based on solid ground; both imply a contradiction. Let us dare finally to put aside as secondary and extremely elusive these questions [of God's nature], condemned by the very manner in which one must expound them never to receive a solution. Let us dare to say that they matter very little to religion. From the moment one believes in man's freedom, in spirit, one believes in God. To love God, to know God, is to love what is beautiful and good, to know what is true. The religious man is he who knows how to find the divine in everything, not he who professes about Divinity some arid and unintelligible formula [*DFP*, I, 711].*

This passage reads well and has an accent of fervor. But where, after breaking away with such daring from the allegedly occult regions of theology, does Renan lead us? Into a cloud-cuckoo-land of his own. "Freedom"—some philosophers have devoted volumes to the problem of free will and determinism, but Renan glides over it. No clear definition emerges from his work to tell us what "spirit" is, and as for God, he has provided so many contradictory definitions that little more than the word remains. How, one asks, can the "religious man" (what, specifically, makes him religious?) find the "divine" in everything if he has no reasonably clear notion of what he is searching for? As for the beautiful, the good, and the true, we have seen how much concrete meaning these could have for Renan the *moraliste*, the author of the *Essais de morale et de critique*. Here in his speculative thought they have little.

One begins to suspect that by "arid and unintelligible formulas" Renan really meant any precisely defined idea with which critical analysis can come to grips, just as by "system" he really meant any reasonably clear and coherent structure of thought. His treatment of metaphysical systems is of a piece with his treatment of Catholicism and other well-defined creeds: to liberate speculation about God from the one and "religious feeling" from the other was his ambition. But a number of questions persist. Is "re-

* Renan, *Dialogues et fragments philosophiques*, I, 711, quoted by permission of Calmann-Lévy, publishers.

ligious feeling" any the less crude an expression of belief in an ineffable God than dogmatic theology? Is an excessively rationalistic, systematic approach to metaphysical questions a greater error than systematic vagueness? Has not Renan replaced "arid and unintelligible formulas" with what we might call "arid and unintelligible obscurities"?

In justice to Renan, it must be said that this vagueness was a taint he had inherited from some very distinguished ancestors, from Cousin, whose stamp is on the passage just quoted, from Lamartine and George Sand, whose works are filled with vast acres of nebulous religious feeling, from Madame de Staël, who had proclaimed that the best part of religion was in fact *"le vague."* Yet Renan was a man of supreme intelligence and a great scholar. How could he tolerate in philosophy a verbalism he scrupulously avoided, for the most part, in scholarship and history? Partly because he felt that vagueness was the best one could hope to achieve in dealing with transcendent questions: "We must admit what is obscure as obscure" (*DFP*, I, 714). Undoubtedly also (and here his position is much less tenable) because he felt that philosophical thought should be no more subject to rational analysis than poetry. But if such was his understanding, he failed to realize that poetry is not language devoid of meaning, but language charged to the utmost with meaning. With Renan, the old metaphysical language is there, but with little reality behind the words. Yet he refused to give the words up. "God, providence, soul, these are so many good old words," he wrote, "a bit heavy, but expressive and respectable, which science will explain but never replace to advantage" (*AS*, III, 1108).

Toward the end of the *Dialogues philosophiques*, having listened to Théoctiste's consoling dreams of a God who may quite possibly exist, Eudoxe remarks: "That's just about the way priests talk; but their words are different" (*DFP*, I, 632). Some of their words are different; but many Renan himself uses. Much of his religious thought is a matter of Christian vocabulary. Yet from these diluted remnants, these leftover verbal fragments of Christian theology, he seemed to derive his own form of sustenance, as did many of his readers, for whom this vague religious philosophy was better than none at all. He was resigned to this vagueness and uncertainty, but far from happy in it. "To do good so that God, if He exists, will be pleased with us, will seem to some a rather empty formula. We live on the shadow of a shadow. What will men live on after us?" (*DFP*, I, 557). "Nous vivons de l'ombre d'une ombre." In a letter of sympathy to Princess Julie, whose daughter had died shortly before (in 1865), he reaffirmed his belief in the truth of the *sentiment religieux*, "the basis of religion," but added a very revealing lament: "But when will we succeed in finding expression for that *infini* which dazzles and overwhelms us, rather than giving us warmth and light? It is painful to be obliged to put off into the future the satisfaction of the most urgent needs of our hearts." [22] The "evolving God" was not easy to worship.

In Renan's effort to maintain intact the elaborate edifice of compromise he had built out of the contradictory beliefs of his time, there is an interesting play of ideas, but there is also a personal drama of some poignancy. Of this drama, the "Examen de conscience philosophique," even more than the works in dramatic or quasi-dramatic form, is the faithful mirror. For all its considerable scientific information and reasoning, its share of plausible hypotheses, its genuine religious sense, it may perhaps best be defined in the end as a sincere form of evasion. In the narrow chamber of positivism, Renan shuts himself up, only to spring a trap door beneath, through which we fall into an infinity where God and the soul may be true. Yet this *échappatoire* is constructed with such scrupulousness and care that one is fascinated by it, and some readers will be moved to sympathy. Should it not be judged, after all, as highly personal writing, not only because it is an *examen de conscience*, but also because it is an essay, and all essays are confessions? Renan once wrote that sentences are bound to raise objections because they have definite limits, whereas hymns, "*harmonies*," have nothing dialectical about them and need take no decisive stand. (*DFP*, I, 712). Is this not one of his own hymns, sung with mingled notes of Pascal and Littré, blending positivism and spiritualism, to help him gather strength in the approaching darkness of old age and death?

Chapter 7

The Last Harvest
and *Renanisme*

"Except for cases of national disaster, allow for a smile and for the hypothesis that this world may not be anything very serious."–*Discours et conférences*

"His attitude as a writer deceives us as to the true content of his thought." – MAURICE BARRÈS, *Huit jours chez M. Renan*

RENAN'S last four collections of essays, the *Mélanges d'histoire et de voyages* (1878), the *Nouvelles études d'histoire religieuse* (1884), the *Discours et conférences* (1887), and the *Feuilles détachées* (1892),[1] contain some new and excellent things, but on the whole they show certain symptoms of decline, especially an increasing repetitiousness and a dangerous facility of style. The extent and the causes of this decline, however, should be made clear. It was by no means part of any general weakening of his literary powers in the postwar period. His creativity asserted itself with renewed strength in the *Dialogues philosophiques* and *Drames philosophiques*, to which we have referred briefly, in the

Souvenirs d'enfance et de jeunesse, which ranks high in the great tradition of French autobiographies from Montaigne to André Gide, and in such superlative volumes of his historical work as *L'Antéchrist* (1873) and *Marc-Aurèle* (1882). The essay tended to suffer, not only from the competition of these other works, but also from his diminishing faith in its possibilities—in its artistic possibilities, that is, for its commercial possibilities interested him more than ever, and like many of our contemporaries whom we call, much less rightly than Renan, "essayists," he was willing to fill out salable books with ephemeral pieces of all kinds, dipping at times close to the bottom of his intellectual stock. Such a procedure, though there is nothing shameful in it, was not conducive to the fine literary craftsmanship which had produced, for example, the *Essais de morale et de critique.*

Many of these last essays are by-products of his historical work, of that vast undertaking which, it is too often forgotten, was the real center of his existence, nothing less than the duty and purpose of his life. Again and again, in his last letters, occurs the refrain: "I must finish my Israel," "I am growing old and must complete my Israel." The only *boulevardiers* with whom he had time to be acquainted were Isaiah and Jeremiah.[2] To this work he devoted himself with extraordinary industry and tenacity, against odds which certainly would have caused a lesser man to abandon the task altogether. Rheumatism, the villain in the last act of his life, subjected his *"vieille machine"* to a violent exercise of patience, attacking now a wrist, now a leg, sometimes crippling his whole body and forcing him to lie prone, dictating his work to his son Ary or his daughter Noémi. To draw his energies away from "his Israel" there were many other

scholarly duties, remote from that particular field of research, and many academic responsibilities, such as teaching
again after 1870 and administering the Collège de France
from 1884 onward. And there were speeches, the best of
them collected in the *Discours et conférences*, speeches for
gay occasions such as the *Dîners celtiques* and for solemn
ones such as addressing the Académie Française, to which
he had been elected in 1878, or pronouncing funeral orations
for less robust Frenchmen. Finally, there were political distractions, his electoral campaign of 1878, but even more
that deep, intangible concern for his country's fate which
led him to compare all his scholarly labors to precision work
being carried out on the deck of a ship in distress.[3]

With such labors and preoccupations and distractions,
what is surprising is not that Renan failed to write many
more great essays, but that he managed to complete his
Histoire du peuple d'Israël (death overtook him as he prepared the last two volumes for publication) and to turn
out several literary masterpieces to boot. There is, however, another reason why his essay work in the 1870's and
1880's shows a greater number of charming trifles and mis-
cellaneous bits of erudition (the first not without their own
minor kind of beauty) and a smaller number of polished,
deliberate essays. He seemed to feel that the *grand article*,
as he called it, had seen its day. The *Journal des débats* and
the *Revue des deux mondes,* for which he had produced
some of his greatest prewar essays, he no longer considered
congenial to this kind of literary art. The former displeased
him with its violent attacks on the fallen imperial family.
Journalism in general he feared had discredited itself. It was
undoubtedly such considerations, as well as the lack of time,
which made him renounce writing the major articles on

Taine and Gambetta, and perhaps on other subjects, which might have ranked with his greatest essays.[4]

In surveying briefly the *Mélanges d'histoire et de voyages* and the *Discours et conférences*, my purpose will be to single out from the miscellany what I regard as the most impressive essays. As for the *Nouvelles études d'histoire religieuse* and the *Feuilles détachées*, the most fruitful approach to them, I believe, is to consider them as manifestations of that complex, perplexing attitude which dominates Renan's last work and which literary historians have baptized with a name of its own: *renanisme*.

The *Mélanges d'histoire et de voyages* is a highly readable, unjustly neglected book in the best Renanian tradition of humanized scholarship. Composed less of true essays than of *comptes rendus*, many of them dating from the 1840's and 50's, it has less real unity than the thematically arranged earlier volumes, but much more than the general run of such *mélanges* which mushroomed wildly from nineteenth-century French printing presses. No deliberate esthetic structure, such as we found in the *Essais de morale et de critique*, holds these pieces together, but they have a unifying theme, which a contemporary essayist might have indicated somehow in the title; it is one of Renan's greatest themes, "the taste for historical truth and for the methods enabling us to discover it" (*MHV*, II, 307).

On the magic carpet of Renan's learning we are carried aloft, and from there, kept airborne by his charming, rapid, conversational style, we survey several areas of philological, archeological, and historical knowledge. With varying degrees of authority, but always with intelligence and contagious fervor, he treats such questions as the extent and the significance of the Roman emperors' wickedness, the

Cid's claim to nobility, the origins of grammatical study in France and in China, the discovery of Nineveh, and medieval French architecture.[5] Of such breadth, the essayist's birthright, Renan always took full advantage. More impressive than this, however, are the unfailing zest for learning and the soundness of a historical method which places equally high value on precise technical scholarship and the cultivation of a broad philosophical viewpoint.

From this rich feast, I would single out two articles, "Joseph Victor Le Clerc" and "Vingt jours en Sicile," as giving off the special resonance of Renan's greatest essays. Neither fits exactly into the category of *mises au point* of learning in a given field to which most of the articles belong.

Less striking than the portraits of Thierry, Cousin, or Burnouf, but in perfect conformity with its subject, the portrait of the famous Sorbonne professor, one of the last survivors of a magnificent generation of teachers, conveys a peculiar kind of greatness. Through his faults, the shallow rhetoric of his early career (he had been mildly ridiculed in the *Cahiers de jeunesse* as the "*type classique universitaire*"), his narrow rationalism and nationalistic approach to literature, Renan makes Le Clerc's unusual virtues shine with a light not brilliant but clear and steady: the courage with which he left his classical scholar's niche in mid-career to assume the enormous task of directing the *Histoire littéraire de la France;* his prodding study of dusty texts which in due time gave forth many valuable discoveries ("that precious virtue," remarks Renan, "which makes the scholar indifferent to the beauty or dullness of the text he is studying"); and finally, his accomplishment, as Dean of the Faculty of Letters, in transforming routine *soutenances de thèses* into "feasts of the mind." All this is splendidly evoked by Renan.

Even the neoclassic vocabulary he uses to describe the world of the Sorbonne which, after his mother's death, became Le Clerc's whole universe—"the *majestueux pavillons*," the "*nobles portiques*," the "*solitude, peuplée par le souvenir*" —is beautifully adapted to the subject. In this curiously moving moral portrait, Renan has once again shown his skill in communicating an unusual, difficult critical theme, the austere beauty and joy of the scholarly life.

"Vingt jours en Sicile" grew out of his voyage to Palermo in 1875 to attend a congress of Italian scholars.[6] Toward Italy, we know, he felt the love of an artistic soul first fully awakened to beauty by that incomparable country, and now to this feeling another is joined, the grateful love of a rheumatic body which found relief from pain in the waters of the bay of Ischia. The learned congress became his excuse for a dazzling excursion through Sicily, during which there was little time for sleep or little time for his stiff leg and dragging foot to remind him that they existed. The record of this trip makes one of Renan's most beautiful and most personal essays. In an admirably chaste manner he reveals the innermost feelings of a man whose youth is abandoning him limb by limb. Fifteen years earlier the little island of Maritimo had appeared to him "radiant with sunlight, adorned with green by the October rains," but now, he sees it as arid and without dew. "Parts of me have died since then; we die, to tell the truth, in fragments" (*MHV*, II, 391).

But the essay is far from a lament. It is one of his most sensuous, a recapturing of his youth which recalls Montaigne's "Sur des vers de Virgile," or, rather, a rediscovery of his unalterable youthfulness of spirit. In an unusually colorful style, he describes the Sicilian landscape, the population, the marvelously rich historical and legendary associations of this island where so many cultures met and mingled. Like the Sicilian vineyards, the essay itself overflows with intoxicating joy, the joy of scholarly discovery which never left Renan. And yet, what makes the essay so strangely moving is that the thought of death is never far away. It looms up in the midst of a pleasant picnic lunch and concert given for the scholars in the ruins of ancient Epipole, when the historian recalls the disastrous expedition of 413 in which thousands of Athenians perished from hunger on that very spot; it suddenly appears again as he contemplates the abyss named for the nymph Cyanea, whose tears for the abducted Proserpina transformed her into a deep pool. Here in this coolness the unwary traveler may contract a fatal fever; as he stands beside this chasm, even the sound of a joyful hymn to nature drifting across the reeds from a shepherd's flute cannot exorcise from Renan's mind the grim thought that nature is never more caressing than when she destroys (*MHV*, II, 401). Reflections on history, vivid descriptions, delicate personal feeling, intimations of death— all these combine to make this one of Renan's most unforgettable essays.[7]

Only by extending the term essay to cover the published speech, or "oral essay" as it has sometimes been called, does the *Discours et conférences*, one of Renan's best-known works, come within our field of inquiry. In this book, composed largely in the 1880's and published in 1887, he acquired a new literary distinction: he became one of the few members of the Académie Française whose speeches before that august body can be read for pleasure. In *La réforme intellectuelle et morale*, he had first begun the practice of incorporating speeches into his essay work, with his electoral address on the educative roles of family and state. Now, in his last books, such "oral essays" are numerous, and it becomes difficult, in fact, to distinguish between his "oral style" in discourses and his "written style" in periodical articles. The same virtues and faults are present in both: a facile, graceful wit, a simple, well-documented eloquence, spoiled far too often by the repetition of ideas now worn thin, by a certain banality, and by an unconsciously pontifical tone. The author well knew that many of these speeches were "words thrown to the wind" (*DC*, I, 719), for which no great literary merit could be claimed. Marvelously witty and intelligent words they often are, but not quite as captivating on the printed page as they must have been when Pasteur, Victor Cherbuliez, or Ferdinand de Lesseps were welcomed by them into the Academy, when prizes were distributed at the Lycée Louis-le-Grand, when the beloved Turgenev's remains were dispatched to Russia from the Gare du Nord, or when champagne was drunk at a banquet in honor of Berthelot.

Among the most substantial pieces in the *Discours et conférences* are the exposition of some truths and errors about nationalism, the justly famous "Qu'est-ce qu'une nation?" which Renan himself singled out as worthy of survival, and the "Discours de réception à l'Académie Française" (April 3, 1879) or eulogy of the great physiologist Claude Bernard. In this last, although writing with obvious fervor and joy, he modestly effaced himself before the greatness of his subject—a life entirely devoted to science. The language is technical yet graceful. More often it is Bernard himself who speaks, through superbly chosen quotations. And there is a truly dramatic quality in Renan's description of the revolutionary experiments carried out by this pioneer of modern medicine upon diseased animals in dark, musty cellars, often at the risk of a hideous death. The speech itself is a fine example of another kind of triumph, Renan's triumph over the element of conventionality, even of falseness, inherent in the genre of the *discours de réception*.[8]

Parts of the *Discours et conférences*, like the tribute to Bernard, are marked by a serious, affirmative tone. But elsewhere in the book there is a curious note of irreverence and frivolity, an alarming light-headedness, all the more alarming if one has followed the course of Renan's essays up to this point. A new form of skepticism and irony seems to be pushing its way into the foreground. To a group of young students, for example, the author of some of the most fervently idealistic works in the French language, a merciless critic of the *esprit gaulois*, suggests that they allow for the possibility that the world is not a very serious matter and recommends that they not be anxious to correct "the old Gallic gaiety" (*DC*, I, 867–868). To his fellow Academicians he confesses that his own laborious youth has taught him the lesson of Ecclesiastes, that all is vanity; but he would amend the lesson to read that "a great many vain things are worth long savoring" (*DC*, I, 729).

Disturbing the pattern of fundamental seriousness to which his work so far has accustomed us, the ironic smile of *renanisme* here confronts us and challenges us to interpret it. The challenge is perhaps the most difficult one the critic of Renan has to meet.

Renanisme is a term often applied to the frivolous skepticism derived from the work of Renan by such famous disciples as Anatole France, Jules Lemaître, and Maurice Barrès (in an early phase), as well as many lesser-known figures. One must not assume that *renanisme* in this sense, a widespread attitude in the last years of the nineteenth century and the early years of the twentieth, reflects Renan's true spirit or essential contribution any more accurately than *cartésianisme* does Descartes's or *voltairianisme* Voltaire's. It may be true that to understand the influence he exercised, even though some of his disciples may have distorted his work, will help us to understand Renan himself; but our primary concern, in any case, is with *renanisme* in another sense: the "philosophy" (so he would have it appear) of the master himself in his last twenty years.

The point of view he would impress upon us—whether it was his true belief or a pose is a question for later discussion—may be briefly summarized. The world is a vast joke, lacking in purpose. It is impossible to know truth; we can but entertain illusions. But we must not weep over this irrational universe; we must respond to its cosmic irony with irony of our own. Detached, irreverent, irresponsible like the force which created us, we must resign ourselves to the enjoyment of life as a spectacle, not committing ourselves, amusing ourselves, "as a connoisseur appraises a rare wine or a precious stone." [9] By means of this *"gaieté philosophique"* we constantly remind nature that we take her no more seriously than she takes us (*FD*, II, 1159–1160). Through this "touch of irony" (to which, according to Renan, the French language is especially well suited), we "enter into the intentions of the Eternal," conforming ourselves to the fundamental lack of seriousness of things (*FD*, II, 1091).

This is the quintessence of *renanisme*. For all its playful dilettantism, it may be seen to be, at bottom, a form of grim disillusionment. The mocking phrase *"l'Eternel"* suggests that the disillusionment may above all be of a religious nature. Indeed, *renanisme* is best known, whether in Renan or Anatole France, in its application to religion, which produced some of the most curious literary effects on record, above all the *tour de force* by means of which the *renaniste* manages to respect and to undermine religious faith at one and the same time. Of this implausible mixture of unctuousness and blasphemy, the *Nouvelles études d'histoire religieuse* is one of the most puzzling examples.

Renan would have us believe, in his preface, that this work is a sequel to the *Etudes d'histoire religieuse*, and it would seem an obvious fact. Nothing, however, could be further from the truth. Between the essays in which, as a young scholar, he had searched for a valid religion unencumbered by the supernatural and these, offered to an adoring public by a celebrated, amusing academic figure, there is an immense distance. There are, it is true, superficial resemblances: the familiar breadth of interest, from the Buddha to Spinoza, the same preoccupation with religion as the most significant fact of human existence. There are others which go below the surface. Some of the affirmative, idealistic spirit of the first *Etudes* has remained intact. The embers of the fire are still warm, he tells us; even though the days on which one does not suffer have become rare, the dream of a spiritual reality still consoles him. Alluding to recent explorers of the sea who had found life in its darkest depths, he is willing to make the affirmation (the "secret affirmation," it should be noted) that absolute night itself is perhaps not "without warmth and life" (*NEHR*, p. xvii) —a most revealing confidence which shows that Renan still withstands, as he always will, the temptation of total nihilism.

The note of affirmation remains strong, for example, in his sympathetic, at times moving, portrait of Francis of Assisi, perhaps the most popular of all Roman Catholic saints with unbelievers, and in his praise of the hidden moral worth, the obscure spiritual heroism of the ascetics of Port-Royal. The note of reverence is strongest of all in his famous commemorative speech in honor of the unsupernatural saint, admired by so many moderns who crave sanctity without benefit of a personal God, Benedict Spinoza. This last is, indeed, despite its occasionally pompous and artificial tone, one of his finest essays, a well-rounded tribute, written with admiration of Spinoza and yet with critical awareness of the defects of his "church filled with a harsh light, like all the constructions of the seventeenth century, cold because it has too many windows, sad because it is clear" (*NEHR*, p. v).

But the dominant tone of the book, unlike that of its predecessor, is one of mockery. The handful of religious heroes, natural and supernatural, are almost completely obscured by the atmosphere of superstition, credulity, morbidity, clerical intrigue, and persecution of thought with which supernatural faith is surrounded in this most Voltairian of Renan's works.[10] In this garden the flowers are strange ones; the heroes in this gallery are almost all seriously ill (p. iv). However, as much as the mockery reminds us of Voltaire (that old eighteenth-century war horse, the fraud-and-imposture theory of the origin of religion, is even put back into harness), there is an essential difference, and it stems precisely from the unique character of *renanisme*. Renan's mockery, unlike Voltaire's, is not clear-cut. It confuses sacred and frivolous matters almost inextricably, sugaring the pill of unbelief with an unctuousness unknown to the author of *Candide*. One feels this from the first pages of the preface, in the anecdote about the Capuchin monk who said Renan's essay on St. Francis would expiate the crime of the *Vie de Jésus*, in the defense of the atheist's blasphemies as against the prayers of the devout, and above all in the crowning jest—almost sufficient to undo all Renan's serious religious thought as well as our respect for him—which is a proposal that a selection of "pious readings" be made from his collected works and placed, a new missal, in delicately gloved hands. Of such subtle blasphemies Voltaire might have been capable, but to sprinkle over them, as though to exorcise them, passages from the Mass and from St. Francis' Sermon to the Birds—this would have been beyond him.

Renanisme reveals another of its distinctive traits in the author's ambiguous, noncommittal approach to his subject. Renan neither believes nor disbelieves, neither loves nor hates. Once again, we are far removed from the *Etudes d'histoire religieuse*, the *Essais de morale et de critique*, or, indeed, Renan's best work in general, where critical sense and a certain skepticism do not exclude subtly expressed convictions and real enthusiasm. Here there is no true detachment, no calm skepticism which might win our respect. There is something radically different, self-destructive irony. It is not pleasant to be buffetted about by these contrary winds of disillusionment and idealism, nor is it agreeable to see a great idealist undermining his own idealism.

Renan is not content, for example, to conclude his essay on Port-Royal, which shows an almost defiant respect for moral integrity, by quoting Sainte-Beuve's famous epilogue to his own *Port-Royal*, with its suggestion that history itself is an illusion "in the bosom of the Infinite Illusion": he must seek Biblical sanction for *renanisme* in the Preacher's "All is vanity." Patiently, almost with affection, he pieces together the historical image of an obscure Scandinavian nun of the Middle Ages, Christina of Stommeln, only to con-

clude that her mysticism was of pathological origin. To
Joachim of Floris and the Franciscans of the *Evangile éternel*
he devotes a long study leading to an anticlimax which dismisses them as insignificant visionaries.[11] One can take, and
even find amusing, the deliberate mystification of "La
méthode expérimentale en religion," but the withering
ironic smile is another matter. It is the most painful aspect
of this strange collection which, with its incredible mixture
of blasphemous quips and respectful portraits of saints, of
cynical witticisms and sensitive insights into religious faith,
is the least satisfactory of Renan's essay works and one of
his least worthy books.

At this point one feels compelled to ask: Is this the same
Renan who twenty years earlier told his colleagues at the
Collège de France that the ideal historian of religion, even
though a skeptic, will dutifully preserve an attitude of
gravity and respect when writing of the faith of others?
(*QC*, I, 148). Is this the same man who once said that only
negation and frivolity have the sad privilege of being beyond attack, whereas the true critic, in his seriousness and
conviction, should be proud to brave the laughter of skeptics? (*AS*, III, 1081). What lies behind this apparently
violent change? How can we explain *renanisme?*

Let us, to begin with, put aside as oversimplified the interpretations which identify this frivolous skepticism with
the whole of Renan's work, either to condemn it or to
praise it. Many sweeping attacks by Catholic commentators
come under this heading, but so also, surprisingly enough,
does the starry-eyed veneration of the otherwise sensitive
critic, Anatole France. Dedicating the controversial statue
to Renan at Tréguier in 1903, reviewing his career, which
he saw as one long, delicate, disillusioned smile from be-

ginning to end, he canonized him as the favorite son of Pallas Athena, the saint of the anticlerical Third Republic, comparable to Christ. Far less than with valid biography or criticism, we are dealing here with a highly personal, prejudiced cult. Almost as though in a vision, Renan, the supreme artist-skeptic-historian, had appeared to Anatole France to absolve him from the responsibility of forming convictions, to bless his estheticism, and to allow him to "dream anew the dream of the ages of faith," to give himself "the illusion of living beliefs." [12] The apotheosis of Renan has now passed; *renanisme*, partly because it is so out of keeping with various forms of the modern temper but partly also because it is such an obvious distortion of his work, has very few followers today.[13]

The soundest interpreters of *renanisme* have clearly recognized a fact which I hope our study of his essays has further illuminated, namely, that it is a final phase, not the dominant factor, of his work, and that it should be carefully distinguished from his morally serious, idealistic youth and maturity. Various explanations of the apparent turnabout have been suggested, and although they all have an element of truth, none seems to me to go to the bottom of the matter. Bourget knew Renan well enough to look for a serious philosophical cause of his final *légèreté*, which he calls "*dilettantisme*" (a term related to *renanisme*, which is a special form of dilettantism). The germ lay, claims Bourget, in his "*esprit cosmique*," his detached view of things as without consequence in the light of eternity.[14] But this "*esprit cosmique*" bears too great a resemblance to the world view of Spinoza or Einstein to be, at least in itself, the cause of frivolous skepticism. Faguet, in an inconsistent, rather abstract, but often penetrating essay, argues that Renan's insistence on seeing all the points of view in a given question, his desire to experience "all the conditions of the mind," led him to become a kind of intellectual vagrant in search of ever-novel cerebral pleasures, an "intellectual epicurean"—a phrase and an interpretation which have had widespread influence.[15] But does the admission that every "yea" has its "nay" and that there is truth in both lead one inevitably to become an intellectual voluptuary? What was it precisely that led Renan and not, for example, Edmond Schérer, in many ways a more devout Hegelian than he was, to such a position? Once again, a distinct special cause of *renanisme*, meaningful in terms of his own biography and his own evolution, seems to have eluded us.

The most convincing explanation—although not entirely so, in my opinion—is to be found in the sober and well-documented *"essai de biographie psychologique"* by the philosopher Gabriel Séailles. Renan's undoing, in his view, was caused by his indifference to philosophical truth, by his long-standing cult of "facts" and of history which, when his hopes based upon them deceived him (*"le démenti des faits"*), proved too feeble a reed to lean on.[16] The strongest part of this analysis by Séailles is that he takes account of the earlier serious idealism, emphasizes Renan's gradual disillusionment and surrender to irony, and, dating the first full-blown appearance of *renanisme* from the *Dialogues et fragments philosophiques* of 1876, thereby establishes the fact that it is (to use another critic's term) "the flower of a late, long-germinating disillusion." [17] Where I disagree with Séailles is in believing that it was less Renan's denial of philosophical truth which brought him to his final giddiness—or affectation of giddiness—than a long series of disappointed ideals, combined with too heady a dose of popularity. Renan, it is quite clear, always had a penchant for skepticism. It had contributed to the disintegration of his faith. But in his reconstructed philosophy, as we have seen, skepticism was curiously hedged in by a number of dogmatic assumptions; it was never allowed to disturb his practical moral idealism; and it was seldom frivolous. Even in speculative questions, it was not truth which he disbelieved in, but absolute truth. He defined his position very clearly in *L'avenir de la science:* "We reject both frivolous skepticism and scholastic dogmatism: we are critical dogmatists. We believe in truth, although we do not pretend to possess absolute truth" (*AS*, III, 1084). His taste for nuances, for contradictions, his Hegelian, eclectic relativism, much more a part of his whole intellectual climate than has been recognized, were not sufficient, in my opinion, to undermine his "critical dogmatism." What, then, were the real causes of the irresponsible manner which first becomes conspicuous, as Séailles rightly pointed out, in the preface of the *Dialogues et fragments philosophiques?* [18]

The most important cause, I feel, was his increasing fear of being duped. It is a familiar theme in French literature, a reflection of what many, including Renan himself, believe to be a distinctive national trait. In the nineteenth century —"this nineteenth century," as Sainte-Beuve wrote, "which will go down in great part as the century of literary, humanitarian, eclectic, neo-Catholic, and other kinds of charlatanism" [19]—the fear of being duped seemed especially strong. In Renan's own generation, it expressed itself often as a recoil from the high-flown eloquence and idealism of the romantics, for to experience this fear in its noblest form one must be not a cynic but an idealist unsure of himself. From the *Cahiers de jeunesse* to the *Feuilles détachées*, *"l'horreur d'être dupe"* runs through Renan's work, gradually becoming deeper and more philosophical in character. A few critics have called attention to it,[20] but no one has examined it in all its psychological import and particularly in its relation to *renanisme*.

The roots of this fear probably lay in the young seminarian's humble provincial origin and social awkwardness. He was subject, as he recalled many years later, to "threefold ridicule as a runaway seminarian, a defrocked cleric, and a thick-shelled pedant" (*SEJ*, II, 905), reason enough to make him want to put on a "breastplate against ridicule" (*AS*, III, 1079). His idealist's sensitivity to the *"rire des sceptiques"* we have already noted. It was a deeper form of the fear of ridicule than his uneasiness in society, which disappeared as he matured and made his brilliant reputation. Gradually, aggravated by the frustration of many of his hopes, this deeper fear assumed such proportions that he came to look upon himself, and indeed the whole of mankind, as the plaything of a cruel God.

Was not his loss of faith the first such great frustration? Such is clearly the implication of the curious concluding paragraph of *L'avenir de la science*, in which he kneels before the altar of the ruined temple, the brass altar against which all prayer is broken, and chides God for having deceived him (*AS*, III, 1121). Allusions to the "deceiving God" occur in works much later than this, as late, indeed, as the year of his death. That the shadow of this first disillusionment never entirely lifted is clear from the intimate notes published for the first time by Henriette Psichari, and especially from the haunting remark, perhaps the most revealing thing Renan ever wrote: "All I have done is nothing but a brilliant sepulcher for my lost faith." [21]

But there were other *démentis*—the failure of the dream of 1848, the dream of progress in a rational democratic society; the reaction of 1850–1851; the vanished hope of Franco-German co-operation. In the wake of this series of harsh blows, from which he never fully recovered, there took shape in Renan's mind a grim notion of "the Eternal," related to the pessimism of Schopenhauer and Hartmann, and even more to that of Vigny. Alongside the set of synonyms we earlier examined, those of God the Ideal and God the *"nisus profond"* or unconscious striving, we must now place a third, God the Duper, the deceiving demon (*RIM*, I, 541), the "transcendent scientist" who blunders about in his laboratory universe (*FD*, II, 1168), the "superior egoism" of which men are the playthings (*DFP*, I, 573). Having no *Docteur noir* such as Vigny's evil prompter to whisper the blackest thoughts into his ear, Renan hoped that the mysterious experiment had meaning and purpose; he found some consolation in resignation to it, in being, at least, a "voluntary dupe" of its Machiavellianism (*DFP*, I, 581). But at other moments he adopted a more flippant attitude. Unlike the proud Vigny, who rendered to the "cruel God" silence for silence, Renan chose to render *boutade* for *boutade*. "We owe to the Eternal," he wrote, "the practice of virtue; but we have the right to add, by way of personal reprisal, our irony. In that manner we pay back to whomever it may concern joke for joke; we play the trick which has been played on us" (*FD*, II, 1160).

It is obvious that profound, cumulative disillusionment

underlies the *"gaieté philosophique"* of *renanisme.* And it
is perfectly in keeping with Renan's character that even his
frivolity should be in this way related to his basic seriousness and idealism. Frivolity was the mask intended to conceal the fact that he had been duped. It is most significant
that *renanisme* is conspicuous in the more popular works
of Renan—the *Dialogues* and *Drames philosophiques,* the
Discours et conférences, the *Souvenirs d'enfance et de
jeunesse* and its sequel, the *Feuilles détachées* (I would also
include the *Nouvelles études d'histoire religieuse*)—but
barely present in his serious historical work or in his teaching, and totally absent from his private moral outlook and
practice. With his public he played a game of hide and
seek, encouraging the legend of himself as a frivolous skeptic, but never completely withdrawing clues to his deeper,
more serious self. And this legend, which his popularity
allowed him to publish far and wide, in turn increased that
popularity. Thousands cheered as he thumbed his nose at
"the Eternal." He even exploited his earlier reputation and
his present position in favor of the legend, for half the
amusement of his audiences was derived from the fact that
this was no ordinary cynic who juggled ideas so deftly, but
an aging academic celebrity, noted for the austere idealism
of his youth.

To illustrate and give further support to my interpretation of *renanisme,* I would refer to the essay on "Henri-
Frédéric Amiel" in the *Feuilles détachées.* In this final book
there is much else of interest, including estimates of George
Sand and Victor Hugo, two small essays of delicate humor
(without the ambiguity of *renanisme*), "Madame Hortense
Cornu" and "Souvenirs du *Journal des débats,*" and the

important "Examen de conscience philosophique," which serves as a ballast for much that is trifling. One is justified, however, in concentrating on the essay on Amiel, since all the essential traits of *renanisme* are crystallized in it: the apparent mockery of moral seriousness, the allusion to *duperie*, the seeming invitation to total skepticism. Moreover, from beneath the camouflage of frivolity, a stubborn affirmation of purposiveness and responsibility breaks through, reminding us of Barrès' remark that this frivolity was an *"attitude d'écrivain"* designed to hide the true character of his thought.

It was the peculiar nature of the subject—Amiel, of the famous *Journal intime*, the symbol of sterile conflict between creativeness and criticism, the victim of the "malady of the ideal," who "sat like a spider in a kind of cosmic web spun from his own body" [22]—which provoked Renan into giving away his game. In the first half of the essay ("Premier article," September 30, 1884), with a few decisive pen strokes, he separates himself from the whole contemporary tribe of pessimists, the Amiels, the Schopenhauers, the Lecontes de Lisle, all those who had sought release from life's problems in the extinction of the will. Against the example of Amiel he reacts with all the vigor of his strong will to life, all his old belief in the inexhaustible beauty and interest of the world. In his impatience with *"l'affreux égoïsme contemporain,"* he even goes so far as to condemn the very genre of the *journal intime* as a cowardly retreat from the responsibility of delving further into the secrets of history and nature (*FD*, II, 1141–1142). This robust voice, calling us to "take up the pick and set to work," is the true voice of Renan.

But into the "Deuxième article" (October 7, 1884) creeps

the familiar levity, growing cleverer and stronger until it conjures away this sober credo and leaves what seems to be a defense against Amiel of the value of immorality. For having revealed the source of his own courage and cheer, his own enthusiasm for life, Renan seems a bit ashamed. And so he must taunt the departed shade of Amiel with the suggestion that for others less fortunate there are the consolations of luxury or women, morphine or alcohol (*FD*, II, 1153). To Amiel's attack on his irony and *persiflage*, he replies that this constitutes true wisdom. It is as though he suddenly recalled, in the midst of his serious refutation of Amiel's pessimism, the amusing role his public liked him to play, the requirements of his myth. The fear of being duped rears its ugly head. Thinking perhaps of someone like that "indifferent and mocking spectator" who peered constantly over the shoulder of Mérimée,[23] he puts on the protective armor of skepticism—no, let us not dignify it with that name—of grim frivolity. "*In utrumque paratus!*" he concludes. "To be prepared for everything, that is perhaps real wisdom. To abandon oneself, according to one's moods, to hope, skepticism, optimism, irony, is the best means of being sure that one has at least now and then been in the right" (*FD*, II, 1159).[24] But such a remark only confirms the rightness of Amiel's charge that he believed nothing—"appeared to believe nothing" would have been more accurate—in order never to be found in the wrong, and desired nothing so much as intellectual safety. Between the paralyzed will he attributes to Amiel and his own fear of being duped, there is little to choose.

To summarize: *Renanisme* in its creator is an attitude of frivolous skepticism conspicuous in the more popular writings and speeches of the last two decades of his life. Its germs lay to some extent in his earlier, more sober unwillingness to commit himself on many philosophical questions. Had the circumstances of his life been different, he might have enjoyed to the end the reputation of a serious, straightforward critic. But under the impact of much disillusionment, unable to withstand the corrupting influence of great popularity, his skepticism became exaggerated and amusing and took on the form of a pose, a complex defense mechanism against the possibility of being duped even further. To conceal his own persistent idealism, he affected that chameleonlike behavior recommended by Prospero in *L'eau de Jouvence* and defined by him as "arranging oneself so that, whatever hypothesis happens to be true, one will not have been too absurd" (*DP*, III, 480).

The most convincing proof that Renan's seriousness of purpose, his spirit of "world-and-life affirmation" (to borrow a phrase from Schweitzer) remained substantially unchanged despite *renanisme* is to be found not in the many revealing passages of his later work or in his unfailing devotion to scholarship, but in the long-delayed publication of *L'avenir de la science* two years before his death—"flesh of my flesh and bone of my bone," an extraordinary reaffirmation, perhaps without parallel in literary history, of his faith in human reason. To uncover this faith from beneath his shell of frivolity and to understand the real and terrible causes of the disillusionment which almost destroyed it, however, is not to absolve him from the grave sin of irresponsibility toward his readers. Had his irreverence been designed solely, as was Philalèthe's in the *Dialogues philosophiques*, to shock postwar *bien pensants* and pharisees by a kind of affectation of vice (*DFP*, I, 582), it might have been excusable. But the mystification he practiced is the most dangerous kind of all for an author, the betrayal—even though in his case it was only apparent—of his own best work. His frequent reminders to his readers to take him with a grain of salt, since he does not mean all the blasphemous things he says, are of little help. In such moments of "perilous abandonment" (*"périlleux abandons,"* Renan himself called them), he admitted that his literary conscience hesitated and his hand trembled; but on he wrote, to the applause of thousands of frivolous readers (*SEJ*, II, 897). He plunged clear-eyed into this literary sin.

It is unfortunate that our survey of Renan's essay work must end on such a painful note. If one can forget for a moment the weakened sense of moral responsibility, the large degree of dissimulation, involved in *renanisme*, it is not without its more palatable aspects. The laughter, the famous *sourire renanien*, often spring from something more sound—a robust cheerfulness and gaiety which, despite much physical suffering and grimly pessimistic moments, remained one of Renan's fundamental traits, distinguishing his smile from the somewhat more artful, literary one of an Anatole France or a Jules Lemaître. The play of ideas, which he compared to the manipulation of lanterns with changing lights or to a billiard game, has a certain fascination. In much of the irreverence there is a healthy, bracing wit, like that of more forthright iconoclasts, Voltaire, Shaw, or, perhaps most of all, Mencken. If all this is decadence, it is, as Faguet observed, "astonishingly brilliant decadence." [25] But in our enjoyment of it, we are apt to be haunted by another Renan, the Renan of *L'avenir de la sci-*

ence or the *Essais de morale et de critique,* the *Cahiers de jeunesse* or *Marc-Aurèle,* the "Vingt jours en Sicile" or the "Examen de conscience philosophique." Sensitive to this presence, we cannot but feel that *renanisme* must weigh more heavily on the debit than on the credit side of his work.

Chapter 8

Renan and the Art of the Essay

"I am false sometimes and think of appearances.
And yet there is also a great fund of truth in me."
— *Nouveaux cahiers de jeunesse*

ONE of the outstanding facts in the history of literature within the last thirty years has been the decline of the essay. Our world at mid-century has not been wanting in able journalists, critics, and scholars. But well-written articles, even those of permanent value, are not necessarily essays. It is merely using the term loosely to assign them to the great tradition which for over three hundred years, from Montaigne to Max Beerbohm, brought joy to our ancestors— the tradition of the brief, highly polished prose work, conveying a view (usually very personal) of almost any conceivable subject and worth rereading again and again. To identify almost any piece of nonfictional prose with the essay, furthermore, is to be unjust to the few who have remembered the tradition and still keep it alive, such true

essayists as E. M. Forster or E. B. White, T. S. Eliot or
Edmund Wilson. Even in France, where the relation between journalism and literary art has long been close, there
are few today who are *essayistes* in quite the same way as,
several generations ago, Paul Valéry or Alain or Remy de
Gourmont.

To the decline of the essay as a distinct form, many
causes have contributed. For many English-speaking readers, the essay has become associated with memories of school-
room chores, of the forced labor of "themes," those artificial
expressions of unreal sentiments.[1] A more universal factor
undermining the vitality of the essay has been the growth
of specialization, with its accompanying diminution in that
general competence, that urbanity, which are the soul of
the essay. "The art of the essay," it has been pointed out,
"like that of conversation, has declined in the last century
because there are too few people who know enough about
enough matters to afford an audience for the attractive
discussion which is expert without being specialized." [2]
Even in France, where, as we have said, there is relatively
little consciousness of the essay as a distinct genre, the publisher Kra noted in 1929, without great enthusiasm, that
specialization seemed to be a characteristic trait of contemporary essayists.[3] The drought of knowing more and
more about less and less has touched the land *par excellence*
of broad humane culture.

There are deeper reasons, however, for the essay's weakened hold on readers. One would think that the essay's
brevity might have been in its favor. But we suffer not so
much from the lack of time to read as from the disinclina-
tion to read carefully, and the essay, like the short-story
and the poem, fellow exiles from best-seller lists, calls for

attentive reading, for a certain amount of pondering and savoring. And it is precisely this willingness to savor subtle works of art, in a spirit of meditation and reflectiveness, that has become increasingly rare today. Perhaps it is significant that the essay began to become unpopular about the time, after the First World War, when, as Schweitzer tells us, the spirit of reflectiveness, the awareness of men as whole beings, individual personalities (an awareness also essential to the health of the essay), began to give way to the spirit of totalitarianism. Man the collective being, the faceless statistic, the thinking machine manipulated by propaganda, is, at least, alien to the very spirit of the essay.

Something of this growing unreflectiveness, in writer and reader alike, was perceived by Virginia Woolf to be the underlying cause of the essay's decline. The eloquent thoughts she recorded on the subject in "The Modern Essay," in 1925, will serve both to enlighten us on the essay in general and to link us up again with Renan and his time. Herself a member of a great generation of essayists, which included Max Beerbohm, Lytton Strachey, and John Middleton Murry; one of the last perfectionists, in her *Common Reader*, of that difficult art, she makes perfectly clear the distinction between the true essay and the modern ersatz product. It is the distinction between "the shapely silver drop, that held the sky in it and so many bright little visions of human life," on one hand, and, on the other, "a hold-all, knobbed with luggage packed in a hurry," or, even worse, "journalism embalmed in a book." [4]

Whetting our appetites for the old masters—for Montaigne, Bacon, Addison, Lamb, Hazlitt, Hunt, De Quincey, Carlyle, Ruskin, Arnold, Pater, Newman, Bagehot—Virginia Woolf makes us feel how great an art we are in danger of losing. Of the Victorians in particular, Renan's contemporaries, she writes: "It was worth while to speak out upon serious matters in an essay; and there was nothing absurd in writing as well as one possibly could when, in a month or two, the same public which had welcomed the essay in a magazine would carefully read it once more in a book." Now (how much more true this is today than in 1925 when she wrote it!), "a common greyness silvers everything. Beauty and courage are dangerous spirits to battle in a column and a half; and thought, like a brown paper parcel in a waistcoat pocket, has a way of spoiling the symmetry of an article." [5]

The nineteenth-century French essay, with Sainte-Beuve as its brilliant pioneer and Renan as perhaps its most versatile representative, flowed through the same channel from periodical to book, was based upon the same premise of broad culture in writer and reader, and professed the same serious literary aim as its English counterpart, described by Virginia Woolf. But there were important differences. The French product admitted of much less variety in form and content; it tended to be critical in nature, whether it treated of politics, history, or literature—critical and much less personal, at least directly personal, much less whimsical and poetic. However, though less luxuriant than its English cousin, the French critical essay, within these limitations, was capable of great diversity, and few writers proved this as successfully as Renan. Few, indeed, possessed the breadth of interests and the flexible command of French prose which made him so well suited to the task.

In the essay Renan found the happiest means—apart, that is, from the writing of history, which remained closest to his heart—for the expression of his personality. Unlike

Montaigne and so many of his disciples, especially his English disciples, unlike the romantics, he disliked speaking freely and directly of himself. The *Cahiers de jeunesse*, that dialogue of the young thinker with himself and himself alone, a dialogue which, as Charles Du Bos pointed out, surpasses even the intimate journal in unstudied frankness,[6] is quite exceptional in his total work. For the *journal intime* as a literary genre, we have seen that he felt only distaste. It stemmed from his natural reticence—despite the *Souvenirs d'enfance et de jeunesse*, more often misleading than revealing, he was a reticent man—and from his training in seventeenth-century *honnêteté*, re-enforced by the lessons of Henriette and Sacy. "*Confessions*" he was not loathe to make, but "*confidences*" (this important distinction is applied to Guizot in QC, I, 32) he withheld. The critical essay, like history, was beautifully suited to this type of modesty, for it allowed him to give generously of his thought and feeling and yet to keep them within the framework of critical restraint, under the sober control of scholarship.

In some ways his essay work seems narrow in scope. Rarely do the "shapely silver drop," the color and poetry of the world around us, the all-important trivia (in Logan Pearsall Smith's sense) of our lives, find a place in it. Only rarely, as in the "Souvenirs d'un vieux professeur allemand" or an occasional *feuille détachée*, does he lend himself to whimsical humor. For a Frenchman, his relative indifference to literary criticism, to questions of art, might almost be called neglect. It is in the *Dialogues philosophiques* and the *Drames philosophiques*, rather than in the essays, that he approaches that spirit of delightfully free and unpredictable reverie we admire in so many essayists. On the other hand, the field of the critical essay, as he explored it, was wonderfully wide and fruitful. Breadth is one of his greatest virtues. And although most of the nineteenth-century essayists possessed this gift, so rare today, few writers anywhere have ever equaled Renan in breadth and solidity of culture. On subjects ranging from ancient Greek myths to the memoirs of Guizot, from the Buddha to the Franco-Prussian War, from Isaiah to the metaphysics of Vacherot, he cast the light of his great learning and intelligence. The results he achieved, though all interesting, are not all equally successful, and some attempt should now be made to arrange them in an ascending hierarchy of excellence.

The philosophical essays, as distinguished from the more brilliant *dialogues* and *drames*, seem to me the least durable. In this perhaps most difficult of all the essay forms, Renan is the inferior of Emerson or Santayana or Bertrand Russell. It was no mean feat to condense the whole of his intellectual drama in the extraordinarily rich and subtle "Examen de conscience philosophique." But his philosophical thought in general suffers from evasiveness: instead of coming to grips firmly with his terrible dilemma, with the basic contradiction of his mind, namely, emotional attachment to a religion whose truth his intellect denied, he glossed over the problem with vague phrases, proposing a compromise between positivism and spiritualism which, designed to please scientific as well as religious minds, ended up satisfying neither.[7] This was the price he paid for his faithfulness to eclecticism, for he was its star pupil and the greatest demonstrator of its essential futility.

In his historical essays, on the other hand, he gives us solid meat. He takes his rightful place with Montaigne and Pascal, Montesquieu, Fontenelle, Voltaire, and Sainte-

Beuve, as a master of that difficult art, in which the French above all have excelled, the art of *vulgarisation*. Like Saturn devouring and digesting the rocks or, to descend to our human level, like Montesquieu "unraveling the chaos of Ripuarian, Visigothic, and Burgundian laws" (*MHV*, II, 624), he turned highly technical knowledge into nourishment for the common reader. To have extracted the "poetry of history" from his own researches and from those of his contemporaries; to have emerged from communion with dead documents, uncontaminated with pedantry and ready to tell of the living things he had seen—this was no small achievement. One need not accept all his views in order to recognize that in his hands the essay in religious history became a source of artistic pleasure as well as of enlightenment, and this is what makes the *Etudes d'histoire religieuse* a major landmark in the history of the French essay. May scholars who are too faint-hearted to risk being called "popularizers" be encouraged by his example: he practiced this art of humanizing learning with no sacrifice of scholarly integrity. He was, in one and the same man, without split personality, the scholar who taught extremely specialized lessons in Hebrew epigraphy and directed the Corpus Inscriptionum Semiticarum and the sensitive prose artist of "L'histoire du peuple d'Israël." "Let us not blame him too much," said Alfred Loisy, "for having been a marvelous writer as well as a scholar. There will always be enough learned men who write badly." [8]

On an equally high plane with his explorations of our religious past are his essays in the political problems, conceived in the broad French manner, of his own time. He understood, to recall a haunting phrase of Virginia Woolf's, that "reverence for the dead is vitally connected with understanding of the living." As a political essayist, in the best of the *Questions contemporaines* and *La réforme intellectuelle et morale*, he ranks with Walter Bagehot or Lord Acton. The latter work, in great part a gloomy, violent attack on democracy, is to be admired not least of all for its power to provoke. Its prefascist vision of order was, however, only a temporary aberration of his pessimism in the 1870's. Despite some confusion and inconsistency, his mature political philosophy may be defined as an intelligent conservatism, a belief in liberal constitutional monarchy which did not exclude the possibility of a future working democracy for France. The point is that his essays abound in historical insight, in shrewd wisdom, and in the sense, not especially common in scholars, of political responsibility and readiness to act if called upon. His greatest tour de force was his ability to place these ephemeral questions in a broad moral and historical context which gives them permanent interest; it was simply not his habit, as he remarked with justifiable pride, to treat any subjects in a narrow manner (*QC*, I, 159).

At the summit of Renan's essay work, in my opinion, stands his *Essais de morale et de critique*, with its condemnation of materialism and bureaucracy, of the cult of mediocrity, in the modern world and its affirmation of idealism. Less perceptive than Sainte-Beuve or Taine as a literary critic, Renan nevertheless brought unusual understanding to figures on the margin of literature, seeking to illuminate his own time through the study of such predecessors as Cousin, Thierry, Lamennais, Tosti, Sacy, and, elsewhere, Guizot, Burnouf, Le Clerc. Here he practiced with great skill the traditional French *portrait moral*, delicately but firmly passing judgment upon an older generation, seeking to learn from their virtues and errors. But the most remarkable feature of these essays is the manner in which he lets his thoughts crystallize in rich patterns around the subjects he treats, while never allowing us to lose sight of the subjects themselves. The themes which emerge—critically controlled enthusiasm for life and learning, detached but interested participation in the political life of one's time, reaffirmation of poetic and spiritual values, mediation between past and present—make up one of the strongest messages he has left us. One could argue, without absurdity, that this is his true masterpiece.

For each of the major divisions of his essay work, Renan used a different kind of style, and this is an appropriate point to sum up our scattered observations on that subject. Much of what we say should apply to his style in general, for we have come into contact with an incomplete, but nevertheless very substantial, area of his prose.

That diversity of style is as much a feature of his work as diversity of subject matter has not always been recognized. For too long the misconception has been abroad—with few critics to combat it [9]—that *le style de Renan* is almost exclusively a form of poetic prose. The highly artificial lyricism of the "Prière sur l'Acropole" or of parts of the *Vie de Jésus* has been assumed by many to be his strong point, and the assumption has done more harm than good to his reputation. The fact is that this type of writing is much less characteristic of Renan than it is supposed to be. His style usually lacks the vivid color, the abundance of images and metaphors, and especially the marked, self-conscious rhythms of poetic prose. Like all great prose, it is, at its best, clear and forceful, spontaneous and self-effacing. Poetic feeling was but one of its ingredients. Nor, to continue for a moment this negative approach, can we accept the equally widespread error that Renan was an impeccable model of French prose, a legend which has frightened many readers away and challenged others, Jean-Paul Sartre, for example, to prick the bubble, by exposing "baseness" and "ugliness" everywhere.[10] Much more sensible is Brunetière's sober observation that Renan did not always write correctly or purely and sometimes wrote carelessly.[11]

The vagueness which was one of his permanent weaknesses, the excessive facility and the bad taste which mar so much of his last work—reflecting, we dare say, the moral slackness of *renanisme* itself, for Renan has taught us the moral significance of style—these are his real faults. Revealing that he was aware of perhaps an even more serious one, which he blamed on certain limitations he found inherent in French prose itself, he declared: "What, indeed, does it mean to write well, as we understand it in France? It means constantly to sacrifice sudden flashes of wit (*saillie*) and often frankness to the moderation (*mesure*) of the language. It means to say at the most half of what we think, and at least a quarter of what we do not think" (*MHV*, II, 523).[12] We certainly need not regret that he refined the crude vigorous metal of his youthful prose into such a marvelously subtle critical instrument. But we may well regret, along with Renan, that the sacrifice of frankness went too far. Above all, we may regret that the subtle critical instrument became an instrument of equivocation.

Once we have squarely recognized these faults, we can proceed to the definition of what is truly beautiful in his style. He wrote in several keys, each with its peculiar excellence, and yet his style as a whole has its distinctive seal. To begin with his diversity, it may be explained in part by the rich variety of influences he absorbed: the lyricism of prose poets like Fénelon and Chateaubriand, the simplicity and restraint of classicism, the austere touch of Port-Royal and Sacy, the polemical vigor of Maistre and of the *Liberté de penser*, the sober descriptive power of Thierry, the learned but graceful precision of scholars like Burnouf. At his best his style represents a fusion of all these influences. He began with the aggressive, frank, often harsh manner of his essays for the *Liberté de penser*. In *L'avenir de la science* he was wild and feverish and verbose in his idealism. Much of this early vigor, restrained and sharpened but still virile, passed into his political essays, which are characterized by an incisive, energetic style, fertile in aphorisms. Here there is none of that "softness" and "uncertainty," that "flaccidity" and "lack of muscle" André Gide complained of in the *Souvenirs d'enfance et de jeunesse* and *L'abbesse de Jouarre*.[13] Renan was of course an adept in what Matthew Arnold called the "Attic style," "*lenis minimèque pertinax*" ("easy and not too violently insisting"), and with him this style of delicate insinuation developed undeniable signs of flabbiness. But he could also be perfectly direct and firm; he could even be violent.

His better-known style, however, is the more subtle one first appearing in the *Averroès* and then in the *Études d'histoire religieuse* and the *Essais de morale et de critique*. Impelled by his need to harmonize the conflicting intellectual gifts he had received, to unite them in "parallel existences," and inspired by Cousin's vision of an age of synthesis, he sought to become a microcosm of the manifold talents of humanity itself, blending in his work critical poise and moral and religious fervor, scientific accuracy and poetic feeling. But "poetry" was only one of the strands making up the pattern: "I have a certain reflective and psychological turn of mind which keeps coming back and which prevents me from being abundantly or easily poetic" (*CJ*, p. 391). Except for a few essays like "Les religions de l'antiquité," the poetic element was not particularly sensuous or colorful. Little realism entered into this art. Although a member of the first generation of realists and Parnassians, Renan remained, in esthetics, an anti-realist, a spiritualist.

This brings us to what may well be the most distinctive feature of his style, and the true secret of its greatness, namely, the effect it gives of moral intensity achieved by the most conservative means, of spontaneous grace within a framework of order and harmony. His sentences reflect his compelling drive toward regularity, toward a balanced, harmonious view of life, and yet this *"ensemble harmonieux"* did not exclude a certain underlying unrest, a trembling of irony. It is this which gives moral life to his style, but it is perhaps even more the fact that unlike Flaubert or Walter Pater, he did not cultivate form for its own sake or strain after effect. Naturally, we except the artificial tricks of *renanisme*. At his best, he was a highly conscious artist who happily failed to polish all the spontaneity out of his art.

In 1923, comparing him with Taine and Flaubert and estimating their relative chances of survival as living writers, Albert Thibaudet pointed out how wise Renan was to avoid Taine's more obviously oratorical style and Flaubert's cult of art. The special mark of his style, wrote Thibaudet,

is that of probity, delicacy, and sobriety. Those who believe that style has a value in itself found little favor with him, and, although Flaubert never expressed his opinion on this score, he must have asked himself in astonishment what one could possibly find to admire in Renan's style. What we admire are precisely those spontaneous aspects of the French language which are most foreign to the willful character of Flaubert's own style.[14]

In singling out Renan's essays for detailed study, I have made no claim that they are necessarily superior to the rest of his work or that they reveal what a French critic might call his *vrai visage*. I have tried to avoid isolating them from his other works. Much of the criticism of Renan, however, has suffered from the failure to take his essays into account at all. In them, on the whole, we discover the strong, affirmative side of his nature also expressed, though with much less artistry, in the *Cahiers de jeunesse, L'avenir de la science*, and the correspondence with Berthelot. And this *visage*, in all probability, is a truer one than that of the arch equivocator, the dissolver of our sense of truth and error, which has stuck in the minds of so many readers. In summing up the image that emerges from his essays, let us try to separate the gold from the dross.

The most serious of Renan's flaws, I would say, was a certain lack of forthrightness. One cannot deny that at times he demonstrated admirable courage, as when he made a clean break from Saint-Sulpice or defined his stand at the Collège de France in 1862 or probed the national conscience in his unpopular prophetic essays of the war and postwar years. But the weakness of his religious position, his inability to face up to the consequences of his repudiation of Christianity, weigh heavily against him. He who so dreaded being duped deceived himself—or perhaps did, for this intimate side of his thought is not very well known [15]—into believing he had not in fact repudiated Christianity at all. He is the most outstanding example of the widespread nineteenth-century error, defined and attacked by Santayana, in his

Winds of Doctrine (1913), as "archeological piety," that vague sentimental clinging to the memory of Christianity, to its historical beauty, when one's reason has rejected it. To modern readers, Renan's religiosity, once considered a virtue, is more likely to appear a most obnoxious vice. Would that he had applied to his own work the critical remark he made of "liberal Catholics," namely, that truth, as Bacon said, is more apt to emerge from error than from confusion—"Malheur au vague! Mieux vaut le faux" (*SEJ*, II, 829).

An even more serious manifestation of Renan's lack of straightforwardness, however, was the weakening of his sense of responsibility toward his readers in the last twenty years or so of his life. He had reason enough to be disillusioned, to be skeptical: the promise of the Revolution, the great dream of a free society ordering its fate with the help of scientific and historical knowledge and an inspired reason, the great dream of 1848, had collapsed, owing, he believed, to the naïve bungling of the romantic generation.[16] What we must reproach him for is not that he was disenchanted, but that he assumed a mask of frivolity, the mask of *renanisme*, designed to convince his readers that, however much of an idealist he had once been, he was now a wise old cynic, safely detached from the search for truth, protected forever from the danger of having beliefs. No longer subject to the restraining moral influences of his sister, of Thierry or Sacy, the voice of his conscience drowned out by popular applause, he succeeded only too well, and in more senses than one, in this mystification. It is precisely this self-refutation of his own best side, this pleading against his own deeply moral nature (see his remarks in the *Avant-propos* of *Le prêtre de Némi—DP*, III, 526), which must be put down as his gravest failing.

But these defects, however serious, should not be allowed, as has too often happened, to obscure his real virtues. Of the vast number of Renan's critics, there have always been some, though they seem to be in a minority, who have suspected that, despite the conspicuous lapse of the last years, he preserved intact to the end his fundamentally moral and idealistic nature. Even critics who have exaggerated his skepticism have had their moments of insight into this stubbornly affirmative core of his being. Barrès, as we have seen, was one of them, and so also, surprisingly, was Anatole France; toward the beginning of his speech canonizing Renan as the saint of skeptics, we find this striking sentence, which seems very much out of place: "Those who believed him to be irresolute and fickle had not taken the trouble to observe the world of his thoughts. It was like the region from which he came, where clouds move swiftly overhead in a troubled sky, but the soil is made of granite, and into it oak trees plunge their deep roots." [17]

Lanson called this inner strength *"douce inflexibilité,"* [18] and Du Bos, a critic whose deeply moral nature no one will deny, was drawn to it, for he wrote that beneath the ironic smile, the surface wrinkles of *"dédaigneuse bonhomie,"* "le fond est demeuré, et demeure, inattaqué." It would indeed have been incredible had that quality of *sérieux* which we find in Renan's youth, and which Du Bos calls "peut-être la plus belle et la plus pure de tout le XIXᵉ siècle français," [19] disappeared altogether. That it survived and that it is unmistakably present in the greater part of his essay work, I hope my study has shown.

For one thing, the continuing presence in Renan's work of these deep roots, these "essential affirmations," as Irving Babbitt called them, is shown in his persistent philosophical view of the universe as an orderly system of laws (whose "immutability" he in fact exaggerated), moving toward moral perfection with an unconscious striving which it is man's duty to interpret and to render ever more conscious. Naïve much of this may seem, but certainly not fickle. Nor should we forget his stubborn pursuit of historical truth, for, despite his belittling of history as a composite of *"petites sciences conjecturales"* (*SEJ*, II, 852), he devoted his life to it, seeking out the truth about the past, compelled to arrange his materials in some kind of coherent, rational picture, even if it meant embracing hypotheses which more cautious historians would have kept at a distance.

Du Bos's phrase *"fond inattaqué"* certainly referred also to the moral probity of the private man, the *personne* as distinguished from the *personnage*, the devoted husband and father, the conscientious scholar and teacher, the citizen solicitous for his country's welfare. In a well-established French tradition which goes back to Descartes if not to Montaigne, Renan's skepticism remained a speculative affair hardly touching his practical moral life. Despite his occasional pessimism and grimness, there was no despair, no *acedia*, in him. From his quietly troubled and brilliant youth down to his death in his apartment of the Collège de France, he never, so far as I know, uttered a word in condemnation of life. To the last, it held its inexhaustible interest for him. Beside him, Flaubert, with his prescription of art as medicine against hysteria, perhaps even Taine, for whom work was a "slow and intelligent form of suicide," appear sickly indeed.

He possessed to a remarkable degree a quality which is of great help to any artist, but which is, as an English essayist has reminded us, indispensable to the creator of the essay —gusto.[20] His critical sense strengthened rather than weakened this enthusiasm for life. But because his enthusiasm was intellectual in nature, nourishing itself on learning, more than one critic has misunderstood it. Hippolyte Parigot, for example, apparently insensitive to this kind of sober scholarly emotion, accused Renan of lack of feeling, and also of "egotism." But even if it were true that Renan sacrificed some of his personal warmth in the interests of his pursuit of knowledge (Parigot offers only the incomplete evidence of a certain harshness toward Henriette), he would thereby find himself in the company of many a great creative spirit. Some egotism would seem to be the unavoidable price many great writers must pay in order to give us their works.

Parigot failed to see, furthermore, that it was precisely Renan's immense interest in life which saved him from egotism in the sense of self-centeredness. Renan is one of the great teachers of curiosity, of that curiosity which turns us outward from morbid preoccupation with self toward participation in the world around us. "Assuredly," he once wrote, "we must not speak ill of curiosity" (*DFP*, I, 697). Perhaps the very term which has been used to curse him with—the word "dilettante"—should be rehabilitated as an honorable epithet.[21] If to be a dilettante means to skim the surface of life, to grasp nothing firmly, he was no dilettante. Whatever the spirit of shallower writers who fancied themselves his disciples, his own spirit was to know and to love many things as deeply as our brief existence will allow. This spirit shines with special brightness through his essay work.

If this be dilettantism, it may be the antidote we need for too much specialization. We need also, in our age of violent and senseless action, which inculcates the use of things and persons merely as means to ends, something of the contemplative spirit which permeates Renan's essays, something of his interest in, his respect for, things and persons in themselves.

Renan deserves a better fate than has befallen him. He deserves more than to be admired from afar, a curious idol preserved by literary historians. His work, despite many dead branches that need clearing away, is still very much alive. That it is a rich and complex work one would suspect simply from the extraordinary variety of temperaments which it has influenced—dabblers in irony as well as scholars and educators of the utmost probity, frivolous dilettantes as well as serious moralists, critics as different as Matthew Arnold and Jules Lemaître, atheists and heretics, agnostics and converts. In the minds of some he sowed doubt and in the minds of others he awakened a sympathy for Christianity after the long dry spell of uncomprehending rationalism. A study of this influence in all its complex fecundity would be revealing, as would a careful exploration, much more thorough than mine has been, of his prose style. The heart of his work, his vast reconstruction of Judeo-Christian history from the shadowy origins of the Jews to the death of Marcus Aurelius, still awaits the historian competent enough as a scholar and yet sensitive enough as an artist to interpret it worthily.

We have approached Renan through a sizable and significant aspect of his work, the nine books of essays he produced between the age of thirty-four and his death at sixty-nine. They fall into three main periods: the inartistic, dogmatic faith in science (or historical scholarship) and the equally inartistic combative journalism of the 1840's; the mature critical art, in history, moral and political problems, and philosophy, of the 1850's, 1860's, and early 1870's; the disillusionment and affected frivolity of *renanisme*, from about 1876 to his death in 1892. Like most Frenchmen, Renan the mature artist prized, above all, order and clarity of composition, and this admirable national prejudice caused his essays to lose something in pleasurable unpredictability. He rarely took advantage of the essay's unique privilege of being "a loose sally of the mind," as Doctor Johnson put it, even though it was a Frenchman who had invented this delightful art of disorderly order, with its *"allure poétique, à sauts et à gambades."* His essay structure—often the total architecture of the book—is clear but subtle, firmer than Sainte-Beuve's (whose *causerie* is closer to Montaigne and perhaps to the English essay), but not so rigid and artificial as Taine's. He knew how to relax with *"feuilles légères," "fantaisies sans conséquence,"* but these pieces, though often charming, fail to capture the light, penetrating humor so common in the English essay.

Where Renan was at his best was in ranging out over history and contemporary events, over broad moral and political questions, and to the treatment of these in essay form he gave new authority and new luster. To these varied themes, he adapted his style with great skill, achieving now a rare combination of scholarly accuracy, poetic sensibility, and critical acumen, now a clear, direct, vigorous prose for political argument, now a note of rarefied moral feeling, expressed with the simplest and most sober means. He reveals himself in his essays as a scholar of genius, devoted to the enlightenment of his public, a keen and responsible political observer, an unsuccessful conciliator of religion and positivism, a vague and devious philosopher, a man of unusual moral probity (despite the lapses of *renanisme*)—"*un honnête homme à qui manque la grâce.*" [22] With Montaigne and Sainte-Beuve, in the still largely unexplored territory of the French essay—whose modern luminaries, from Bourget and Gourmont to Alain and Valéry, have not been few—he holds an assured and eminent place. His finest essays—"L'histoire du peuple d'Israël," "M. Augustin Thierry," "M. de Lamennais" (indeed, most of the *Essais de morale et de critique*), "Vingt jours en Sicile," "Examen de conscience philosophique"—are worthy of the greatest in any language. They have the qualities defined by Virginia Woolf as the special virtues of the essay: the delicate harmony of all their parts, the power of creating a single impression within a variety of perceptions, above all, the power to draw a magic curtain round us.

Renan is not, in my opinion, either in his essays or in his other works, a writer of the very first order; he is a great *second*. Like Ariel, in *L'eau de Jouvence*, he lacked a certain fire; but like Ariel also, he had light and air in abundance (*DP*, III, 451). To read his essays is to experience something of Henry James's feeling when he opened Emerson and Goethe, the "sense of moving in large intellectual space." [23] Du Bos, who was aware of Renan's serious weaknesses, tells us how, one evening, he took up the *Essais de morale et de critique* and read the essay on Lamennais for the first time, and how it led him to rediscover Renan's breadth of vision and his tranquillity, his brightness of outlook. Only the Renan of the end, he wrote, "the only one naturally who 'founded a school,'" failed to satisfy him completely. "Beside him," noted Du Bos, "there are hardly any Frenchmen of the nineteenth century who do not seem at times lacking in intelligence." [24]

It is always gratifying to find our literary judgments confirmed by a sensitive critic. It was his contact with this same beautiful book which first aroused the present writer's interest in Renan's essays and drew him across the barrier of prejudice and misunderstanding surrounding the subject of Renan and into the citadel of his work. He can only hope that he may have persuaded other readers to make a similar journey.

In Virginia Woolf's lament for the passing of the essay's heyday, there was much more than literary antiquarianism. The nineteenth, like all centuries, had its share of errors and absurdities, its own forms of barbarism, and from some of these we may have freed ourselves. But it was also a century of deep humanism, of a humanism which found one of its truest expressions in the essay, conceived as a work of art. In our own age of narrow specialization, of the fear of individualism, of growing unreflectiveness and insensitivity to language, we need the lightness and common sense, the breadth and freedom, the thoughtfulness and eccentricity and polish, of the essay. From the more often wise than foolish voice of Renan, speaking to us in the form of this most modest and perhaps most humane of all the literary arts, we have much to learn.

Appendix

Illustrative Passages

1. "Les religions de l'antiquité," in Renan's Etudes
d'histoire religieuse, *pp.* 20–23

Un des mythes qui me semblent les plus propres à faire com-
prendre cette extrême complexité, ces aspects fuyants, ces in-
nombrables contradictions des fables antiques, est celui de
Glaucus, mythe humble pourtant, mythe de pauvres gens, mais
ayant par là même mieux conservé son caractère primitif et
populaire. Ceux qui ont passé leur enfance sur les bords de la
mer savent combien d'associations d'idées profondes et poéti-
ques se forment en présence du spectacle animé qu'offre le
rivage. Glaucus est la personnification et le résumé de ces
croyances et de ces impressions, un dieu créé par des matelots,
en qui se résume toute la poésie de la vie marine, telle qu'elle
apparaît à de pauvres gens. La vieillesse l'accable; en proie au
désespoir, il se précipite dans la mer et devient prophète; prophète de malheur, triste vieillard, on le rencontre parfois, le
corps tout appauvri par l'action des eaux, couvert de co-
quillages et de plantes marines. Selon d'autres, il se précipita
dans les vagues pour n'avoir pu prouver à personne son immortalité. Depuis ce temps, il revient chaque année visiter les

rivages et les îles. Le soir, quand le vent s'annonce, Glaucus (c'est-à-dire le flot de couleur glauque) s'élève en prononçant de bruyants oracles. Les pêcheurs se couchent au fond de leur barque, et cherchent par des jeûnes, des prières et de l'encens à détourner les maux qui les attendent. Glaucus cependant, monté sur un rocher, menace en langue éolique leurs champs et leurs troupeaux, et se lamente sur son immortalité. On contait aussi ses amours, amours tristes, malheureux, finissant comme un mauvais rêve. Il aima une belle vierge de mer, nommée Scylla; un jour, espérant la toucher, il lui apporta des coquilles et de jeunes alcyons sans plumes pour l'amuser. Elle vit ses larmes et en eut pitié; mais Circé, par jalousie, empoisonna le bain de la jeune fille, et elle devint un monstre aboyant, personnification de l'horreur naturelle qu'inspirent les squales et des dangers de la mer de Sicile. Le pauvre Glaucus, en ce moment, resta toujours gauche, méchant, murmurant, malveillant. On le voit sur les monuments, avec sa barbe d'algues marines, le regard fixe, les sourcils contractés. Les Amours s'égayent à ses dépens: l'un lui tire les cheveux, l'autre lui donne un soufflet. Quelquefois il est *Glaucé*, c'est-à-dire cette teinte tirant sur le vert et le bleu que revêt la mer dans les endroits où elle repose peu profonde sur un sable blanc: la couleur de la mer devient aussi une femme, comme le sommet moutonnant des vagues devient la tête blanche des *Grées* (vieilles femmes), qui font peur aux matelots. Quelquefois il est *Lamie*, qui attire les hommes et les séduit par ses attraits; d'autres fois, un épervier qui plonge en tournoyant sur sa proie, puis une sirène insatiable tenant un jeune homme de chaque main.—Jetez pêle-mêle toutes les idées des gens de mer, amalgamez les branches éparses des rêves d'un matelot, vous aurez le mythe de Glaucus: préoccupation mélancolique, songes pénibles et difformes, sensation vive de tous les phénomènes qui naissent dans les flots, inquiétude perpétuelle, le danger partout, la séduction partout, l'avenir incertain, grande impression de fatalité. Glaucus est à la fois la couleur et le bruit de la mer, le flot qui blanchit, le reflet du ciel sur le dos des vagues, le vent du soir qui prédit la tempête du lendemain, le mouvement du plongeur, les formes rabougries de l'homme de mer, les désirs impuissants, les tristes retours de la vie solitaire, le doute, la dispute, le désespoir, le long ennui d'une certitude s'épuisant contre le sophisme, et la triste immortalité qui ne peut ni s'assurer ni se délivrer d'elle-même; énigme pénible, écho de ce sentiment mélancolique qui parle à l'homme de son origine inconnue et de sa destinée divine, vérité que pour son malheur il lui est impossible de prouver, car elle est supérieure à l'entendement, et l'homme ne saurait ni la démontrer ni s'y soustraire.

2. *"L'histoire du peuple d'Israël,"* in Renan's Etudes d'histoire religieuse, *pp. 113–114*

Pendant qu'au sein de Jérusalem s'agitaient ces délicates questions, d'où dépendait l'avenir religieux du monde, s'établissaient en Orient d'immenses et toutes-puissantes monarchies, auxquelles la destruction du royaume de Juda devait à peine coûter un effort. Les Hébreux, avec leurs idées si simples en fait d'organisation politique et militaire, éprouvèrent une vive impression d'étonnement et de terreur, quand ils se trouvèrent pour la première fois en présence de cette redoutable organisation de la force, de ce matérialisme impie et brutal, de ce despotisme où le roi usurpait la place de Dieu. Les prophètes, aveugles selon la chair, clairvoyants selon l'esprit, ne cessaient de repousser la seule politique qui pût sauver Israël, de battre en brèche la royauté et d'exciter par leurs menaces et leur puritanisme des agitations intérieures. On les vit sur les ruines de Jérusalem maintenir leur obstination et triompher presque des désastres qui réalisaient leurs prédictions. Une politique vulgaire les condamnerait et les rendrait en grande partie responsables des malheurs de leur patrie; mais le rôle religieux du peuple juif devait toujours être fatal à son rôle politique. Israël devait avoir le sort des peuples voués à une idée, et promener son martyre à travers les dédains du monde, en attendant que le monde rallié vint lui demander en supplice une place dans Jérusalem.

3. "La monarchie constitutionnelle en France," in Renan's La réforme intellectuelle et morale, *I, 478*

C'est dans cet esprit que nous voudrions proposer quelques observations sur les graves événements accomplis en cette année 1869. La philosophie que nous porterons dans cet examen n'est pas celle de l'indifférence. Nous ne nous exagérons pas la part de la réflexion dans la conduite des choses humaines; nous ne croyons pas cependant que le temps soit déjà venu de déserter la vie publique et d'abandonner les affaires de ce monde à l'intrigue et à la violence. Un reproche peut toujours être adressé à celui qui critique les affaires de son siècle sans avoir consenti à s'en mêler; mais celui qui a fait ce qu'un honnête homme peut faire, celui qui a dit ce qu'il pense sans souci de plaire ou de déplaire à personne, celui-là peut avoir la conscience merveilleusement à l'aise. Nous ne devons pas à notre patrie de trahir pour elle la vérité, de manquer pour elle de goût et de tact; nous ne lui devons pas de suivre ses caprices ni de nous convertir à la thèse qui réussit; nous lui devons de dire bien exactement, et sans le sacrifice d'une nuance, ce que nous croyons être la vérité.*

4. "Nouvelle lettre à M. Strauss," in Renan's La réforme intellectuelle et morale, *I, 451–452, 454*

Je ne crois pas à la durée des choses menées à l'extême, et je serais bien surpris si une foi aussi absolue en la vertu d'une race que celle que professent M. de Bismarck et M. de Moltke n'aboutissait pas à une déconvenue. L'Allemagne, en se livrant

* Quoted by permission of Calmann-Lévy, publishers.

aux hommes d'Etat et aux hommes de guerre de la Prusse, a
monté un cheval fringant, qui la mènera où elle ne veut pas.
Vous jouez trop gros jeu. A quoi ressemble votre conduite?
Exactement à celle de la France à l'époque qu'on lui reproche
le plus. En 1792, les puissances européennes provoquent la
France; la France bat les puissances, ce qui était bien son droit;
puis elle pousse ses victoires à l'outrance, en quoi elle avait
tort. L'outrance est mauvaise; l'orgueil est le seul vice qui soit
puni en ce monde. Triompher est toujours une faute et en tout
cas quelque chose de bien peu philosophique. *Debemur morti
nos nostraque.*

. . . . . .

L'Alsace est maintenant un pays germanique de langue et de
race; mais, avant d'être envahie par la race germanique, l'Alsace
était un pays celtique, ainsi qu'une partie de l'Allemagne du
Sud. Nous ne concluons pas de là que l'Allemagne du Sud
doive être française, mais qu'on ne vienne pas non plus soutenir
que, par droit ancien, Metz et Luxembourg doivent être allemands. Nul ne peut dire où cette archéologie s'arrêterait.
Presque partout où les patriotes fougueux de l'Allemagne ré-
clament un droit germanique, nous pourrions réclamer un droit
celtique antérieur, et, avant la période celtique, il y avait, dit-
on, les Allophyles, les Finnois, les Lapons; et avant les Lapons,
il y eut les hommes des cavernes; et avant les hommes des cavernes, il y eut les orangs-outans. Avec cette philosophie de
l'histoire, il n'y aura de légitime dans le monde que le droit
des orangs-outans, injustement dépossédés par la perfidie des
civilisés.*

5. *"La monarchie constitutionnelle en France," in* Renan's La réforme intellectuelle et morale, *I, 488*

La France avait créé un huitième sacrement, qui ne s'admi-
nistrait qu'à Reims, le sacrement de la royauté. Le roi sacré
fait des miracles; il est revêtu d'un «ordre»: c'est un person-

* Quoted by permission of Calmann-Lévy, publishers.

nage ecclésiastique de premier rang. Au pape, qui l'interpelle au nom de Dieu, il répond en montrant son onction: «Moi aussi, je suis de Dieu!» Il se permet avec le successeur de Pierre des libertés sans égales. Une fois, il le fait arrêter et déclarer hérétique; une autre fois, il le menace de le faire brûler; appuyé sur ses docteurs de Sorbonne, il le semonce, le dépose. Nonobstant cela, son type le plus parfait est un roi canonisé, saint Louis, si pur, si humble, si simple et si fort. Il a ses adorateurs mystiques; la bonne Jeanne d'Arc ne le sépare pas de saint Michel et de sainte Catherine; cette pauvre fille vécut à la lettre de la religion de Reims. Légende incomparable! fable sainte! C'est le vulgaire couteau destiné à faire tomber la tête des criminels qu'on lève contre elle! Le meurtre du 21 janvier est, au point de vue de l'idéaliste, l'acte de matérialisme le plus hideux, la plus honteuse profession qu'on ait jamais faite d'ingratitude et de bassesse, de roturière vilenie et d'oubli du passé.*

6. Some pithy sayings of Renan: From Questions contemporaines

Le Pape est bon juge en matière de foi catholique. (p. 22)

La plus grande gloire des gouvernements est dans ce qu'ils laissent faire. (p. 45)

La royauté ne sort pas d'un hôtel de ville. (p. 50)

(Cf. "On ne se taille pas un justaucorps dans le manteau de Louis XIV" in *RIM*.)

D'une part, en effet, la vérité ne se démontre qu'à des auditeurs libres; d'une autre, la possibilité de mal faire est la condition essentielle du bien. (p. 67)

[On miracles:] Nous ne nions pas, nous attendons. (p. 164)

[On the too facile French gift for writing:] Les Allemands n'écrivent pas; ils cherchent et ils pensent. (p. 182)

Jamais on n'a pensé avec moins d'originalité que depuis qu'on a été libre de le faire. (p. 212)

* Quoted by permission of Calmann-Lévy, publishers.

La France est le pays du monde le plus orthodoxe, car c'est
le pays du monde le moins religieux. (p. 228)
L'indifférence et l'orthodoxie se touchent. (p. 228)
Rien de ce qui est de l'humanité n'est à dédaigner, mais rien
non plus n'est à embrasser d'une manière absolue. (p. 278) *

From La réforme intellectuelle et morale

La France était une grande société d'actionnaires formée par
un spéculateur de premier ordre, la maison capétienne.
(p. 338)
Le hasard de la naissance est moindre que le hasard du scrutin.
(p. 360)
On peut être royaliste sans admettre le droit divin, comme
on peut être catholique sans croire à l'infaillibilité du pape,
chrétien sans croire au surnaturel et à la divinité de Jésus-
Christ. (p. 380)
La Prusse passera, l'Allemagne restera. (p. 432)
On ne combat le fanatisme que par un fanatisme opposé.
(p. 438)
Ce qui fait entrer dans le Walhalla est ce qui exclut du
royaume de Dieu. (p. 447)
Le péché originel de toute institution démocratique, ce sont
les sacrifices qu'on est obligé de faire à l'esprit superficiel
de la foule. (p. 467)
Un pays ne se sauve que par des actes de foi et de confiance
en l'intelligence et en la vertu de quelques citoyens.
(p. 470)
La société est une hiérarchie. (p. 482)
Le gouvernement personnel ne se maintient qu'à la condition
d'avoir toujours et partout gloire et succès. (p. 500)
La vie des nations, comme celle des individus, est un com-
promis entre des contradictions. (p. 518)
L'État doit maintenir un niveau, non l'imposer. (p. 533) *

* Quoted by permission of Calmann-Lévy, publishers.

7. *"Examen de conscience philosophique,"* in Renan's Feuilles détachées, *II, 1162, 1181–1182*

Le premier devoir de l'homme sincère est de ne pas influer sur ses propres opinions, de laisser la réalité se refléter en lui comme en la chambre noire du photographe, et d'assister en spectateur aux batailles intérieures que se livrent les idées au fond de sa conscience. On ne doit pas intervenir dans ce travail spontané; devant les modifications internes de notre rétine intellectuelle, nous devons rester passifs. Non que le résultat de l'évolution inconsciente nous soit indifférent et qu'il ne doive entraîner de graves conséquences; mais nous n'avons pas le droit d'avoir un désir, quand la raison nous parle; nous devons écouter, rien de plus; prêts à nous laisser traîner pieds et poings liés où les meilleurs arguments nous entraînent. La production de la vérité est un phénomène objectif, étranger au moi, qui se passe en nous sans nous, une sorte de précipité chimique que nous devons nous contenter de regarder avec curiosité. De temps en temps, il est bon de s'arrêter, de se recueillir en quelque sorte, pour voir en quoi la façon dont on envisage le monde a pu se modifier, quelle marche, dans l'échelle de la probabilité à la certitude, ont pu suivre les propositions dont on a fait la base de sa vie.

· · · · ·

L'huître à perles me paraît la meilleure image de l'univers et du degré de conscience qu'il faut supposer dans l'ensemble. Au fond de l'abîme, des germes obscurs créent une conscience singulièrement mal servie par les organes, prodigieusement habile cependant pour atteindre ses fins. Ce qu'on appelle une maladie de ce petit *cosmos* vivant amène une sécrétion d'une beauté idéale, que les hommes s'arrachent à prix d'or. La vie générale de l'univers est, comme celle de l'huître, vague, obscure, singulièrement gênée, lente par conséquent. La souffrance crée l'esprit, le mouvement intellectuel et moral. Maladie du monde, si l'on veut, en réalité perle du monde, l'esprit est le but, la cause finale, le résultat dernier et, certes, le plus brillant de l'univers que nous habitons. Il est bien probable que, s'il y a des résultantes ultérieures, elles sont d'un ordre infiniment plus élevé.*

* Quoted by permission of Calmann-Lévy, publishers.

Notes

Introduction

1. *Histoire de la littérature française*, p. 1078.
2. Edmund Wilson, *The Triple Thinkers*, p. 183.
3. For periodicals during the Second Empire, see René Dumesnil, *L'époque réaliste et naturaliste*, chs. x and xiii.
4. *The Pathos of Distance*, p. 303.
5. *Histoire de la littérature française de 1789 à nos jours*, p. 55.
6. *Nouveaux lundis*, II, 383.
7. *Renan, Taine, et Michelet, les maîtres de l'histoire*, p. 15.

Chapter 1

1. *Nouveaux lundis*, II, 390.
2. See *FIR*, esp. letters to Liart of Jan. 24, 1842, and May 3, 1842, and "Principes de conduite" (Dec. 1843).
3. *CRB*, p. 29, Renan to Berthelot, Sept. 16, 1847.
4. *Correspondance*, I, 130, quoted (in his translation) in Irving Babbitt, *Masters of Modern French Criticism*, p. 104.
5. *Matthew Arnold*, p. 23. See also p. 24, on Coleridge.
6. *AS*, III, 935, 974. See also Mariette Soman, *La formation philosophique d'Ernest Renan*, pp. 72-73.
7. *Evocations littéraires*, pp. 258-260.
8. See also *EMC*, II, 162 ("Dom Luigi Tosti") and *QC*, III, 229 ("Réflexions sur l'état des esprits, [1849]").

Notes

9. *EMC*, II, 87; also *NCJ*, pp. 154–156, 245, 262–264, and *AS*, III, 1038.

10. *AS*, III, 1143, note 136. See Henri Peyre, "Renan et Lamartine," in *Essays in Honor of Albert Feuillerat*, pp. 211–230.

11. For further light on Renan's relationship with Sainte-Beuve see "Lettres de Renan à Sainte-Beuve," published with commentary by Victor Giraud, *Revue des deux mondes*, XIII (Jan.–Feb. 1923), 789–806; Henri Peyre, "Ernest Renan critique littéraire," *PMLA*, XLIV (1929), 288–308; and the author's "Renan and Sainte-Beuve," *Romanic Review*, XLIV (April 1953), 127–135.

12. *NCJ*, p. 36, *EMC*, II ("M. Cousin," esp. p. 61), *FD*, II ("M. Cousin"). See also Soman, *op. cit.*

13. See Renan's tribute to Fauriel in *AS*, III, 964, and *Mélanges religieux et historiques*.

14. *Nouvelles lettres intimes*, p. 66, Renan to Henriette, April 12, 1847.

15. *Ibid.*, p. 301, Renan to Henriette, Jan. 28, 1849.

16. *De l'Allemagne*, pt. ɪ, ch. xiii. See also pt. ɪɪ, ch. xxx, on Herder, and pt. ɪɪɪ, ch. x.

17. *Lettres intimes*, pp. 300–301, Renan to Henriette, Sept. 22, 1845. For Renan's own summary of his views on German scholarship, see *EMC*, II ("Souvenirs d'un vieux professeur allemand," on Creuzer).

Chapter 2

1. *EHR*, preface; Sainte-Beuve, *Nouveaux lundis*, II, 394–395.

2. Lewis F. Mott, *Ernest Renan*, p. 444; Georg Brandes, *Eminent Authors of the Nineteenth Century*, pp. 162–163; Jean Psichari, *Ernest Renan, jugements et souvenirs*, p. 77.

3. *Vie et correspondance*, II, 242.

4. See also Jean Pommier, *La jeunesse cléricale d'Ernest Renan*, pp. 660–661, and Michel Mohrt, "Renan et Veuillot," in *Les intellectuels devant la défaite, 1870*.

5. *Histoire du peuple d'Israël*, I, xv, note 1.

6. This article first appeared in *LP*, III (March and April 1849), 365–384, 437–470.

7. Entitled "Qu'est-ce que la religion dans la nouvelle philosophie allemande?" it appeared in *LP*, VI (Sept. 1850), 341–349.

8. This first appeared in *LP*, I (May 1848), 510–531.

9. Entitled "L'activité intellectuelle en France en 1849," it appeared in *LP*, IV (July 1849), 126–147.

10. Pommier, *Renan et Strasbourg*, pp. 65–77, and Mott, *op. cit.*, pp. 74–84.

11. *Nouvelles lettres intimes*, pp. 214, 283. See also pp. 176, 222, 272, and Henri Peyre, "Renan et Lamartine," in *Essays in Honor of Albert Feuillerat*.

12. The famous *Loi Falloux*, sponsored by the Minister of Public Instruction and promulgated in March 1850, was supposedly designed to grant freedom of education, but actually extended clerical control over it. "Liberal" clerical candidates played a conspicuous role in the elections to the National Assembly in April 1848.

13. See J. A. Ryan and F. J. Boland, *Catholic Principles of Politics*.

14. *QC*, I, 286–287, notes 1 and 2. See also pp. 46–47, where authority for the revolt against Charles X (1830) is found in St. Thomas Aquinas' definition of the seditious tyrant.

15. It appeared in *LP*, III (Jan. 1849), 148–164, and was later reprinted in *NEHR*.

16. Renan had won Chateaubriand's *Itinéraire de Paris à Jérusalem* as his *prix de mémoire* at the Tréguier school when he was thirteen. See Pommier, *Ernest Renan, travaux de jeunesse*, p. 262.

17. Mott, *op. cit.*, p. 83.

18. *Renan d'après lui-même*, p. 119.

19. Renan's first contribution to the *Journal des débats*, "Les séances de Hariri," appeared on June 8, 1853, and was later reprinted in *EMC*. Sacy was a descendant of Pascal's famous interlocutor at Port-Royal, Louis-Isaac Lemaistre de Sacy, and the son of the great orientalist and founder of Arabic studies in France, Isaac Silvestre de Sacy.

20. Doctoral thesis, defended on Aug. 11, 1852, published in 1852 and in subsequent revised and enlarged editions in 1861 and 1866. The complementary thesis was the Latin *De philosophia peripatetica apud Syros*.

21. See, e.g., *Averroès et l'averroïsme*, III, 234–235, on the representation of hell in a painting by Andrea Orcagna.

22. *Ibid.*, III, 249. Cf. *AS*, III, 848, for criticism of Auguste Comte as lacking the essential faculty for an understanding of the human spirit, "*la délicatesse du tour (c'est le tour d'ordinaire qui exprime le plus), la ténuité des aperçus, le contraire en un mot de l'esprit géométrique.*"

23. See Abel Lefranc, *Ernest Renan en Italie, sa mission scien-*

Notes

tifique et littéraire (*juillet 1849–juillet 1850*), and René Dussaud, *L'oeuvre scientifique d'Ernest Renan.*

24. E.g., *AS*, III, 904–905, *De l'origine du langage*, pp. 231–232.

25. *CRB*, p. 98, Renan to Berthelot, Feb. 17, 1850.

26. *Ibid.*, pp. 41–50, Renan to Berthelot, Nov. 9, 1849.

27. The periodical was the *Journal des jeunes personnes*, directed by Mlle Ulliac, and Renan's first contribution to it "Enigme historique, Valentine de Milan" (1846). See Jean Psichari, *op. cit.*, "La première prose imprimée de M. Renan."

28. *Ma soeur Henriette*, pp. 35–37.

29. *Nouvelles lettres intimes*, pp. 20, 108.

30. See also *AS*, preface, III, 716–717, and *EMC*, II, "M. Augustin Thierry."

31. Augustin Thierry, *Dix ans d'études historiques*, in *Oeuvres*, II, 13.

32. *Ibid.*, p. 22. Cf. *AS*, preface, III, 718.

33. Renan's criticism of *éclectisme* parallels very closely that of Baudelaire the same year, in "De l'éclectisme et du doute" ("Salon de 1846") in *Curiosités esthétiques.*

Chapter 3

1. *Essais de critique religieuse*, p. xliii. See also in that work the chapter entitled "De la renaissance des études religieuses en France," reprinted from the *Revue des deux mondes*, XXIV (Nov. 1859), 68–99. For excellent background material, see Camille Jullian, *Extraits des historiens français du XIXᵉ siècle*, introduction, pp. i–cxxviii.

2. This was perhaps not always true, for Renan himself had to combat a prejudice according to which interesting general philosophical ideas belonged to the *gens du monde*, while precise knowledge was the property of heavy, unreadable pedants. See *AS*, III, 910, and *DFP*, I, 700–701.

3. *Culture and Anarchy*, p. 70.

4. Renan's whole emphasis, contrary to that of Strauss, was on the concrete historical reality of Jesus. Like Edgar Quinet (in "De *La Vie de Jésus* du Docteur Strauss," *Revue des deux mondes*, XVI, Dec. 1838, 585–629), he approved of higher criticism in general, but rejected the more extreme theories of the *mythologues*. See Albert Houtin, *La question biblique chez les catholiques de France au XIXᵉ*

siècle, pp. 36–45, and Albert Schweitzer, *The Quest of the Historical Jesus.*

5. See esp. the article of Théodore Jouffroy, "Comment les dogmes finissent," *Le Globe,* II (May 24, 1825), 565–568, reprinted in *Mélanges philosophiques,* Paulin, 1833, and *Le Cahier Vert,* Poux, 1923.

6. *Essays in Criticism,* 2d ser., p. 2.

7. *EHR,* p. 73, *EMC,* II, 117, *SEJ,* II, 830. For a defense of Chateaubriand against at least one of these charges (faulty erudition in the field of Greek), see Marcel Duchemin, *Chateaubriand, essais de critique et d'histoire littéraire,* pp. 455–461.

8. Emery Neff, *The Poetry of History,* p. 23; Renan, *EMC,* II, 264.

9. *EHR,* pp. 20–23; see our Appendix 1.

10. *Ma soeur Henriette,* pp. 65–66.

11. "L'art religieux," *Journal des débats,* May 20, 1858; reprinted in *NEHR* (see esp. p. 411).

12. "Lettre à M. Gustave Flaubert sur *La tentation de Saint Antoine*" (dated Sept. 8, 1874, from Venice), in *FD,* II, 1137.

13. Scheffer, the uncle of Renan's wife, was a painter of Dutch descent whose works ("La mort de Géricault," "Saint Augustin et Sainte Monique," "Francesca da Rimini," and others) are pseudo-classical in form and lean heavily toward romantic moral sentimentalism in spirit.

14. Cf. Baudelaire, "De M. Ary Scheffer et des singes du sentiment," in *Curiosités esthétiques,* which may go to the opposite extreme.

15. The only metaphor of Renan's own wording, "Israël a été la tige sur laquelle s'est greffée la foi du genre humain" (*EHR,* p. 131), is adapted from St. Paul, *Epistle to the Romans,* ch. 11.

16. *L'art de la prose,* pp. 239 *et seq.*

17. *EHR,* pp. 113–114. See Appendix 2.

18. *Essais de politique et de littérature,* p. 260.

19. Ferdinand Brunetière, *Cinq lettres sur Ernest Renan,* p. 87.

20. See Thierry, *Dix ans d'études historiques,* preface, and esp. Taine, *Essai sur Tite-Live,* p. 190. See also Pierre Moreau, *L'histoire en France au XIXe siècle,* and Neff, *The Poetry of History.*

21. George M. Trevelyan, *Clio, a Muse;* Allan Nevins, "The Struggle to Make the Past Alive," *New York Times Book Review,* Jan. 13, 1952.

22. For both pro and con on the subject of Renan's erudition, see Henri Tronchon, *Ernest Renan et l'étranger*, pp. 41, 80, 149. A very able summary of Renan's achievement has been written by the chronicler of the Académie des Inscriptions et Belles-Lettres and historian of Phoenician art, René Dussaud, *L'oeuvre scientifique d'Ernest Renan*. See the Bibliography for other works on this topic.

23. In L. Petit de Julleville's *Histoire de la langue et de la littérature française*, VIII, 259.

24. *Histoire de la littérature française*, p. 1079.

25. *EHR*, esp. pp. 12, 19, 70. See also *De l'origine du langage*, and for modern arguments similar to Renan's, Suzanne Langer, *Philosophy in a New Key*, pp. 39–40.

Chapter 4

1. For the rehabilitation of Napoleon III, see two recent works, Albert Guérard, *Napoleon III: A Great Life in Brief* (New York, 1955) and J. M. Thompson, *Louis Napoleon and the Second Empire* (New York, 1955).

2. René Dumesnil, *L'époque réaliste et naturaliste*, p. 39.

3. *Nouveaux lundis*, III, 15. Bourget's *Essais de psychologie contemporaine* and Faguet's *Politiques et moralistes du dix-neuvième siècle* (3d ser.), despite their bias against Second Empire writers and their somewhat negative approach, remain perhaps the best general studies of the moral thought of the period. See also Albert Guérard, *French Prophets of Yesterday*.

4. *Politiques et moralistes du dix-neuvième siècle*, 3d ser., p. xxii.

5. See Félix Hémon, *Bersot et ses amis*, for a moving account of Bersot's plight. The friends included Renan.

6. See Alphonse Roche, *Les idées traditionalistes en France de Rivarol à Charles Maurras*, pp. 77–83.

7. Hémon, *op. cit.*, p. 104, letter of Renan to Bersot, Jan. 1852.

8. "La morale sociale," first published in *Journal de l'instruction publique*, XX (May 10, 1851), 218–219, and reprinted in *Mélanges religieux et historiques*.

9. *Souvenirs personnels 1848–1851*, p. 244: "Jamais on n'a vu sortir une idée de sa tête, cette outre sonore."

10. For some remarks on the sources of this widespread nineteenth-century notion, see Camille Jullian, *Extraits des historiens français du XIXe siècle*, p. v.

11. These expositions were the prototype of the "world's fairs."

The London Exposition of 1851 had inaugurated the idea, and the first French Exposition Universelle had been held in 1855 in Paris, when Napoleon III's prestige was at its height.

12. Souvestre's *Le monde tel qu'il sera* is not mentioned in *EMC* but is referred to several times in *CJ*. See Mariette Soman, *La formation philosophique d'Ernest Renan*, p. 124.

13. *Essays*, 2d ser., in *The Complete Essays and Other Writings of Ralph Waldo Emerson*, p. 338.

14. *FIR*, pp. 159–160, letter of Renan to Liart, Feb. 5, 1841. For marginal notes of Renan on Victor Le Clerc's *Rhétorique*, see Jules Wogue, "Les idées littéraires de Renan, 1843–1844," *Revue bleue*, XLII (1905), 797–799, 827–831.

15. Octave Gréard, *Prévost-Paradol*, p. 155.

16. Renan himself distinguished between "*romantisme de la forme*," which he calls an error, and his own "*romantisme de l'âme et de l'imagination*" (*SEJ*, II, 767).

17. "Souvenirs du *Journal des débats*," in *FD*, II, 1026.

18. *Histoire littéraire du sentiment religieux en France*, IV, ch. i, "Du prétendu style janséniste."

19. *Evocations littéraires*, p. 252.

20. Gustave Lanson, *L'art de la prose*, p. 269.

21. For Biblical metaphors, see *EMC*, II, 72, 93, 108, 186; for Dantesque ones, *EMC*, II, 147, 173, 184, 240, 252; for the perfume metaphors, *EMC*, II, 13, 78, 130, 295.

22. Renan followed to some extent here the teaching of Ozanam (see *CJ*, p. 170). See also Henri Tronchon, *Ernest Renan et l'étranger*, p. 368.

23. *The Irish Tradition*, pp. 109–111.

24. For further discussion of this question, see René Galand, "La genèse du thème celtique chez Renan," *La nouvelle revue de Bretagne*, VII (1953), 166–176.

25. Myles Dillon, *Early Irish Literature*, p. 124.

26. *Essais de politique et de littérature*, p. 268 (in his review of *EHR*).

Chapter 5

1. See Frederick Bliss, "Renan and His Contemporaries," in *The Development of Palestine Exploration*, and René Dussaud, *L'oeuvre scientifique d'Ernest Renan*.

2. Among the best criticisms of the *Vie de Jésus* (on which there

is a vast literature, much of it worthless) are M.-J. Lagrange, *La vie de Jésus d'après Renan*, and Albert Schweitzer in *The Quest of the Historical Jesus*. Sainte-Beuve's "La Vie de Jésus" in *Nouveaux lundis*, VI, and Taine's brief remarks in his *Vie et correspondance*, III, 245, are also penetrating. See the Bibliography for further titles.

3. This *discours d'ouverture* is reprinted in *MHV* as "De la part des peuples sémitiques dans l'histoire de la civilisation." The comparison to a bishop is from Taine, who was an eyewitness (see his *Vie et correspondance*, II, 227–228).

4. "Destitution d'un professeur au Collège de France," "La chaire d'hébreu au Collège de France. Explications à mes collègues," and "Trois professeurs au Collège de France" (the essay on Pierre Ramus).

5. This essay first appeared in the *Revue des deux mondes*, LXXXIV (Nov. 1, 1869), 71–104, and was reprinted in *RIM*.

6. *CRB*, pp. 181, 183, Berthelot to Renan, Oct. 25 and Oct. 30, 1860.

7. See also "Du protestantisme libéral," *Journal des débats*, Sept. 23, 1876 (reprinted in *Mélanges religieux et historiques*), which gives Renan's judgment of the revival of Protestant thought in the 1860's and the 1870's with Edgar Quinet, Samuel Vincent, Athanase Coquerel fils, the Ecole de Strasbourg, and others.

8. *Renan et la guerre de 70*, p. 114.

9. "La part de la famille et de l'état dans l'éducation," a lecture of April 1869, published in the *Journal des débats* (April 19, 1869), and "La monarchie constitutionnelle en France," *Revue des deux mondes*, LXXXIV (Nov. 1, 1869), 71–104.

10. *Le système historique de Renan*, p. 36.

11. "M. Renan," apropos of *RIM*, in *Essays in Criticism*, 3d ser., p. 159.

12. *Op. cit.*, p. 21. For Renan's political activity, see Gaston Strauss, *La politique de Renan*.

13. Psichari, *op. cit.*, p. 114.

14. See *RIM*, I, 431, 432, 439, 451, 500, and esp. the two letters to Strauss. See also *Correspondance* (1846–1871), I, 341, Renan to Charles Ritter, March 11, 1871. Ritter was the Swiss theologian who had arranged Renan's debate with Strauss and in this letter Renan confessed to him: "Tout ce que j'avais rêvé, désiré, prêché se trouve chimérique. J'avais fait le but de ma vie de travailler

à l'union intellectuelle, morale, et politique de l'Allemagne et de la France."

15. "Des meurtrissures qui ne guérissent pas" (*Correspondance*, I, 355, Renan to Dr. Suquet, July 17, 1871).

16. See the essays on Channing, Calvin, and Mohammed in *EHR*, for example, or *QC*, I, 224–225.

17. "Un mandat législatif ne peut être ni recherché ni refusé" (*L'Antéchrist*, p. xlix). See the similar statement in *DFP*, preface, I, 557.

18. *La philosophie politique de Renan*, p. x.

19. For Renan the administrator and the reforms he effected, see Psichari, *op. cit.*, p. 147, and Gaston Paris, *Penseurs et poètes*.

20. *Essais de psychologie contemporaine*, I, 113.

21. See for example "La chaire d'hébreu au Collège de France," *QC*, I, 168, or the long paragraph of "L'avenir religieux des sociétés modernes" beginning "*Le dogmatisme, qui croit posséder la formule éternelle du vrai*" in *QC*, I, 278, which seems extremely obscure.

22. Buloz tried unsuccessfully to have Renan rewrite "La monarchie constitutionnelle en France" to make it less offensive to the *parti démocratique* and to French national pride in general. See Psichari, *op. cit.*, pp. 36–41. Whether for similar reasons, or simply because of haste, the far bolder title essay passed through no periodical.

23. "L'instruction publique en France jugée par les Allemands," which first appeared in *Journal de l'instruction publique*, XVIII (April 25 and 28, 1849), 176–178, 182–184.

24. For Renan's influence and Duruy's reforms, see Albert Guérard, *French Civilization in the XIXth Century*, ch. vii. For Renan's contribution to the strengthening of scientific research in France (which was in great part made posthumously, through the delayed influence of *L'avenir de la science*), see Henry E. Guerlac, "Science and French National Strength," in *Modern France, Problems of the Third and Fourth Republics*, ed. by Edward M. Earle, pp. 89–90.

25. See esp. "Nouvelle lettre à M. Strauss" and "La guerre entre la France et l'Allemagne," *RIM*, I, 430–432, 456–459. For further details, see the author's "Renan as Prophet of the European and World Future," *The American Society Legion of Honor Magazine*, XXII (1951), 299–309.

26. Edmond de Goncourt was the most notable figure to accuse Renan of defeatism. The most elaborate attempt to make a collaborationist *avant la lettre* of Renan is Louis Vié's *Renan, la guerre de 70, et la 'Réforme' de la France.* See the Bibliography for my comment on this book.

27. From an unpublished draft of a letter written apropos of the Goncourt charges; quoted by Psichari, *op. cit.*, p. 220.

28. *French Political Thought in the Nineteenth Century*, p. 220.

29. *CRB*, p. 442, Renan to Berthelot, July 27, 1875.

30. *Ibid.*, p. 477, Renan to Berthelot, Aug. 17, 1879 (from Ischia). Renan remained on the whole faithful to the view he expressed in *AS*, III, 747: "The French Revolution is the first attempt of the human race to take its reins in its own hands and guide itself."

Chapter 6

1. Emile Bréhier, *Histoire de la philosophie*, II, fasc. 4, ch. i. For some important articles on Renan's relation to the spiritualist, idealist, and also vitalist currents of thought of his time, see our Bibliography under René Berthelot and Raymond Lenoir.

2. For Renan and Bergsonism, see D. Parodi, "Ernest Renan et la philosophie contemporaine," *Revue de métaphysique et de morale*, XXVI (Jan.–Feb. 1919), 41–66.

3. Quoted in L. Halphen and P. Sagnac, *Peuples et civilisations*, XVII, 296.

4. *History of Modern Philosophy in France*, p. 403.

5. *Ibid.*, pp. 400–401.

6. "La philosophie écossaise, son influence sur la nôtre," published posthumously in *Journal de psychologie normale et pathologique*, XX (1923). The quotations are from pp. 288, 291.

7. In the *Journal des débats*, March 29, 1870, in a brief article introducing the preface of Taine's work, which was shortly to be published.

8. See *CRB*, pp. 292–293, Renan to Berthelot, Aug. 4, 1863. Renan is actually referring to an earlier essay, but his remark might well be applied to the "Examen de conscience philosophique" also.

9. *Ibid.*, p. 528, Renan to Berthelot, July 7, 1889.

10. Halphen and Sagnac, *op. cit.*, XVII, 289.

11. See the conclusion of *AS*, the prefaces of *EHR* and *Les apôtres*, and *SEJ*, II, 796, for further evidence of Renan's awareness of the sacrifice he had made.

12. Renan had used a similar metaphor in his "Essai psychologique sur Jésus-Christ," written in May 1845 and first published by Jean Pommier in the *Revue de Paris*, Année 27, tome 5 (Sept. 15, 1920), 225–261: "Avant tout, il faut une science de bonne foi, qui se mette à genoux devant les faits, et se laisse traîner par eux où ils pourront la mener" (p. 228).

13. It would take a whole page to list the passages in which Renan denies the possibility of miracles; but see, for example, *CJ*, p. 40, *AS*, III, 863, *DFP*, I, 637, *SEJ*, II, 839, 861, *NEHR*, p. 11. He frequently links with his denial of miracles Malebranche's formula according to which God does not act by *"volontés particulières."*

14. *FIR*, pp. 197–198.

15. For further light on Renan and Pascal, see Jean Pommier, *La jeunesse cléricale d'Ernest Renan*, Henri Tronchon, *Ernest Renan et l'étranger* (pp. 15, 140, on the *"pari"*), and Paul Bourget, "Pascal et Renan," in *Quelques témoignages*.

16. *Correspondance* (1846–1871), I, 231, undated letter of Renan to George Sand.

17. George Sand, *Spiridion*, in *Oeuvres*, VII, 300. See also pp. 268 and 362, on the *"horizons infinis,"* the limitations of science, the *"certain"* and the *"possible,"* and other ideas to which Renan may well have owed some of his inspiration in the "Examen de conscience philosophique."

18. See Gabriel Séailles, *Ernest Renan*, pp. 244–245.

19. *La crise philosophique*, pp. 86–87.

20. *Nouveaux lundis*, II, 397–398, 409 *et seq.* Cf. p. 384, "M. Renan dissout et dissémine le *divin*, mais il ne le détruit pas."

21. *Op. cit.*, p. 58.

22. *Correspondance*, I, 267–268, Renan to Princess Julie, July 26, 1865.

Chapter 7

1. The posthumously published *Mélanges religieux et historiques* (1904) adds little to Renan's stature as an essayist.

2. *Correspondance* (1872–1892), II, 105, 179, 322.

3. *Ibid.*, p. 123.

4. *Ibid.*, pp. 19, 179, 273.

5. An interesting critique of Renan's treatment of this last subject, in his "L'art du moyen âge et les causes de sa décadence," was published by the famous architect Viollet-le-Duc in the *Revue*

archéologique, VII (Jan.–June 1863), 103–118, 184–193, 250–258.

6. Renan was accompanied by two younger scholars, Joseph de Laborde and the now-famous medievalist Gaston Paris. His essay, written at Ischia and dated Sept. 20, 1875, appeared two months later in the *Revue des deux mondes* in the form of a letter to the director.

7. The only other voyage essay in the book, "L'ancienne Egypte," recording the trip Renan took in 1864 with the great archeologist Mariette, is interesting, though much less a work of art.

8. See *Correspondance*, II, 157.

9. Holbrook Jackson, "The Irony of Irony," *Golden Galleon*, II (Spring 1925), 34.

10. This harsh appraisal of supernaturalism colors much of Renan's work in the 1880's, especially *Le prêtre de Némi* (1885) in *DP*.

11. The same effect of anticlimax, of a subject carefully delineated only to be conjured away, may be found in the *Vie de Jésus* and *Saint Paul*.

12. Preface, *Les noces corinthiennes*, in *Oeuvres complètes illustrées*, I, 249. The "Discours prononcé à l'inauguration de la statue d'Ernest Renan à Tréguier le 13 septembre 1903" was published by Calmann-Lévy in 1903.

13. A recent example of such uncritical admiration is Emile Buré's introduction to his *Ernest Renan et l'Allemagne, textes recueillis et commentés*. Anatole France's "Discours à Tréguier" may be found therein.

14. *Essais de psychologie contemporaine*, I, 124.

15. *Politiques et moralistes du dix-neuvième siècle*, 3d ser., pp. 359 *et seq.* Hippolyte Parigot, in his *Renan, l'égoïsme intellectuel*, also stresses the sensuous play with ideas, but is much less just than Faguet toward Renan.

16. Gabriel Séailles, *Ernest Renan*, p. viii.

17. Haakon M. Chevalier, *The Ironic Temper, Anatole France and His Time*, p. 46. The author makes some useful distinctions between various types of irony from Socrates to Renan and Anatole France.

18. Although there are isolated passages of mockery in some of the earlier works of Renan, including such fundamentally serious ones as the *Vie de Jésus* and the *EMC*, none is frivolous in quite the same way as the preface of the *DFP*, with its reference to a God moved "by the moral refinement of Prussian soldiers and the

unquestionable excellence of Prussian shells" and its anecdote about the *bon curé* who told his congregation not to weep too much at the story of the Passion, since it happened long ago and may not have been true anyway.

19. *Nouveaux lundis*, V, 253. Cf. Renan: "Ce dont on a le plus horreur en France, c'est d'être dupe" (*AS*, III, 1083); Baudelaire: "Cette humeur française qui craint surtout d'être dupe" ("Salon de 1859," *Oeuvres*, ed. by Le Dantec, p. 774); Amiel: "La naïveté tue dans la patrie de Voltaire" (*Fragments d'un journal intime*, I, 132).

20. Notably Amiel, *op. cit.*, I, 277–278, II, 25–26, and Gabriel Monod, *Renan, Taine, et Michelet*, p. xiii. It is also touched upon by Jean Pommier, *Renan d'après des documents inédits*, p. xiii, and Charles Du Bos, *Approximations*, 3d ser., pp. 54–55.

21. *Renan d'après lui-même*, p. 276: "Tout ce que j'ai fait n'est qu'une brillante sépulture de ma foi perdue." For further references to the "deceiving God," see *AS*, III, 1084, *SEJ*, II, 878, *FD*, II, 1160. Renan's fear of being judged a dupe is expressed in *EMC*, II, 162, *QC*, I, 229, *DFP*, I, 581, *Marc-Aurèle*, p. 263, *Conférences d'Angleterre*, pp. 234–235, *L'eau de Jouvence* in *DP*, III, 480, *AS*, preface, III, 727, *FD*, II, 1159.

22. Van Wyck Brooks, *The Malady of the Ideal*, p. 77.

23. Hippolyte Taine, *Essais de critique et d'histoire*, p. 434.

24. See also *Marc-Aurèle*, p. 263, and *Conférences d'Angleterre*, pp. 234–235.

25. *Op. cit.*, p. 369.

Chapter 8

1. See Cyril Connolly, *Enemies of Promise*, pp. 11, 13, 131. He blames the teaching of Addison's and Lamb's "whimsical" essays, but perhaps is unjust toward the writers themselves. He predicts, wrongly, I hope, that the essay will survive only in the form of the long critical article.

2. David Daiches, *A Century of the Essay*, p. 4.

3. *Anthologie des essayistes français contemporains*, p. 10.

4. *The Common Reader*, pp. 150, 290.

5. *Ibid.*, pp. 299, 304–305.

6. *Journal 1921–1923*, I, 186.

7. Félix Ravaisson, *La philosophie en France au XIXᵉ siècle*, p. 31, apropos of eclecticism in general.

Notes

8. *Choses passées*, p. 373.

9. Among the few critics who have emphasized Renan's variety of styles are Albert Thibaudet, *Histoire de la littérature française*, p. 358, and Maurice Weiler, *La pensée de Renan*, ch. vi.

10. See Jean-Paul Sartre, *Situations II*, p. 163. In almost the same breath with which he disposes of Renan's *"beau style"* he dismisses Taine as *"un cuistre."*

11. *Cinq lettres sur Ernest Renan*, p. 80.

12. See also the remark in *AS*, preface, III, 718, referred to in the conclusion of our Chapter 2: "Si des critiques soutiennent un jour que la *Revue des deux mondes* et le *Journal des débats* me gâtèrent, en m'apprenant à écrire, c'est-à-dire à me borner, à émousser sans cesse ma pensée, à surveiller mes défauts, ils aimeront peut-être ces pages." Cf. *NCJ*, p. 78: "La phrase régulière est-elle la vraie forme de la pensée, ou n'est-elle pas un moule gênant qui lui est imposé? Et ne serait-il pas plus commode d'aller *lege solutus* pourvu qu'on se fît entendre?"

13. *Journal 1889–1939*, pp. 659, 959, 1134. Like Sartre, Gide was surprised that Renan *"passe encore pour un maître de la langue française"* but his criticism, except for the fact that he seemed to overlook Renan's vigor and exaggerate his *"aménité,"* was much more just.

14. *Réflexions sur la littérature*, p. 204. Note that Thibaudet does not seem to share Renan's view that correct, elegant French prose was a hindrance to his freedom of thought, to spontaneity.

15. He seemed aware, for example, that spiritualism was a poor substitute for religion. See Henriette Psichari, *Renan d'après lui-même*, pp. 274–275.

16. See *CRB*, p. 445, Renan to Berthelot, Aug. 10, 1875: "Avons-nous été victimés par le sort! Jusqu'au bout, les fautes de la génération qui nous a précédés nous poursuivront et pèseront sur nous."

17. "Discours prononcé à Tréguier," in Emile Buré, *Ernest Renan et l'Allemagne*, p. 207.

18. *Histoire de la littérature française*, p. 1079.

19. *Approximations*, 3d ser., p. 54 (referring specifically to the *sérieux* of the *Cahiers de jeunesse*).

20. A. C. Benson, "The Art of the Essayist," in *Types and Times in the Essay*, p. 3.

21. Matthew Arnold, in so many respects the heir of the best in Renan, defended curiosity as part of the "disinterested love of a

free play of the mind on all subjects, for its own sake" which makes up "real criticism" (*Essays in Criticism*, 1st ser., p. 16). See also Irving Babbitt, *Masters of Modern French Criticism*, pp. 291–292.

22. Albert Thibaudet, *Réflexions sur la littérature*, p. 202.

23. Quoted in Edmund Wilson, *The Triple Thinkers*, p. 115.

24. *Journal 1921–1923*, pp. 185–186.

Bibliography

~~~~~~

PART I consists of works bearing wholly or in part on Renan. What is intended is not an exhaustive list but a guide to works which the author has found especially helpful in interpreting Renan's essays. Descriptive or critical remarks have frequently been added. A few titles not referred to in the course of the study have been included, in the hope that they might increase the general usefulness of the bibliography.

Part II gives more complete information about other works consulted than that provided in the notes.

The place of publication is Paris unless otherwise stated.

I. Works Wholly or in Part on Renan

Albalat, Antoine. *La Vie de Jésus d'Ernest Renan.* Malfère, 1933. Preparation, composition, publication, and so forth, of the work, treated here as a *"grand événement littéraire."*

Alfaric, Prosper. *Les manuscrits de la Vie de Jésus d'Ernest Renan.* Les Belles-Lettres, 1939.

Allier, Raoul. *La philosophie d'Ernest Renan.* Alcan, 1895. One of the earliest over-all treatments of the subject, in part superseded by later works; sober, often penetrating criticism.

Amiel, Henri-Frédéric. In his: *Fragments d'un journal intime.* Stock, 1927. I, 277–278, II, 25–26; emphasizes Renan's fear of being duped.

Arnold, Matthew. "M. Renan." In his: *Essays in Criticism.* 3d ser. Boston: Ball Publishing Co., 1910. Pp. 153–179; criticism of *RIM.*

Babbitt, Irving. "Renan." In his: *Masters of Modern French Criticism.* Boston and New York: Houghton Mifflin, 1912. Pp. 257–297; probably the best brief general treatment of Renan in English, on the whole sound in its critical judgment. This essay was earlier printed as the introduction to Babbitt's fine edition of *SEJ,* D. C. Heath, 1902.

Barrès, Maurice. *Huit jours chez M. Renan.* Plon, 1913.

——. "Renan." In his: *Taine et Renan, pages perdues.* Ed. by Victor Giraud. Bossard, 1922. Pp. 27–62. In these and other works on Renan, Barrès shows progress from ridicule and injustice toward deeper understanding of the master's work.

——. "Le centenaire d'Ernest Renan. Discours prononcé à la Sorbonne au nom de l'Académie Française le 28 février 1923." In his: *Les maîtres.* Plon, 1927. Pp. 297–310.

Bersot, Ernest. "Renan." In his: *Un moraliste.* Hachette, 1882. Pp. 82–101; good article on *EMC.*

Berthelot, René. "La pensée philosophique de Renan," *Revue de métaphysique et de morale,* XXX (1923), 365–388. Stresses scientific basis; useful but largely uncritical.

Bliss, Frederick. "Renan and His Contemporaries." In his: *The Development of Palestine Exploration.* London: Hodder and Stoughton, 1906. Pp. 241–254; points out Renan's mistakes but recognizes his valuable pioneer work as an archeologist.

Boulenger, Jacques. *Renan et ses critiques.* Editions du siècle, 1925. Better in its criticism of Henri Massis', Jacques Maritain's, and Pierre Lasserre's interpretations of Renan than in its positive views.

Bourget, Paul. "M. Ernest Renan." In his: *Essais de psychologie contemporaine.* Plon, 1926. I, 37–96. The essay (dated 1882) stresses "dilettantism," while two important appendixes, B ("A propos du *Prêtre de Némi*," pp. 97–107, dated 1885) and C ("La correspondance de MM. Renan et Berthelot," pp. 108–125, dated 1898), record Bourget's later discovery of Renan's fundamental moral strength.

――. "Pascal et Renan." In his: *Quelques témoignages.* Plon, 1928. Pp. 111–130; interesting comparison of their views of human destiny.

Brandes, Georg. "Ernest Renan." In his: *Eminent Authors of the Nineteenth Century.* New York: Crowell, 1886. Pp. 147–167; interview with Renan in 1870.

Bréhier, Emile. In his: *Histoire de la philosophie.* Tome II, fasc. 4. Les Presses Universitaires de France, 1948. Ch. i, "Positivisme et néo-criticisme"; provides good background, but not especially acute on Renan.

Brunet, Gabriel. "Renan." In his: *Evocations littéraires.* Prométhée, 1930. Pp. 249–297; 298–303; full of penetrating insights into Renan's thought and style and into method and spirit of *AS* in particular.

Brunetière, Ferdinand. *Cinq lettres sur Ernest Renan.* Perrin, 1910. May also be found in *Pages sur Ernest Renan*, Perrin, 1924, along with other essays on Renan. Polemical in tone, often unjust, but deeply appreciative of Renan as *vulgarisateur* in the field of religious history. Calmer and fairer judgments may be found in his *Nouvelles questions de critique*, Calmann-Lévy, 1890, pp. 246–249, *Manuel de l'histoire de la littérature française*, 2d ed., Delagrave, 1899, pp. 510–516, and *Histoire de la littérature française*, 4th ed., Delagrave, 1926, IV, 336–352.

Buré, Emile. *Ernest Renan et l'Allemagne, textes recueillis et commentés*. New York: Brentano's, 1945. Timely, but marred by its superficial introduction, mentioned here only as an example of the cult of Renan at its worst.

Caro, Elme. "L'école critique. M. Renan." In his: *L'idée de Dieu et ses nouveaux critiques*. Hachette, 1864. Pp. 59–169; perceptive criticism of Renan's philosophy, though largely negative.

Chadbourne, Richard. "Renan or the Contemptuous Approach to Literature," *Yale French Studies*, II (1949), 96–104. Renan's method as a literary critic, illustrated by "M. Cousin" (*EMC*).

——. "Renan as Prophet of the European and World Future," *The American Society Legion of Honor Magazine*, XXII (1951), 299–309.

——. "Renan and Sainte-Beuve," *Romanic Review*, XLIV (April 1953), 127–135. Sainte-Beuve's influence on Renan less great than has been claimed; Renan's reservations.

Darmesteter, James. "Ernest Renan," *The New World*, II (1893), 401–433. Valuable portrait of Renan as scholar and teacher by eminent fellow orientalist.

Darmesteter, Mary James. *La vie d'Ernest Renan*. Calmann-Lévy, 1898. One of earliest biographies, by close friend of the Renan family from about 1880 on; largely superseded by later and better works.

Du Bos, Charles. In his: *Approximations*. 3d ser. Arras: Le rouge et le noir, 1929. Pp. 54–55; brief but penetrating comparison of Renan and Mérimée in their use of irony.

——. In his: *Journal 1921–1923*. Corrêa, 1946. I, 14, 41, 185–186. Fervent admiration for *CJ;* praise for all except "*Renan de la fin*."

Dubreuil, Léon. *Rosmapamon*. Ariane, 1946. Renan *vieillard* in his Breton summer home; occasionally dithyrambic in tone.

Duchemin, Marcel. "Renan et Chateaubriand." In his: *Cha-*

teaubriand, essais de critique et d'histoire littéraire. Vrin, 1938. Pp. 455–461; defends Chateaubriand against Renan's charge he was a poor Hellenist.

Dussaud, René. *L'oeuvre scientifique d'Ernest Renan.* P. Geuthner, 1951. Valuable survey of Renan's learned works.

Faguet, Emile. "Ernest Renan." In his: *Politiques et moralistes du dix-neuvième siècle.* 6th ed. 3d ser. Société Française d'Imprimerie et de Librairie, 1903. Pp. 315–379; Renan seen as an "intellectual epicurean"; a doubtful and inconsistent interpretation but stimulating and often perceptive.

Flint, Robert. In his: *Historical Philosophy in France.* New York: Scribner's, 1894. Pp. 622–627; generally favorable to Renan as a historian, but denies he had any serious or deep understanding of religion.

Flower, Robin. In his: *The Irish Tradition.* Oxford: The Clarendon Press, 1947. Pp. 109–111; questions Renan's picture of Celtic peoples and provides critical perspective on "La poésie des races celtiques."

France, Anatole. *Discours prononcé à l'inauguration de la statue d'Ernest Renan à Tréguier le 13 septembre 1903.* Calmann-Lévy, 1903. Cult of Renan, patron saint of skeptics.

——. "M. Ernest Renan, historien des origines" and "Histoire du peuple d'Israël." In his: *La vie littéraire,* in *Oeuvres complètes illustrées.* Calmann-Lévy, 1950. VI, 286–291, 618–624; Renan presented as the ideal historian of religion. In general, Anatole France exaggerates Renan's skepticism.

Galand, René. "La genèse du thème celtique chez Renan," *La nouvelle revue de Bretagne,* VII (1953), 166–176. Excellent *mise au point* of this question.

Gide, André. In his: *Journal 1889–1939.* Gallimard, 1939. Pp. 659, 959, 1134; critical remarks on Renan's style, valid on the whole but limited in scope.

Girard, Henri, and Moncel, Henri. *Bibliographie des oeuvres d'Ernest Renan.* Les Presses Universitaires de France, 1923. Indispensable; includes original dates and places of publication of all Renan's articles.

Giraud, Victor. "Lettres de Renan à Sainte-Beuve," *Revue des deux mondes,* XIII (Jan.–Feb. 1923), 789–806. Letters of the two authors, with valuable commentary by Giraud on their relations; he tends, however, to exaggerate Sainte-Beuve's influence on Renan.

——. "La crise religieuse de Renan." In his: *Portraits d'âmes.* Firmin-Didot, 1929. Pp. 108–127; despite questionable thesis, developed from Barrès, that real *crise religieuse* never occurred, contains some good insights. Reprinted substantially in same author's *La critique littéraire,* Aubier, 1945, pp. 163–176.

Gooch, G. P. In his: *History and Historians in the Nineteenth Century.* London: Longmans, Green, 1913. Pp. 527–530; finds Renan's historical work needs some correction, but calls it fascinating "literary" history with "foundation of solid learning."

Guérard, Albert. "Renan." In his: *French Prophets of Yesterday.* London and Leipzig: T. Fisher Unwin, 1913. Pp. 224–255; excellent background for Second Empire; summary of Renan's work good but perhaps insufficiently critical.

Hémon, Félix. In his: *Bersot et ses amis.* Hachette, 1911. Contains interesting letters of Renan to Bersot, not published elsewhere. See especially chs. viii and xiii.

Huret, Jules. "M. Renan." In his: *Enquête sur l'évolution littéraire.* Fasquelle, 1901. Pp. 419–422; Renan's views on contemporary literature (including symbolism and naturalism) expressed to a reporter in an interview for the *Echo de Paris* in 1891.

Janet, Paul. "La philosophie de M. Renan." In his: *La crise philosophique.* Baillière, 1865. Pp. 53–92; some excellent criticism of Renan's philosophical thought by an astute contemporary.

Jaspar, Marcel. *Renan, le génie libéral de la France.* New York: Moretus, 1942. Defense of Renan's "liberalism" conceived in broad sense; useful, but marred by oversimplification and by inaccuracy in quotations. Published earlier as *Ernest Renan et sa république,* Editions Albert, 1934.

Jullian, Camille. In his: *Extraits des historiens français du XIXᵉ siècle.* Hachette, 1896. Pp. lxxxviii–xci, xcvii–ci; good estimate of Renan the historian; whole introduction provides valuable background material on history in nineteenth century.

Lagrange, M.-J. (Père). *La vie de Jésus d'après Renan.* Gabalda, 1923. Severe judgment by an orthodox Catholic Biblical scholar; recognizes merits and originality of the work, however.

Lanson, Gustave. "Ernest Renan." In his: *Histoire de la littérature française.* Hachette, 1898. Pp. 1078–1082; brief estimate which remains on the whole admirably just and sound; stresses Renan's fundamental seriousness and his strength of will. Recent edition (1952) revised and completed by Paul Tuffrau makes only minor changes.

Lasserre, Pierre. *Renan et nous.* Grasset, 1923. Brief, sympathetic general study.

——. *La jeunesse d'Ernest Renan.* Vols. I, II, Garnier, 1925. Vol. III, Calmann-Lévy, 1932. Places Renan's religious crisis on broad background of the "*histoire de la crise religieuse au XIXᵉ siècle*"; valuable when it does not stray too far into the history of western philosophy.

——. "Ernest Renan." In: *Cent ans de vie française à la Revue des deux mondes.* Hachette, 1929. The originality and historical significance of Renan's first contributions to this periodical, particularly "Mahomet et les origines de l'Islamisme."

Lefranc, Abel. *Ernest Renan en Italie, sa mission scientifique et littéraire (juillet 1849–juillet 1850).* Nouvelle revue critique, 1938.

Lenoir, Raymond. "La conception de la religion chez Renan," *Revue philosophique,* LXXXIII (Jan.–June 1917), 547–572. Renan's religious thought considered as one of many *"variations spiritualistes"* in the nineteenth century.

——. "Renan et l'étude de l'humanité," *Journal de psychologie normale et pathologique,* XX (1923), 355–388. Role of political events in shaping Renan's conception of humanity.

Lévy-Bruhl, Lucien. "Renan and Taine." In his: *History of Modern Philosophy in France.* Chicago: Open Court, 1899. Pp. 397–435; stresses limits to Renan's skepticism.

——. "La religion de Renan," *Journal de psychologie normale et pathologique,* XX (April 1923), 335–344. Renan's religion seen as a consistent personal faith, based on moral probity and love of truth.

Loisy, Alfred. In his: *Choses passées.* Nourry, 1913. Pp. 64–67, 372–375; reminiscences of Renan's *cours d'hébreu* at the Collège de France and interesting judgments of his work by the famous modernist leader. Repeated almost verbatim in interview for *Les nouvelles littéraires* (Feb. 24, 1923) published in Frédéric Lefèvre's *Une heure avec,* 1st ser., Editions de la Nouvelle Revue Française, 1924, pp. 193–197.

Meyer, Eugène. "L'art et le style de Renan," *Revue des cours et conférences,* XXIV¹ (1922–1923), 602–613; 673–689. Renan's progress in style shown by close study of passages of *AS* as revised for "Réflexions sur l'état des esprits (1849)," *QC.*

——. *La philosophie politique de Renan.* Boivin, 1925. Doubtful "ivory tower" interpretation.

Mohrt, Michel. "Renan et Veuillot." In his: *Les intellectuels devant la défaite, 1870.* Corrêa, 1942. Paradoxical, interesting *rapprochement.*

Bibliography

Monod, Gabriel. *Renan, Taine, et Michelet, les maîtres de l'histoire.* Calmann-Lévy, 1894. Brief, sober, just general estimate; brings out *"optimisme volontaire de l'homme d'action."*

Mott, Lewis F. *Ernest Renan.* New York and London: D. Appleton and Century, 1921. Most reliable and complete study in English, but somewhat inconclusive and lacking in critical forcefulness.

Neff, Emery. "History as Art: Renan, Burckhardt, Green." In his: *The Poetry of History.* New York: Columbia University Press, 1947. Ch. vii.

Noonan, John T. "Renan's *Life of Jesus:* A Re-examination," *The Catholic Biblical Quarterly,* XI (Jan. 1949), 26–39. Compares Renan's *Vie de Jésus* with Santayana's *Idea of Christ in the Gospels,* to Santayana's disadvantage.

Parigot, Hippolyte. *Renan, l'égoïsme intellectuel.* Flammarion, [n.d.]. Important work, containing much valid criticism to counteract the cultists, but exaggerates Renan's selfishness and irresponsibility and almost completely overlooks his basic seriousness and idealism.

Paris, Gaston. "Ernest Renan." In his: *Penseurs et poètes.* Calmann-Lévy, 1896. Pp. 324–339; fine tribute to Renan as teacher and administrator.

Parodi, D. "Ernest Renan et la philosophie contemporaine," *Revue de métaphysique et de morale,* XXVI (Jan.–Feb. 1919), 41–66. Renan as precursor of Bergson; important article.

Peyre, Henri. "Ernest Renan critique littéraire," *PMLA,* XLIV (1929), 288–308. His original contribution and his limitations.

——. "Renan et Lamartine," in *Essays in Honor of Albert Feuillerat.* New Haven: Yale University Press, 1943. Pp. 211–230.

246

Pommier, Jean. *Renan d'après des documents inédits.* Perrin, 1923. Essential reference work, by an eminent Renan authority; one of best biographies, but, as in other works on Renan by author, somewhat inconclusive.

———. *La pensée religieuse de Renan.* Rieder, 1925. Definitions of major terms used by Renan in the formulation of his religious thought.

———. *Renan et Strasbourg.* Alcan, 1926. Detailed study of Renan's relations with great center of liberal Protestant thought.

———. *Ernest Renan, travaux de jeunesse 1843–1844.* Les Belles-Lettres, 1931.

———. *La jeunesse cléricale d'Ernest Renan, Saint-Sulpice.* Les Belles-Lettres, 1933. This and preceding work indispensable for knowledge of early period.

Prévost-Paradol, Lucien. "M. Renan." In his: *Essais de politique et de littérature.* Michel Lévy, 1859. Pp. 259–276; good essay on the *EHR.*

Psichari, Henriette. *Renan d'après lui-même.* Plon, 1937. Excellent moral and spiritual portrait by Renan's granddaughter; contains some revealing *pensées inédites.*

———. *Renan et la guerre de 70.* Albin Michel, 1947. Many valuable insights into the man and his work; a vigorous defense which, like the preceding study, nevertheless retains a sense of critical detachment.

Psichari, Jean. *Ernest Renan, jugements et souvenirs.* Editions du monde moderne, 1925. Some interesting personal testimony, but on the whole superficial.

Ravaisson, Félix. In his: *La philosophie en France au XIXᵉ siècle.* 2d ed. Hachette, 1885. Pp. 105–110; more valuable for placing Renan in context of his times than for brief sketch of his thought.

Renard, Edmond (Père). *Renan, les étapes de sa pensée.*

Bloud et Gay, 1928. Severe, not always well documented, sometimes unjust; grants Renan *"une assez grande part de bonne foi."*

Réville, Albert. "De la renaissance des études religieuses en France." In his: *Essais de critique religieuse.* Paris and Geneva: Cherbuliez, 1869. Defines Renan's contribution to the rebirth of religious studies, as of 1859. Reprinted from *Revue des deux mondes,* XXIV (Nov. 1859), 68–99.

Roche, Alphonse. In his: *Les idées traditionalistes en France de Rivarol à Charles Maurras.* Urbana: University of Illinois Press, 1937. Pp. 77–83 deal largely with the influence of *RIM* on *traditionalisme.*

Sainte-Beuve, Charles Augustin. "M. Ernest Renan." In his: *Nouveaux lundis.* 3d ed. Michel Lévy, 1870. II, 381–420.

———. *"Vie de Jésus* par M. Ernest Renan." In his: *Nouveaux lundis.* 2d ed. Michel Lévy, 1872. VI, 1–23.

———. "De la liberté de l'enseignement." In his: *Premiers lundis.* 3d ed. Calmann-Lévy, 1883. III, 280–326. Defense in the Senate of Renan's right to teach and refutation of charges made against Renan of *"athéisme," "matérialisme,"* and *"immoralité."* This and preceding articles, all dating from the 1860's, constitute an appraisal of Renan which, given the limitation that it extends only through the *Vie de Jésus,* remains remarkably penetrating.

Schérer, Edmond. "La réception de M. Renan à l'Académie Française." In his: *Etudes sur la littérature contemporaine.* Calmann-Lévy, 1882. VII, 347–352. Brief general estimate of Renan's work, stressing its variety and showing deep appreciation for the *essayiste* and *publiciste.* In other volumes of this work (IV, V, VIII, IX, X) and in his *Mélanges de critique religieuse* and *Mélanges d'histoire religieuse,* Schérer reveals himself a perceptive critic of Renan's religious and philosophical thought.

Schweitzer, Albert. "Renan." In his: *The Quest of the His-*

torical Jesus. New York: Macmillan, 1948. Pp. 180–192; deals devastatingly, and perhaps unjustly, with the *Vie de Jésus.*

Séailles, Gabriel. *Ernest Renan, essai de biographie psychologique.* Perrin, 1923. Isolates thinker from artist a bit too much, but remains one of the most impressive treatments of Renan's thought; good on *renanisme.*

Seignobos, Charles. In: L. Petit de Julleville, *Histoire de la langue et de la littérature française.* Colin, 1899. VIII, 259–267; stresses Renan's solid preparation as a historian.

Soltau, Roger. In his: *French Political Thought in the Nineteenth Century.* New Haven: Yale University Press, 1931. Pp. 215–230; brief summary and critical estimate of Renan's politics, on the whole excellent.

Soman, Mariette. *La formation philosophique d'Ernest Renan jusqu'à L'avenir de la science, d'après des documents inédits.* Emile Larose, 1914. (Diss., Paris.) Valuable study of sources of Renan's thought.

Sorel, Georges. *Le système historique de Renan.* G. Jacques, 1905. Often penetrating in criticism of Renan's historical work, but superficial in psychology and generally too doctrinaire in approach.

Strauss, Gaston. *La politique de Renan, suivie d'une étude sur les candidatures de 1869 et de 1878.* E. Grevin, 1909. (Diss., Paris.) Probably most complete and sound study of Renan's political thought and action, but by no means definitive.

Taine, Hippolyte. In his: *Vie et correspondance.* 3d ed. Hachette, 1908. II, 227–228, 242–244; III, 245; brief but acute remarks on Renan's process of philosophical thought and on the *Vie de Jésus.*

Thibaudet, Albert. "Renan." In his: *Histoire de la littérature française de 1789 à nos jours.* Stock, 1936. Pp. 352–359; fine chapter on Renan.

———. "Renan et Taine." In his: *Réflexions sur la littérature.*

Gallimard, 1938. Largely very interesting comparison of their styles.

Thompson, James W., and Holm, Bernard J. *A History of Historical Writing.* New York: Macmillan, 1942. II, 555–587; admire Renan's powers of synthesis and his blending of science and art, but conclude, somewhat curiously in view of this, that his work is "literature rather than history."

Tronchon, Henri. *Ernest Renan et l'étranger.* Les Belles-Lettres, 1928. Very useful catalogue of references, but difficult to read and lacking in comprehensive view and conclusion.

Van Tieghem, Philippe. *Renan.* (Grands Ecrivains Français.) Hachette, 1948. Good, readable introduction and synthesis, but somewhat conventional in approach.

Vié, Louis. *Renan, la guerre de 70 et la 'Réforme' de la France.* Bloud et Gay, 1949. Mentioned only as example of a prejudiced attack on Renan under the guise of a minutely documented, "impartial" study; Renan viewed as a forerunner of collaborationists; superpatriotic tone.

Weiler, Maurice. *La pensée de Renan.* Grenoble: Bordas Frères, 1945. Good general study.

Wilson, Edmund. "Decline of the Revolutionary Tradition: Renan." In his: *To the Finland Station.* New York: Harcourt, Brace, 1940. Pp. 36–44; considers Renan as incomparable master of the history of "man's formulated ideas," but tends to sacrifice him to admiration for Michelet, master of "organic history."

Wogue, Jules. "Les idées littéraires de Renan, 1843–1844," *Revue bleue (Revue politique et littéraire),* XLII² (1905), 797–799, 827–831. Important for Renan's views on rhetoric.

Ys, René d'. *Ernest Renan en Bretagne.* 3d ed. Emile-Paul, 1904. Valuable documentation on this aspect, but general views of Renan largely uncritical.

II. Other Works Consulted

Arnold, Matthew. *Essays in Criticism.* 2d ser. New York: Macmillan, 1924.

——. *Culture and Anarchy.* Ed. by J. Dover Wilson. Cambridge, Eng.: University Press, 1935.

Baudelaire, Charles. *Oeuvres.* Ed. by Y.-G. Le Dantec. Gallimard, 1951.

Benson, A. C. "The Art of the Essayist," in *Types and Times in the Essay.* Ed. by Warner Taylor. New York and London: Harpers, 1932.

Bremond, Henri. *Histoire littéraire du sentiment religieux en France.* Vol. IV. Bloud et Gay, 1920.

Brooks, Van Wyck. *The Malady of the Ideal.* Philadelphia: University of Pennsylvania Press, 1947.

Chevalier, Haakon. *The Ironic Temper, Anatole France and His Time.* New York: Oxford University Press, 1932.

Connolly, Cyril. *Enemies of Promise.* New York: Macmillan, 1948.

Daiches, David. *A Century of the Essay.* New York: Harcourt, Brace, 1951.

Dillon, Myles. *Early Irish Literature.* Chicago: University of Chicago Press, 1948.

Dumesnil, René. *L'époque réaliste et naturaliste.* Tallandier, 1945.

Emerson, Ralph Waldo. *The Complete Essays and Other Writings.* Ed. by Brooks Atkinson. New York: Modern Library, 1940.

France, Anatole. *Oeuvres complètes illustrées.* Calmann-Lévy, 1950. Vol. I.

Gréard, Octave. *Prévost-Paradol.* Hachette, 1894.

Guérard, Albert. *French Civilization in the Nineteenth Century.* London and Leipzig: T. Fisher Unwin, 1914.

Guerlac, Henry E. "Science and French National Strength,"

in *Modern France, Problems of the Third and Fourth Republics.* Ed. by Edward M. Earle. Princeton: Princeton University Press, 1951.

Halphen, Louis, and Sagnac, Philippe, eds. *Peuples et civilisations.* Vols. XVII and XVIII. Alcan, 1937, 1939.

Houtin, Albert. *La question biblique chez les catholiques de France au XIXe siècle.* Picard, 1902.

Hugo, Victor. *Souvenirs personnels 1848–1851.* Ed. by Henri Guillemin. Gallimard, 1952.

Huneker, James. *The Pathos of Distance.* New York: Scribner's, 1913.

Jackson, Holbrook. "The Irony of Irony," *Golden Galleon,* II, no. 2 (Spring 1925).

Kra, Simon, ed. *Anthologie des essayistes français contemporains.* Editions Kra, 1929.

Langer, Suzanne. *Philosophy in a New Key.* New York: Penguin Books, 1948.

Lanson, Gustave. *L'art de la prose.* Librairie des annales politiques et littéraires, 1911.

Moreau, Pierre. *L'histoire en France au XIXe siècle.* Les Belles-Lettres, [n.d.].

Ryan, J. A., and Boland, F. J. *Catholic Principles of Politics.* New York: Macmillan, 1943.

Sand, George. *Spiridion.* In *Oeuvres,* Vol. VII. Garnier, 1845.

Santayana, George. *Winds of Doctrine.* London: Dent; New York: Scribner's, 1913.

Sartre, Jean-Paul. *Situations II.* 11th ed. Gallimard, 1948.

Staël, Mme de. *De l'Allemagne.* Firmin Didot, 1871.

Taine, Hippolyte. *Essai sur Tite-Live.* 10th ed. Hachette, [n.d.].

——. *Essais de critique et d'histoire.* 7th ed. Hachette, 1896.

Thierry, Augustin. *Dix ans d'études historiques.* In *Oeuvres,* Vol. II. Garnier, 1866.

Trevelyan, George M. *Clio, a Muse, and Other Essays.* London, New York, Toronto: Longmans, Green, 1930.

Trilling, Lionel. *Matthew Arnold.* New York: Columbia University Press; London: George Allen and Unwin, 1949.

Wilson, Edmund. *The Triple Thinkers.* New York: Harcourt, Brace, 1938.

Woolf, Virginia. *The Common Reader.* 1st and 2d ser. New York: Harcourt, Brace, 1948.

Index

Index

Index

Index